AHAD HA - AM

a biography

To Alan Kravitz, on his
Bar Mitzvah, with best
wishes.   The afterguts

AHAD HA-AM: London, 1923

AHAD HA - AM

A S H E R   G I N Z B E R G

a

biography

by

Leon Simon

Philadelphia

The Jewish Publication Society of America

1960-5721

to my grandchildren JESSICA MAYER

HELEN MAYER *and*

ROBERT SIMON MAYER

FOREWORD

The first biography of Ahad Ha-Am, a short Hebrew mono-
graph by M. Glickson, was published in Tel Aviv within a
few months of his death at the beginning of 1927. This was
followed in 1941 by a *Biographical Story,* also in Hebrew,
written by Johanan Tverski and published in New York.
Tverski's book is rather an imaginative reconstruction than
a factual account of Ahad Ha-Am's life; it interweaves fact
and fancy so artistically that the reader is at a loss to know
where the one ends and the other begins. It was not until
many years later that the first attempt was made to produce a
full-scale biography, which should do justice alike to Ahad
Ha-Am's life-story and personality, and to his contribution
to Jewish life and thought. This was a Hebrew book of some
270 pages, entitled *Ahad Ha-Am: The Man, his Work and*

his Teaching, which was written in collaboration by Dr. J. E. Heller and myself, and was published in 1956 by the Hebrew University Press (the Magnes Press) in Jerusalem. It was the second to appear in a series of biographies of nine-teenth-century Hebrew writers for the publication of which a fund had been established by Sir Montagu Burton, of London. Its predecessor in the series, a *Life Of Tchernichow-sky* by Professor Joseph Klausner, had appeared nine years earlier.

While the biography by Dr. Heller and myself was in course of preparation, Dr. Grayzel, the Editor of The Jewish Publication Society of America, suggested that I might write an English life of Ahad Ha-Am for publication by the So-ciety, and I promised to take up this suggestion as soon as I became free to do so. I was engrossed in other concerns for some time after the appearance of the Hebrew volume; and it was not until the end of 1957 that I was ready to pursue the question of an English biography. By that time Dr. Heller was unfortunately no more, having died within a year or so of the appearance of our joint work.

The Hebrew biography, though the responsibility for it was shared by the two authors, fell into two parts, of which the first, dealing with Ahad Ha-Am's life-story, his public work and his personality, was written by myself, and the second, written by Dr. Heller, was concerned with his thought and teaching. This division of labor was adopted by Dr. Heller's wish, on the grounds that the more theoretical aspect of the subject ought to be treated by a single hand, and that I, having had the privilege of Ahad Ha-Am's friend-ship, was the better qualified of the two to handle the bio-graphical aspect. Dr. Heller's contribution to the volume devotes a great deal of space to an analysis and systematiza-tion of Ahad Ha-Am's sociological ideas and beliefs, by way of preparation for the discussion of his views on Judaism and the idea of the national revival. This skillful attempt—the first ever made—to construct a coherent account of Ahad Ha-Am's general philosophy out of the scattered and unco-ordinated statements in his essays is of considerable value for any who may wish to make a study of Ahad Ha-Am's philosophical background and the extent of his debt to con-temporary non-Jewish thinkers; but it is, I think, unlikely to interest the general body of English readers of Jewish books. For that reason among others, the theoretical or ideological section of the Hebrew biography would have needed consid-erable curtailment for the purposes of an English translation of the book; and I did not feel that I had a right to take liberties with Dr. Heller's work after his death. Moreover, the very different cultural background of English readers would have necessitated extensive departure from the Hebrew original to make it intelligible to them. In these circum-stances I came to the conclusion that it would be better, though more troublesome, to start entirely afresh, and pro-duce a new biography of Ahad Ha-Am for English readers, without the somewhat artificial division into two separate sections, which was due solely to the dual authorship of the Hebrew biography. There are one or two short passages in this book which might be regarded as very free translations of corresponding passages in my own section of the Hebrew book; and it contains a few paragraphs which are repro-duced, with the permission of the copyright holders, from a couple of earlier publications of mine. Subject to these small reservations, the present biography, for which I am solely responsible, is a new and independent work.

Ahad Ha-Am's life was neither eventful nor fruitful in practical achievement, and it might be thought—indeed I myself thought many years ago—that his personality and the events of his life are without interest or importance, see-ing that his teaching, which is what really matters, can be distilled from his written work. That idea fits in with his own insistence on hiding his individuality behind a very impersonal pseudonym, and on maintaining a rigid separation between opinions and the personalities of their propounders. It now seems to me, however, that without some knowledge of his personal characteristics, background and early education, his attitude to the problems of Jewish life and Judaism cannot be fully understood, his philosophy being largely, at least in its omissions and emphases, a projection of his personality. His influence, moreover, is due as much to his character as to his ideas. Hence it has seemed to me proper to interweave the presentation of his views with a reasonably detailed account of his life, and of his early life in particular, and to endeavor to throw into relief the points of contact between his personal characteristics and his approach to the interpretation of Judaism and the question of the Jewish future.

As already mentioned, I was on terms of personal friendship with Ahad Ha-Am during the years of his life in London; and although the difference of age and background, as well as his reserved disposition, precluded real intimacy, I was probably as close to him as anybody could be who did not belong to his own generation and his own Odessa circle. I have not allowed that personal relationship, which can scarcely be regarded as a fact of significance for those who read his biography, to be reflected in the pages of this book. But I cannot forgo this opportunity of placing on record my deep sense of personal obligation to him for all that his personality and his ideas have meant to me since I first made acquaintance with his essays in my student days. He not only led me to Zionism, but gave me a new conception of the nature and meaning of Judaism, and of what is involved in being a Jew in the modern world; and, beyond the specifically Jewish field, the Hegelianism which I brought down with me from the Oxford of those remote days has, I think, been somewhat mitigated over the years by the sanity of his more empirical idealism.

Jewish life has undergone vast changes during the last half-century, and the problem of the survival of Jewry and Judaism, which was Ahad Ha-Am's chief concern, now wears superficially a different aspect. But the fundamentals of his teaching have not thereby lost their relevance, and his "spiritual Zionism" is still, I am convinced, as capable as it was fifty years ago of giving inspiration and guidance to assimilated Jews, especially of the younger generation, who are attached to the Jewish people and are capable of taking a serious interest in its problems. If this biography helps in some degree to stimulate interest in him and his work among English-speaking Jews, I shall feel that a fraction of my debt to him is repaid.

I have to thank the Magnes Press of the Hebrew University of Jerusalem for permission to make such use as I might think fit of the Hebrew biography of Ahad Ha-Am by the late Dr. J. E. Heller and myself; the East and West Library, London, for permission to incorporate in this book passages from *Ahad Ha-Am: Essays, Letters, Memoirs* and from my essay on "Ahad Ha-Am and the Future of the Diaspora" included in *Between East and West* (the Bela Horovitz Memorial Volume); and the Zionist Organization of America for similar permission in respect of an article of mine on "Ahad Ha-Am and the Jewish State," which appeared in the (now defunct) *Zionist Quarterly*.

To Rabbi Arthur Hertzberg, of Temple Emanu-El, Englewood, New Jersey, author of *The Zionist Idea,* I am greatly indebted for his kindness in reading through the typescript, and for a number of valuable criticisms and suggestions. To my daughter Aviva, who typed the book for me, I am grateful not only for that service, but for several helpful and challenging observations on my first draft.

For readily given help in the bibliographical field my thanks are due to the Zionist Archives, the Library of Jewish Information of the American Jewish Committee, and the Yivo Institute for Jewish Research, all of New York; to Mr. Josef Fraenkel, the representative in London of the Zionist Central Archives, Jerusalem; and to Mr. Johanan Pograbinski, Librarian of the Beth Ahad Ha-Am, Tel Aviv. (News of Mr. Pograbinski's death reached me after this book had gone to press.)

I have to thank the Jewish Publication Society of America for undertaking the publication of the book, and Dr. Solomon Grayzel and Mr. Lesser Zussman, the Society's Editor and Executive Director respectively, for help of various kinds in the course of its preparation.

Finally, I wish to place on record my deep sense of obligation to my wife, without whose unfailing encouragement and forbearance this book could not have been written.

London, January, 1960.   L. S.

CONTENTS

FOREWORD   vii

CHAPTER   1   *The Furnace of Iron*   3
          2   *Escape to Odessa*   32
          3   *The Wrong Way*   46
          4   *First Visits to Palestine*   57
          5   *Sons of Moses*   76
          6   *At the Crossroads*   95
          7   *The Editorial Chair*   127
          8   *Mission to Paris*   150
          9   *Jewish Humanism*   157
         10   *Political Zionism*   169
         11   *Last Years in Russia*   195
         12   *London Exile*   214
         13   *World War and National
              Home*   248
         14   *Tel Aviv*   267
         15   *Philosophy of Judaism and
              the Spiritual Center*   279
         16   *His Personality and Influence*   299
GLOSSARY OF HEBREW WORDS..............   329
BIBLIOGRAPHICAL NOTE...................   331
NOTES 333
INDEX 341

AHAD HA - AM

a biography

1

THE

FURNACE

OF IRON

In the middle of the eighteenth century a new religious movement came to birth among the Jews of the Carpathian mountains on the borders of Poland. Its founder, one Israel ben Eliezer, reputed a wonder-worker, was known as the Baal-Shem, "Master of the (divine) Name," and became the central figure of a host of legends. Its adherents called themselves Hasidim ("Pious ones"). Hasidism was in essence a revolt against the excessive legalism and intellectualism which had become characteristic of rabbinic Judaism as it was preached and practiced in the great centers of Jewish population in eastern Europe. Without challenging the authority of the ceremonial law, or wishing to modify it except in inessential details, Hasidism stood for a new scale of values, asserting the claims of the heart against the head, and of simple folk against the tyranny of learning. It exalted faith and spontaneous religious emotion above keenness of intellect, and prayer above study; it taught the godliness of joy. Its doctrines and legends brought much-needed hope and comfort to masses of Jews in eastern Europe at a time when their condition was even more than usually depressed, and not surprisingly, it made rapid headway.

The promulgation of this new doctrine alarmed the constituted religious authorities, and the outraged champions of traditional Rabbinism tried by every means in their power to extirpate what they regarded as a dangerous heresy; but neither polemic nor persecution could stem the tide of Hasidism, which in the course of a few decades gained a firm foothold not only in its native Poland, but also in Russia, Rumania and Hungary. The whole of East-European Jewry was thus divided into the two camps of hasidim and mithnaggedim, "opponents"—the name bestowed by the hasidim on those who did not join them, and somewhat oddly adopted by the latter for themselves, as though they, and not the rival sect, had been the dissenters.

It was in accord with the essentially popular character of the new movement, and with its emphasis on feeling, that it fostered a warm emotional attachment to Palestine and to the Jewish people; and this embryonic nationalism was manifested in the high esteem in which it held the religious duty of settlement in the Holy Land. When, in the latter half of the nineteenth century, the undying Jewish aspiration after the return to the ancient homeland began to find organized expression in eastern Europe, the "Love of Zion" (Hibbath Zion) movement numbered many hasidim among its inspirers and faithful adherents.

Mysticism and emotionalism have their dangers no less than formalism; and before long Hasidism fell into disrepute because of the development of some of its less admirable features. If at its highest it soared into the empyrean of saintliness, at its lowest it sank into the abyss of ignorance and superstition. Its emphasis on the joy of life was interpreted by too many of its adherents as a license for insobriety and moral laxity. Worst of all, ambitious and unscrupulous men exploited the hopes and fears of the gullible masses, and among the hasidic rabbis, or rebbes, who were also given the name of Tsaddik ("righteous one"), there were not a few who pretended to possess miraculous powers, and arrogated to themselves the position of intermediary between the worshiper and his God. Many of these were shameless charlatans, who lived in almost regal state on the offerings of their credulous devotees, and founded dynasties in which the privileges and powers of the Tsaddik were handed down from father to son without any regard for personal merit.

The better types of hasidim steered clear of these abuses, and the sect known as Habad (a name formed from the initials of the Hebrew words for Wisdom, Understanding and Knowledge) effected a synthesis between the new emphasis on enthusiastic devotion and the old insistence on the paramountcy of law and study. Some Tsaddiks were justly renowned alike for piety and for learning. But the sect as a whole was gravely compromised by the excesses of its least worthy members. When, in the first half of the nineteenth century, the movement known as Haskalah ("enlightenment," modernism, pursuit of European culture) began to gain ground in East-European Jewry, and a three-cornered struggle developed between hasidim, mithnaggedim, and maskilim, the keenest shafts of the champions of Haskalah were aimed at the hasidim, and especially at their Tsaddiks, who became a byword for ignorance and chicanery. It is only in comparatively recent times that prejudice has given way to a more objective view, which can do justice to the genuine spirituality of Hasidism, and to its value and importance as a strand in the web of Jewish thought and teaching. Today it inspires the religious philosophy of a Martin Buber no less than the fanatical obscurantism of anti-Israel rebbe-worshipers in New York and other cities of the western world.

The Ukraine, in southern Russia, early became one of the strongholds of Hasidism, mostly of the less enlightened type; and it was in that area, in the mainly Jewish townlet of Skvira, not very far from Kiev, that Asher Zvi Ginzberg, afterwards to become famous throughout the Jewish world under his pen-name *Ahad Ha-Am,* ("one of the people"), was born, of hasidic parents, on the 17th of Ab, 5616—the 18th of August, 1856, according to the European calendar (which was then twelve days ahead of the Russian). His birthplace was later described by him in his *Reminiscences* as "one of the most benighted spots in the Hasidic sector of Russia"; and the description is eloquent of the complete breach which reading and reflection early created between him and the environment in which he spent his most impressionable years.

The *Reminiscences*[1] just mentioned, which are one of our two sources of information about his early life, were begun a few years after he settled in Odessa in 1886, when his pen-name was already well known to the Hebrew-reading public, and were apparently intended to be a connected story of his life, though not meant for publication. His object in writing them, he explains in a note, was "to satisfy the need which I sometimes felt to turn away from the world and be alone with my own self, so as to account to that self, and to that self alone, for all my thoughts and actions." But he goes on to say that on reading over the first few pages he felt that the habit of writing for the public had become second nature to such an extent that he was involuntarily writing as though for publication; and he accordingly abandoned the narrative form and added only a few disconnected notes. For some unexplained reason, however, these too were discontinued, and the *Reminiscenses* remained untouched throughout most of his life. Many years afterwards, when he was settled in Tel Aviv, he dictated further notes to his secretary, mainly but not exclusively about his early years, when he felt well enough to do so; and after a time, when his store of memories ran dry, his friends got him to dictate replies to specific questions which they formulated.

The *Reminiscences* are thus, apart from the first few pages, fragmentary and disconnected. They are for the most part devoid of any arrangement, either logical or chronological, and, not surprisingly, there are occasional discrepancies between the earlier and later sections. They

are, moreover, less concerned with external events than with
his intellectual development, his education, his revolt against
the narrowness of his environment, and matters of that kind.
They are, above all, exasperatingly uninformative about
the conditions in which he lived, and especially about his
emotional life and his personal relations with those among
whom his early years were spent.

Fortunately they are supplemented to some extent by the
recollections of his younger sister, Esther, who married a
Dr. Shimkin, and became herself one of the first woman
doctors in Palestine. A little booklet of hers, in Hebrew,
printed in Haifa in 1941, tells something of the family history of the Ginzbergs and of their mode of life in Gopitshitza, the village to which they moved when Asher was
twelve, and in which she herself was born when he was
about twenty. Her booklet was expressly intended to supplement her brother's *Reminiscences* (which had been published many years earlier); but it was printed for private
circulation only, and is very little known. Being so much
his junior, she was naturally dependent on hearsay for what
she wrote about his early years; but her booklet does something to fill in the very sketchy outline provided by the
Reminiscences. Nonetheless many questions about his childhood and youth with which a biographer might be expected
to deal must perforce remain unanswered.

✌ 2 ✌

Asher's father, Isaiah Ginzberg, was born in 1836 of a
better-class hasidic family, which was believed to have
migrated to Russia from Austria in an earlier generation.
The Ginzbergs must have belonged to the less extreme wing
of Hasidism, which did not turn its back on learning, for
Isaiah was a brilliant Talmud student. His father had been
a man of substance, but had lost his money, and thereafter
had moved to a small place in the district of Kiev, where

he had died of tuberculosis at the age of about thirty-five,
leaving his widow and eight children in destitution. Isaiah
grew up to be a very handsome young man, and his good
looks, together with his reputation as a prodigy of learning, would in ordinary course have made him a coveted
prize in the marriage-market. He was, however, narrow-
chested and cadaverous, showing all the symptoms of lung
trouble; and medical advice was naturally against his marriage. This notwithstanding, he was married at eighteen to
Golda, the sixteen-year-old daughter of Jacob and Rachel
Zozovski of Skvira, a pious couple in reduced circumstances, who had lost all their sixteen children except Golda
and an older sister. Golda Zozovski was, according to her
daughter, a comely blonde, with good features, large grey
eyes, and a fine figure, of a gay and lively temperament,
fond of dress and jewelry, and little inclined to trouble her
pretty head about serious matters. She was also extremely
good-natured, and generous to a degree. Asher, the eldest
of her five children, is said to have resembled her more
closely than either of the other two who survived childhood
—Hannah, born in 1862, and Esther, born in or about 1876.
Isaiah and Golda conformed to established custom by
commencing their married life in the home of Golda's parents; and when the time came to set up house for themselves,
they remained at first in Skvira. It was, accordingly, in his
native townlet that Asher's education began; and it was of
course an education of the traditional type. At the tender
age of three he was sent to *heder* to be taught Hebrew reading and *humash*. The child stipulated at the outset that he
was not to be taught more than three lines a day, and protested vigorously and successfully when his *melammed* tried
to overstep that limit. This might suggest that the passion
for justice developed in him earlier than the avidity for
learning, for which in later life he was not less remarkable;
but his intellectual curiosity displayed itself at the age of
eight in a desire to learn the Russian alphabet. This he had

to satisfy surreptitiously, because his maternal grandfather, a rigorist of the most extreme type, had once heard from a great Tsaddik that Jewish eyes were forbidden to look at any characters other than the Hebrew. Fortunately that particular superstition did not bind the common run of hasidim, who used to allow their children to learn the Russian alphabet in order that they might be able in later life to sign their names to official documents when necessary; and Asher persuaded some of his humbler fellow-pupils to impart to him their knowledge of the Russian letters. Thus initiated, he used to spend time on the way home from *heder* trying to read the signs on the shop-fronts, until his late arrival home led to inquiry, and this illicit pastime was forbidden.

Other incidents of his early life recorded in the *Reminiscences* illustrate the almost incredible obscurantism of the surroundings in which he grew up. The story of how he began to learn algebra may serve as an example.

He contracted the habit of smoking at the early age of eleven. This caused his parents great concern, and his father took him to see the celebrated Dr. Pirogov, who told him that unless he gave up smoking he would die. The lad determined to make the required sacrifice; but he felt the need of something to keep his mind off smoking. As luck would have it, he found in his father's library an early eighteenth-century Hebrew book in which the elements of algebra and geometry were explained; and algebra so fascinated him that for the time being cigarettes were forgotten. He had ample time for the study of the new subject in the *heder,* because the teacher used to sleep for a couple of hours in the afternoon, and Asher was already so far advanced in his studies that he had no need to use this interval for recapitulation, as the other pupils did. But in his enthusiasm for the letters which by some magic turned out to be numbers, he took to scribbling algebraic formulae on the doors and windows of his home: whereupon his shocked maternal grandfather told his parents that their son was practising witchcraft. So algebra was forbidden, and smoking resumed.

The young Asher was very far from being a spoiled child: his well-to-do father may even have had some theory of his own about the superiority of the hard way. Even in the depth of the Russian winter the child was escorted to *heder,* at a very early hour in the morning, without having tasted bite or sup, and had to wait a long time in the cold classroom (which incidentally was also the bedroom of the *melammed's* wife) until a cup of tea, no longer warm, reached him from home. Such, at any rate, were the conditions in one of the *hedarim* which he attended; we do not know whether he fared any better in the others at which he successively studied, moving from the less to the more advanced, until his eleventh year, when his father took him away from school and provided him with a private tutor, with whom he studied Talmud and Responsa until he was fifteen. Thereafter he pursued his studies unaided.

In the meantime his father, whose health had improved after his marriage, had given up the student's life and gone into business, for which he displayed considerable aptitude. By 1868, when Asher was eleven or twelve, his father had become possessed of sufficient money to be able to lease from an aristocratic Russian family, the Rzhevutskis, their estate in or near the large village of Gopitshitza. The village was in the neighborhood of Berditchev, the principal town in the district of Volhynia, which had a large Jewish population, and not far from a Jewish townlet with an ancient synagogue. This enterprise, in which Isaiah invested his all, was undertaken against the wishes of his wife, who was loath to leave her family and friends and the pleasures of urban life for a backwoods village; but her husband, acting on what turned out to be the sound advice of his Tsaddik, the famous Rabbi of Sadigura, insisted on having his way.

The Rzhevutski property had been almost ruined by neglect, but the new lessee's capable administration turned it into a flourishing and profitable estate, and he himself became comparatively affluent.

Dr. Shimkin in her booklet waxes lyrical in her description of the "paradise" in which Gopitshitza was situated. It was surrounded, she says, by smiling meadows and dense pine woods, infested by wolves and other wild animals, and the adjoining marshes were covered with white flowers of wonderful beauty (and were probably responsible, adds the lady doctor, for the prevalence in the region of malaria, from which her father suffered till the end of his days). There was a dense cherry-orchard on one bank of the river which flowed through the village and bordered the estate. On the estate itself, in addition to the large house in which the Ginzbergs lived—"the court" as it was called—were numerous other buildings: storehouses full of grain, great stables to house the pedigree horses and the carriages which served the family for traveling and excursions, workshops for the manufacture of brandy and other spirits, more stables for the draught-horses, and stalls for the oxen and cows, which were sent to market every year.

The house itself (in which the family was joined by Golda's father after his wife's death) was a one-story building with sixteen rooms, and had an annex containing four or five more. It stood in a large flower garden (Isaiah was very fond of flowers), and beyond that was an orchard of forty or fifty acres, in which many kinds of fruit grew in abundance. The furniture and appointments of the house were luxurious, and the large dining room, with its parquet floor, was furnished in the style of Louis XVI, with gilt-framed mirrors and highly ornamental tables and chairs. The Ginzbergs had a large staff of domestics, chosen with an eye to their good looks, and kept open house. Their guests often included Gentile neighbors and traveling government officials, as well as rabbis and alms-collecting com·

munal workers, whose appeals for charity never went
unanswered. One neighbor with whom they were on terms
of friendship was Count Ignatiev, later the inspirer of the
notorious May Laws of 1882, in which the anti-Jewish legis-
lation of tsarist Russia reached its climax. Isaiah Ginzberg
himself used to spend two or three months every summer
at one or another of the fashionable watering-places abroad;
his wife paid frequent visits to Skvira, where she was Lady
Bountiful to her poor relations and many others, and spent
some of her time in Kiev and Odessa, where she was able
to indulge her taste for finery.

The relation of the family to their staff and the villagers
was almost patriarchal, and they were looked up to with a
respect and affection such as few Jewish farmers of estates
enjoyed. Even in 1881, when the Russian pogroms were in
spate, and Isaiah removed his household to Brody in Galicia
for safety, he himself was able to return to his village without apprehension, and found the inhabitants deeply hurt by
the lack of confidence in them which he had shown by
evacuating his family. (It seems odd that Asher makes no
allusion to this evacuation in his *Reminiscences,* though he
mentions having been in Brody in the winter of 1881-2 when
on his way to Vienna in search of a University education.)

From Dr. Shimkin's booklet we learn something about
her relations, and hear in particular of an uncle with some
artistic gift, which of course remained uncultivated, and a
cousin, a tall, handsome girl, who wept bitter tears when
she had to sacrifice her luxuriant black hair, in conformity
with custom, before her wedding. The booklet also tells of
its author's early education—how she and a girl cousin had
lessons, commencing at the age of five, from eight in the
morning till seven in the evening on six days a week, when
they would far rather have been playing in the garden with
the numerous dogs belonging to the estate. And there are
one or two glimpses of Asher himself in his boyhood and
adolescence. He had a bedroom and a study of his own in

the large house, with a wide balcony overlooking the garden, and the study lined with bookcases overflowing with the books which were his main interest in life. Even in those early days he had the habit, which he retained in manhood, of rising frequently from his seat at the desk and pacing the room for a while, deep in thought. And in the evening he would be visited by two young friends, employees of his father, with whom he would spend many hours discussing the books he had been reading. (He himself mentions these two friends with affection in the *Reminiscences,* as young men of good education, whose society was his one relief from boredom.) An earlier incident recorded by Dr. Shimkin reveals his deep attachment to his sister Hannah. Their mother used to tell how on one occasion, when he was ten years old, he came home from *heder* and found little Hannah with her hair afire, whereupon, without any fear or hesitation, he ran to her and started to put out the flames with his hands. (This Hannah, who died in Odessa in 1921, grew up to an irregular life of adventure, and was estranged from her family, but was apparently supported by her brother in her last years.) And finally, we learn from Dr. Shimkin that as a youth he was fond of swimming, and that when he was fifteen he got into difficulties while swimming in the river, and would have lost his life if he had not been pulled out by a faithful and intelligent dog.

Life at "the court" was governed strictly by the Jewish tradition, and the visits of the Russian nobility and gentry were not allowed to interfere with the most punctilious observance of the ritual and ceremonial law. The house was remarkable, perhaps even unique, in its combination of rigid Jewish traditionalism with upper-class Russian taste and elegance, and as a point of friendly contact between two worlds built upon entirely different and even antithetic philosophies. The contrast between the two is graphically illustrated by an incident recorded in the *Reminiscences.* Once an important government official stayed the night with the

Ginzbergs, and, as the guest-room which he occupied was
next to young Asher's room, heard the voice of the lad having his Talmud lesson. He asked Isaiah what it was that he
had heard, and was told that it was his host's son learning
the Talmud, and that the boy was very gifted and would
one day, his father hoped, be a rabbi. Thereupon the official said: "If he is so gifted, why do you keep him here and
teach him this old-fashioned stuff? Why don't you send him
to a big city, where he will be able to study at high school
and university and become a real scholar?" When Isaiah
subsequently recounted this to some of his Jewish friends, in
Asher's hearing, he did not say how he had answered the
official's question, but concluded his recital with the words:
"Now go and explain a thing like this to a *goy!*"

Such was the environment, strangely compounded of
disparate elements, in which the future philosopher of
Zionism spent his youth and early manhood. It left its impress on his mind and character. Despite the completeness of
his later revulsion from Hasidism and its beliefs and super-
stitions, the intense piety and patriotism of the hasid reap-
pear, however transmuted, in his almost mystical faith in
the Jewish people, its unique character, and its indissoluble
connection with its ancient homeland. On the other hand,
the easy material circumstances to which he was accustomed
in his early life, so startingly different from the grinding
poverty and squalor of the Lithuanian and Polish ghettoes
in which most of his contemporaries in Hebrew literature
were born and grew up, and the habit of meeting cultured
and well-born non-Jews on equal terms, no doubt contributed to the development of some of the characteristics
which set him apart—his aristocratic morality and independence of mind, his fastidiousness, his regard for form
and style, his rooted dislike of anything vulgar or shabby,
and his strong sense of human dignity.

Although, as has been indicated, the *Reminiscences* say
little about the young Asher's emotional reactions to his sur-

roundings, they leave no doubt that his childhood was not a happy one. He says explicitly that life at home was not pleasant, and he was glad when he was able to spend some time elsewhere. His father, he tells us, was hot-tempered and very exacting, and made things uncomfortable for the children. His mother, too, was sharp-tongued, though not to the same degree. It was his father's custom to examine him every Saturday, after his afternoon sleep, on what he had learned during the week, and the examination invariably ended with his having his ears boxed, with or without reason, whereupon his mother would angrily protest. He also blames his parents for their vanity and snobbishness. But his most serious complaint is of his father's habit of belittling his knowledge and abilities, instead of giving him the encouragement which so diffident a boy badly needed. This seemed to him in retrospect to have been a major cause of the lack of self-confidence which hampered him in practical affairs all his life.

He says not a word about how he felt towards his parents in his boyhood, and there is nothing to suggest that he ever showed active resentment of their behavior towards him. He seems to have been a dutiful son, who always bowed to the wishes of his parents and did not willfully wound or displease them. But there is no evidence of any warmth of filial affection on his part. His attachment to his sister Hannah shows that he was not incapable of affection; but his parents do not seem to have invited or encouraged it, and it is probable that even as a child he was largely shut up in himself. He had no brother, and he lost all his playmates at the age of twelve, when his family moved to Gopitshitza. There, on the great estate, he "had no companions and took part in no childish games," as he laconically puts it. There can be little doubt that he was emotionally starved, and that what may be assumed to have been a congenital inability to "let himself go" was thereby intensified.

❧ 3 ❧

The beauties of Gopitshitza evidently made much less impression on him than on his sister. This is what he writes in the *Reminiscences:*

> Though I spent the best part of my youth in a village, I did not acquire any love of nature. We lived in a large house (formerly occupied by the owner of the estate), which had many large rooms and was surrounded by a large garden going down to the river which passed through the village. But I was occupied with books and study, and paid no attention to the beauties of nature. I did not learn even to ride a horse properly. My only contact with nature was that I used often to walk in the village cornfields.

He was an exceptionally clever and precocious boy, with no interest outside his studies. As a child he had been fond of reading romances, and he records having shed copious tears over those of Kalman Shulman (1819-1899), one of the most distinguished of the early Haskalah writers, including his Hebrew translation of Eugène Sue's *Mystères de Paris;* but there is nothing to indicate that his love of light literature outlasted his childhood.

He had already shown a marked aptitude for talmudic studies, which no doubt encouraged his father in the hope that he would in due course fulfill the most cherished paternal ambition of the traditional Jew by becoming a rabbi. That hope, however, cannot have been other than short-lived, for at an early age the boy exhibited signs of a disposition to think for himself; and he broke away from Hasidism at about the time of the move to Gopitshitza.

The immediate occasion of the breach, paradoxically enough, was his one and only visit to the headquarters of the hasidic group to which his father belonged, that which owed allegiance to R. Abraham Jacob of Sadigura (a Galician village), a son of the famous Tsaddik of Rozhin. The boy had of course been brought up to reverence this holy man as a kind of near-divinity; and when the time approached for him to become *bar-mitzvah,* his father wished him to obtain the rabbi's blessing and spiritual counsel, hoping perhaps that these might help to nip his heretical tendencies in the bud. So when Isaiah went to Sadigura for the Feast of Tabernacles, in the year 1868, he took Asher with him.

The result disappointed whatever expectations the father may have had. Asher was, indeed, greatly impressed by the Tsaddik himself, who was a man of striking presence and personality (and who, it was currently believed, wiped his hand on his long coat after it had touched that of the young heretic). But it so happened that once during the week of their stay his father and he ate in the *sukkah* with a crowd of the smaller fry, among whom were the Tsaddik's eldest son and one of his sons-in-law; and here, to the boy's disgust, the assembled company was regaled by an old Galician Jew with a string of crudely indecent stories, which were received with acclamation. Then all of a sudden somebody called upon a well-known *hazzan* who was present to sing a religious hymn, and this was done in an atmosphere of intense devotion. The abrupt alternation between lewd vulgarity and religious fervor made a highly disagreeable impression on the sensitive boy, and set the seal on his rejection of Hasidism. He became, at the early age of twelve, a mithnagged, applied himself with greater zeal than ever to study of the Bible and medieval Hebrew literature, on which he had embarked even before the visit to Sadigura, and began to observe scrupulously certain *mitzvoth* to which hasidim attached no importance (such as praying at set times). He was especially attracted by the works of the medieval Jewish philosophers, which he studied with great assiduity, and was profoundly influenced by the lucid and logical mind of the great Maimonides, to whom in later life he paid tribute, in one of his most notable essays, as the champion of "the supremacy of reason." Studies of this kind were anathema to the pious hasidim, and he used to have arguments with some of the more courageous of his father's acquaintances— the general run of them did not venture to question the heresies, however pernicious, of the rich man's son—about "external" studies and their relation to the Torah. These discussions, in which he pitted quotations from Maimonides, Ibn-Ezra and other philosophers against those of his adversaries from the dicta of ancient Sages and modern hasidic teachers, sometimes went on all through the night, of course without effect on the opinions of any of the disputants.

But his bent towards intellectual freedom was not satisfied for long by the successful assertion of his right to extend his reading beyond the limits prescribed by hasidic zealotry. The thirst for wider knowledge, which had impelled him as a child to seek to learn the Russian alphabet and algebra, soon drove him into even more reprehensible adventures of the spirit, and from a mere mithnagged he became a maskil, for whom hasidim and mithnaggedim alike were reactionaries, and the differences between them shrank into insignificance beside the gulf that separated the children of Enlightenment from the children of darkness. He had to cultivate his interest in Haskalah literature alone, for there were no maskilim in the benighted village, which he left but rarely, and he was condemned to live in virtual isolation in a world of his own, with practically nobody to whom he could confide his thoughts and aspirations. The only congenial spirit of whom we hear in the *Reminiscences* was one Shalom Rapoport, a maskil of a neighboring townlet, who used to visit his father on business, and of whom he speaks in most appreciative terms.

Isaiah Ginzberg was not so bigoted an enemy of Haskalah and its literature as many other hasidim were—he enjoyed reading Haskalah works of the more serious kind,

like Shulman's *Universal History*—and he made no attempt
at active interference with his son's new interest. Nonetheless, the extent to which Asher was able to indulge his
taste for secular reading was in practice governed by the
rather narrow limits of his father's tolerance: for Isaiah
threatened to remove his well-stocked library from Asher's
room, where it was kept, if Haskalah books of which he disapproved were placed on its shelves, and this threat was
sufficient to win from the boy a promise not to buy such
books. Asher had cause to repent of his promise not long
afterwards, when among the books carried by an itinerant
bookseller (of course there was no bookshop in the village)
he chanced to light on a copy of Isaac Erter's anti-hasidic
satire. *Ha-tsofeh l'veth Israel,* which is one of the classics of
Haskalah literature, and found the temptation to buy it ir-
resistible. Having succumbed, he got out of what might
have been an awkward situation by reading the book right
through in bed that same night, and committing it to the
flames as soon as his bedroom fire was lit in the morning.

Premonitions of his future literary career were not entirely lacking in his early years. As a boy, he tells us, he
did not limit himself to writing notes on the Talmud and
Responsa, but used to compose homilies in the style of the
Akedath Yitzhak, a medieval Hebrew commentary on the
Pentateuch, partly philosophical and partly homiletical in
character, by which he was profoundly impressed. At a later
stage he followed the fashion set by so many maskilim, and
tried his hand at lyric poems. These, however, he never had
the courage to submit to any editor for publication, but kept
to himself and ultimately destroyed, thereby, as he puts it,
making sure that his old age would not have to blush for
the follies of his youth.

❧ 4 ❧

By the age of fifteen, if not earlier, the process of his intellectual emancipation was complete: he had made the journey from implicit acceptance of the doctrine and practice of Hasidism, through the less anti-rational position of the mithnagged, to full freedom of thought. The process had not, however, been accompanied by any overt revolt against the traditional way of life, or any outspoken assault on the traditional pattern of thought. He had remained rooted in the paternal home, and outwardly obedient to its rigorous code; nor, so far as we are aware, did he find any difficulty in the combination of theoretical dissent with practical conformity. His development had been syncretistic: it had not proceeded by a series of stages, each of which had to be abandoned in turn in order that the next might be reached, but rather by the superimposition on one another of a series of different points of view, not all mutually consistent, which by some alchemy of his own he was able to fuse into a single amalgam. At the end of the journey he would have been not less aptly described as a freethinking hasid than as an ex-hasid freethinker.

Thus, while his intellectual horizon was widening, and his appetite for European culture was becoming ever sharper and more insistent, he continued to give most of his time to the study of the Talmud and Responsa, for which he had a private tutor until he was fifteen. He became, like his father before him, an *ilui,* a prodigy of talmudic learning. He was especially expert in the law of the *agunah* (deserted wife), and knew all the Responsa on that subject: and having a boyish ambition to correspond with the greatest rabbi of the day, he concocted a case about an imaginary *agunah,* involving complicated legal questions, wrote a long and learned judgment on it, and sent the case and the judgment to Rabbi Joseph Saul Nathanson of Lemberg, one of the greatest talmudists then living, for his concurrence. The un-suspecting rabbi took Asher's communication at its face value, and replied as one authority to another. This naturally made a great impression on the scholars and rabbis of Asher's neighborhood. They took to consulting the boy on cases involving the law of the *agunah;* and a couple of years after his first letter to the Lemberg rabbi one of them asked him to submit a general case to the same authority. This he did, and again received a reply, which is said to be included in one of the published collections of the Lemberg rabbi's Responsa.

In his sixteenth or seventeenth year, he writes in the *Reminiscences,* when he already had a reputation for rab-binic scholarship, his parents arranged a great feast, accord-ing to custom, to celebrate his completion of the study of the Talmud. By that time he had been betrothed for over a year, and was soon to be married.

Naturally a youth of such brilliant attainments, and of a well-to-do family to boot, was a highly desirable son-in-law, and since his boyhood there had been no lack of compe-tition for such a prize among parents of eligible daughters. When he was fourteen, and his parents felt that it was time for his future to be settled, there were effectively two candi-dates in the field: one the daughter of a man of wealth but no learning, the other the orphaned and dowerless child of the learned hasidic Rabbi of Zhitomir, and a connection of the very distinguished Shneerson family. Asher was required by his parents to choose between these two young ladies, neither of whom was personally known either to them or to him; and his tutor was commissioned to ascertain his views.

For the young man the question was somewhat embar-rassing. He did not want to marry into a pious rabbi's fam-ily, and on that ground would have much preferred the rich man's daughter; but he could scarcely avow the real reason for his choice. At the same time, he did not wish his par-ents to think that he rejected the poor girl for mercenary reasons. So, according to the *Reminiscences,* he avoided giving his tutor a plain answer, and wrapped up his reply in a cryptic talmudic allusion. A well-known passage in the Talmud says: "A man should sell all that he has and take to wife a scholar's daughter"; but a less familiar version substitutes for the last words "and get him shoes for his feet." Asher replied to the fateful question: "A man should sell all that he has, *et cetera,*" meaning to suggest that the existence of two versions of the dictum showed how little importance the Sages attached to marrying a scholar's daughter. This, however, was evidently too subtle for the tutor, who not unnaturally assumed that he was expected to complete the quotation by the more familiar of the two endings, and that the penniless orphan girl was chosen. He reported accordingly to Asher's parents, who worshiped *yihus,* and were overjoyed at the prospect of an alliance with so illustrious a family. In the earlier section of the *Reminiscences* we are told that they did not even think it necessary to go or to send somebody to the distant home of the bride-to-be in order to make sure that she was not blind or deformed; but his sister has a different story, which is confirmed, with some variations, in the later section of the *Reminiscences.* She says that an emissary was in fact sent, without Asher's knowledge, to make the necessary inquiries, and was told, after expressing unqualified approval of the young lady submitted for his inspection, that the actual bride-elect had a cold and could not be seen, but was even more well-favored than this her cousin.

In any case, Asher had to take his future wife on trust; and when they met under the bridal canopy—which was not until two years later, two months before his seventeenth birthday, because the bride's family would not agree to an earlier marriage—he found that he had not fared too badly. "The bride," he writes in the *Reminiscences,* "was neither blind nor deformed, but was a simple Jewish girl, who had had a good religious upbringing, and knew her evening, morning and afternoon prayers and the other things that a Jewish girl has to know. And what more could one want?" He criticizes his parents severely for their vanity and love of showing off, which, he says, frequently caused him embarrassment in his later life; but he has to admit that on this occasion the luck was on his side.

The *Reminiscences* say not a word more on the subject of his marriage or his feelings about it, but clearly he must have regarded it with anything but enthusiasm. There is no mistaking the irony and the suggestion of passive hostility in the words just quoted. The old unromantic Jewish practice of marrying off boys and girls who met for the first time under the bridal canopy no doubt justified itself in practice from the point of view of the stability of family life; but it was unlikely to produce, except by a fortunate accident, the kind of ideal union in which the intimate partnership of husband and wife extends beyond the joint domestic concerns into the realm of the mind and the spirit. Asher Ginzberg was denied that supreme good fortune, and his marriage, though not in the ordinary sense a failure, did not bring him great happiness. His wife, who was his junior by five months, was petite and good-looking, and lacked neither intelligence nor good taste. She kept house for him, ministered to his creature comforts, watched over his health so far as he would allow, and was a good mother to their three children,[2] (in whom he himself began to take an affectionate interest as they emerged from childhood). He on his side gave her no reason to complain of neglect or serious lack of consideration, and she had no rival in his affections, despite his platonic friendship with a handsome and cultured lady who was the wife of one of his close friends in Odessa. But they lived on two different planes. Mrs. Ginzberg was assumed by her husband to be incapable of sharing his deepest interests and playing a part in his work for the Jewish people. It is possible that he took too low a view of her capacities, and that with encouragement and help the "simple Jewish girl" might have been able to take an effective interest in the ideas and problems which occupied his mind. He records with gratitude in his *Reminiscences* that at an early stage in their married life, when he had to fight for freedom to continue his pursuit of western culture, she stood by him and helped him to win his battle. There is, however, no evidence that he ever turned this promising gesture to account by making a serious attempt to broaden her horizon. He was too apt to acquiesce in an unsatisfactory situation, which a man with greater self-confidence and a more optimistic temperament would have made up his mind to change for the better; and it would be like him to resign himself to having a wife from whom he could not expect understanding or intellectual companionship, finding what comfort he could in the reflection that things might have turned out much worse. But his marriage must be supposed to have sharpened, instead of softening, the sense of spiritual loneliness by which he was oppressed and handicapped all through his life.

Two or three months after the wedding, which took place in the bride's home town, the young couple traveled to Gopitshitza and took up their abode with Asher's parents. The circle in which his wife had been brought up was so ultra-pious that even her new home did not come fully up to her standards in some of the subtler refinements of observance; and he was not loath to escape from an atmosphere so uncongenial. But he could not decently maintain a refusal to pay a visit to the village of Tcherkassi to see his wife's paternal grandfather, a celebrated Tsaddik, whose advanced age had prevented him from attending the wedding; and during this visit an odd thing happened, which many years later he thought worthy of record in his *Reminiscences*. The Tsaddik being too old to preside at the Sabbath meal, his place was to be taken on this particular Sabbath by one of his grandsons, who himself afterwards became a Tsaddik;

but the substitute had an accident, which confined him to bed for some days, and it fell to the young Ginzberg to fill the vacant place. So he became for once in his life an acting Tsaddik; and, although his defection from Hasidism was notorious, the assembled devotees nonetheless went through the normal ritual of snatching bits of food from the dish which the Tsaddik had hallowed by his touch. With his usual reticence, he states the facts without comment in the *Reminiscences,* and we are left to guess whether he undertook a function for which he was so unsuited because he was too polite to refuse, or out of a nostalgic attachment to Hasidism. There may be a measure of truth in both theories.

Back in the paternal home, the young man resumed the way of life which had been interrupted for a brief space by his wedding. He had become more and more unhappy at home, and now longed to get away; but at that time, and for many years to come, there was for him no possibility of escape from the "furnace of iron," as he afterwards called it, borrowing an expressive phrase used in the Bible to describe Egyptian bondage. Had he been of an adventurous spirit, he might conceivably have taken his courage in both hands and gone forth into the world with his young wife, to sink or swim; but he was not of those who leap without careful looking. He had not been trained to stand on his own feet; and, what is not less important, he had a very strong sense of duty, and was constitutionally incapable of willingly inflicting pain on those near and dear to him, or of insisting on having his own way in their despite. His parents would certainly have resisted strenuously any suggestion that as a married man he ought to be allowed to set up house for himself; and from a practical point of view his flight from the parental home would have been highly inconvenient, because his father's health necessitated an annual visit to Baden-Baden or some other watering-place, and during his absence it fell to his only son to manage the various undertakings connected with the estate—cultivation of the land, manufacture of spirits, forestry, cattle-breeding and the rest. We are not told how the young recluse had acquired the necessary knowledge and ability, and it must be assumed that he had inherited the practical bent which had enabled his father to become the successful administrator of a large estate.

It was in the early years of his married life, according to the *Reminiscences,* that the "critical and analytical spirit" with which nature had endowed him awoke to full life, and played havoc with his spiritual world. He gave much of his time to the study of religion in all its aspects, and the result was—though he does not state this in so many words—that he became an agnostic. He now devoted himself largely to non-Jewish studies. He mastered Russian and German, and read whatever came to his hand in the literatures of both languages. The haphazard character of his reading, and his exceptional memory, are attested by a footnote in the *Reminiscences,* according to which, when passing through the town of Zhitomir in 1873 or 1874, he dropped into a bookshop to buy Hebrew books, and happened on one or two volumes of the Minutes of the St. Petersburg Academy of Science. He acquired these for use as a textbook of the Russian language and read them so often, and with such concentration, that he knew almost by heart as much of them as he could understand.

In time, he became less omnivorous and more selective in his reading. Following his natural inclination, he concentrated on humanistic subjects, especially history, literature and philosophy, with emphasis on psychology and sociology rather than on abstract metaphysics, for which he had no taste. The positivist philosophy which was in vogue in Russia at that time, and was among the most powerful of the non-Jewish influences that contributed to the shaping of his general outlook on life, blended somewhat uncomfortably with the fundamental Jewishness of his spiritual make-up.

The blending was easier in the case of the British moralists, by whom also, as by British empirical philosophy in general, his thinking was so deeply influenced. His first acquaintance with them was made through German translations of their works; it was only later, when he had left the village and was in his thirties, that he learned English and French. His reading in the field of *belles-lettres,* in which he must have lost interest quite early in life, did not go beyond a few standard writers, like Schiller and Goethe.

It has already been said that Asher appears to have done very little traveling so long as he lived with his parents at Gopitshitza. He records his first visit to Warsaw at the age of twenty-two, when he could not resist a strong desire to become acquainted with the maskilim of that town, which was one of the principal centers of the Haskalah movement, and especially with the aged A. B. Gottlober (1811-1899), one of the most noteworthy of the Hebrew writers of the time. Gottlober was editor of a Hebrew monthly, *The Light of Dawn,* to which Asher was a subscriber. Apparently his father did not object to his bringing Gottlober's paper into the house, in spite of its editor's heretical leanings, possibly because he had at one time taught in a rabbinical school; but in giving his son permission to go to Warsaw he stipulated that he was on no account to import *Hashahar,* "The Dawn," another and more famous Hebrew monthly edited by Peretz Smolenskin (1842-85), one of the pioneers of Jewish nationalism, who was regarded by the pious as the very fountainhead of heresy. This visit to Gottlober was for Asher a disillusioning experience, and helped to confirm him in a determination to desert the Hebrew literature of Haskalah, which was so largely imitative and second-hand, in order to become more thoroughly conversant with the European literature which was the authentic vehicle of modern thought and culture. He was shocked by the discovery that Gottlober edited his paper not in the spacious and

well-furnished editorial sanctum which his imagination had
pictured, but in a dark little attic with no furniture except
a rickety table, chair and bed not remarkable for their clean-
liness; and what survived of his enthusiasm for Haskalah,
which had long ceased to satisfy him, was further damped
by the supercilious attitude adopted by the Warsaw maskilim towards the unknown young man from the country.

In that same year, 1878, he visited Odessa for the first
time in his life, and there struck up an acquaintance with
another young man staying in the same hotel, who turned
out to be educated in the modern sense and well-read in
Russian literature. This chance encounter had momentous
consequences. Though painfully aware of his own lack of
secular education, Asher evidently made an impression on
the unnamed stranger, who after their first conversation
sought him out daily, had long discussions with him, and
introduced him to the critical essays of the positivist philosopher Pisarev, who was then the idol of the young Russian *intelligentsia*. Asher was greatly taken with Pisarev's
ideas, and thought them the acme of that broad culture for
which his soul was athirst. He returned to Odessa fired by
a new and revolutionary resolve: though already in his
twenty-third year, and a married man, he would master the
subjects covered by the high school curriculum, and thereby
qualify for a university education.
    He lost no time in embarking on this rather utopian
scheme. Actual attendance at a *gymnasium* being out of the
question, he had to set about acquiring the necessary school-
boy knowledge by himself, without the aid of a teacher, or
even of a fellow-student. He applied himself, unaided, to the
study of Latin, mathematics and other high school subjects,
and profited at least to the extent of being able to understand and enjoy Latin literature. He was, however, too
grown-up to be able to stomach the mass of intrinsically unimportant details with which grammar school pupils have

to be stuffed in order to pass their examinations; and he had to abandon the idea of matriculation at a Russian university.

He began to think, instead, of the possibility of attending a foreign university, entrance to which might not necessitate so much school-boy knowledge. Realization of this plan had to be postponed for various reasons. His wife had a long illness after the birth of their first child, Leah, in September, 1879; in the following summer his father went abroad, as was his wont, for a cure; and then, in 1881, came the avalanche of Russian pogroms, which burst the bubble of his Haskalah ideology and forced him to re-examine first principles. This was no time for thinking about going to a university; and by the time he had recovered from the shock, there were other (unspecified) private reasons which made it impossible for him to leave his father and the family affairs. So it was not until the winter of 1881-2, when he was twenty-five years of age, that he could attempt to carry out his design. His parents would of course have forbidden him to leave home if he had avowed his real purpose, and he allowed himself to deviate from the truth so far as to say that he was going abroad for six months to improve his knowledge of foreign languages. Having obtained their consent, not without great difficulty, he left for Vienna.

He returned home, defeated, after two or three weeks. His defeat was due to his own lack of self-confidence and of the touch of hardness without which a son cannot deliberately wound his parents. There is nothing to suggest that he had any strong emotional attachment to his father and mother; but he was a dutiful son, and the reproachful letters which he received from home while in Vienna confronted him with the prospect of a constant tug-of-war, for which he had no stomach. Thus predisposed against continuing on the course on which he had embarked after so many postponements, he was able to persuade himself that the objective difficulties in his way were really serious. How could

he, who had never before been thrown on his own resources, and had scarcely even been away from home, live
for years in a strange city, alone and friendless, far from
his young wife and child and all his kith and kin, and
study at the university along with a pack of boys? He could
not, he felt sure, go through with the thing to the bitter end;
and it would be more sensible not to begin at all than to
begin and then give up after six months or so. Back to
Gopitshitza, then, he went.

However, the desire for a university education had become too much of an obsession to be abandoned. His dislike
of the village life, with its complete intellectual barrenness,
had become a positive loathing, and he felt that at all costs
he must escape. So he began to believe that what had driven
him from Vienna was the uncongeniality of that gay city
itself, rather than anything in his own character or circumstances. During the following year or two he went to Breslau, to Berlin, to Vienna again, and to Leipzig in search of
university education; but on each occasion the experience
of the first attempt was repeated. Finally he renounced his
ambition, resigned himself to remaining a self-taught man,
and devoted himself more intensely than ever to his lonely
studies.

These frustrations exacted a fearful toll of spiritual agony,
and the result was a pathetic disparity between the ease of
his external circumstances and the unrest and unhappiness
of his inner life. Thus he writes in the earliest section of
his *Reminiscences:*

Those years [*i.e.,* 1882-3] were the worst years of my life.
The unending struggle within and without, the advances
and retreats, my hatred of the conditions in which I lived,
and my inability to carve out for myself a path suited to
my character and way of thinking—all this overwhelmed
me, embittered my life, and plunged me into the depths
of misery. I had no peace of mind by day or night; I went
about like a ghost, wrapped up in my thoughts and im-

aginings, with nobody to whom I could pour out my heart, nobody who might help me in any way out of my perplexity. All the other members of the household enjoyed the good things of life, and were always happy and cheerful; I alone was wretched in the midst of all this wealth and prosperity, and nobody worried about me. For how could Jews who were practical men of affairs understand that it was possible for the only son of rich parents to suppose himself unhappy and carry a load of grief in his heart, when he had plenty of money and lacked for nothing?

This emotional outburst, to which there are few parallels in the generally matter-of-fact *Reminiscences,* is eloquent of the sufferings endured by the frustrated young man, and of the indelible impression they left on his mind. His bitterness was no doubt all the more intense because he thought, not apparently without justice, that his father was in part responsible for the weakness of will and lack of self-confidence which not only defeated his efforts to obtain a university education, but also hampered him on many occasions in his later life. As we have seen, he did not get from his father the encouragement and stimulus which a youth of his temperament needed so badly to counteract his tendency to skepticism and an unduly pessimistic appraisal of the possibilities of a given situation. Had he been born of a poor family, he would have been compelled by the harsh taskmaster of economic need to develop more self-reliance; but as things were, he had no incentive to try to overcome his natural weakness. He realized all this clearly on reflection, and set it down dispassionately in his *Reminiscences.*

2

ESCAPE
TO
ODESSA

The final abandonment of his university ambitions robbed the unhappy young man of his last defense against the feeling of complete frustration, and made life in the benighted village no longer tolerable. He resolved to gain his freedom at all costs: he would move to one of the big cities, where he could live by commerce and enjoy the society of cultured people. This decision cost him another battle with his parents; but he stuck to his guns, and in the spring of 1884 took his wife and their small child to Odessa. As it turned out, their stay there was of brief duration, because a few months later he was compelled for private reasons to return to the village, where he remained for nearly two years longer before his final emancipation.

The *Reminiscences* give no hint of the nature of the private reasons which compelled his return, nor do they say anything about his efforts to establish himself in business in Odessa. The two paragraphs in which he writes about this first escape deal solely with the ampler facilities for study that Odessa afforded him, and with his first contacts with the maskilim and the early Zionists in that great center of Hebrew literature and the Jewish national movement. He tells us that he quickly acquired sufficient knowledge of the English and French languages to be able to read their literatures, and also began to take an active interest in the movement for settling Jews on the land in Palestine, which went by the name of Hibbath Zion, "Love of Zion," and to which he had felt drawn for some time past. He became a member of the Central Committee of the Lovers of Zion (Hovevé Zion) which was set up in that year (1884) under the presidency of Dr. Leo Pinsker, the Odessa physician who two years earlier had advocated the idea of a Jewish State in his now famous brochure *Auto-Emanzipation;* and although at first the natural diffidence of a young man from the country restrained him from venturing to express an opinion in so august an assembly, he gained courage in time, discovered that even city-bred folk could propound views which were open to challenge, and became a regular and effective contributor to the Committee's discussions. This was a time of feverish activity in preparation for the Kattowitz Convention of 1884, which became a landmark in the history of the Hibbath Zion movement, and we are told of the clash of opinions about the presidential address which was to be delivered by Pinsker. For tactical reasons he was inclined to stress the humanitarian aspect of the Jewish colonization of Palestine, whereas Ginzberg and others favored a more outspoken avowal of its national aims. The protracted debates ended in a compromise satisfactory to neither side.

There is no record of anything that happened during the last two years of Asher's life in the village, except for the birth of his second daughter, Rachel, on July 7, 1885 (24th Tammuz, 5645). The final exodus from the village involved the whole Ginzberg establishment, and was due to circumstances beyond control. Isaiah's lease of the Rzhevutski estate expired in 1886, and as the May Laws of 1882 forbade the leasing of estates to Jews, it could not be renewed in ordinary course. An exception in favor of Isaiah could have been secured through his friendship with Count Ignatiev; but Asher, whose opinion was by this time treated with great deference by all those about him, objected to deriving advantage over other Jews through what we should now call *protektsia,* and so there was nothing for it but to give up the lease and leave the village. His father, who had become attached to life on the land, would have liked to settle in Palestine and take up farming there; but Asher insisted that if they went to Palestine they must become real farmers, not just employers of agricultural laborers, and as that condition could not be fulfilled, the plan was abandoned. Isaiah moved to Odessa with his wife and daughter; Asher and his family remained a short time longer in the village, which they left for Berditchev at the beginning of March, 1886. After about three months there they, too, settled down in Odessa, where Asher was able to take up again the interrupted thread of his Zionist interests and work.

The final escape from Gopitshitza is the occasion for another of those rare examples of self-revelation in the *Reminiscences:*

> So at last came the hour of my escape from that furnace of iron, in which I had spent eighteen years, the best years of my youth, and which had eaten me up and destroyed whatever of worth nature had endowed me with when I was born. I entered it as a boy of twelve, and left it as a man of thirty, with a wife and children; I entered it pure of soul and full of hope, and left it with despair in my soul and a heart torn and weary.

We do not know exactly when this was written, but certainly it was not until some years after he had settled in Odessa, by which time he should have been able to look back on his village life with some degree of detachment. Yet he writes as though his wounds were still fresh, and in terms which, in the light of his subsequent career and achievements, seem grossly exaggerated, to say the least. It may be that there was, apart from his spiritual isolation and the disappointment of his university hopes, some specific reason for his bitterness, at which he does not even hint in his autobiographical notes.

Certainly, whatever cause he may have had for a feeling of frustration and of opportunities irreparably lost, his eighteen years in Gopitshitza had been far from wasted. His intensive study of the Talmud and rabbinic literature had qualified him to achieve distincton as a talmudist if he had had ambitions of that kind. To his proficiency in the studies approved by orthodoxy of the most rigid type he had added a thorough knowledge of the "forbidden" literature of medieval Jewish philosophy. He had devoted much more time than a great many talmudists do to the Bible and Hebrew grammar, and had studied the Hebrew and German works of the pioneers of *Jüdische Wissenschaft,* or the application of modern methods of inquiry and research to the study of the Jewish past. He had read widely outside the Jewish field, devoting particular attention to moral philosophy, psychology, history and sociology. He had studied and assimilated the positivism of Comte as presented by Russian thinkers like Pisarev, and (as yet only in translation) the metaphysical and ethical ideas of the British moralists, and of the British empirical philosophers from Locke and Hume to John Stuart Mill and Huxley. His essentially philosophic mind had digested and co-ordinated a heterogeneous mass of knowledge acquired in the process of self-education. Above all, he had formed definite views on the major problems of the Jewish people at a time which he rightly discerned to be a turning-point in its history, and had reached the conviction that its paramount need was for reunion, both spiritual and physical, with its historic land.

Thus, when he settled in Odessa, towards the end of his thirtieth year, he was well on the way to being fully equipped for the great work that lay before him. In Odessa he gave much time to his English and French reading, and studied the French psychological sociologists—Taine, Paulhan and others—before being launched on his literary career, almost accidentally, by an external stimulus such as

his lack of self-confidence made essential if he was ever to
come out of his shell.

❧ 2 ❧

At this point, on the threshold of his Odessa period, it
will be convenient to glance at a remarkable document in
which some account is obliquely given of the development
of his ideas on the problem of the Jewish future while he
was still immured in the "furnace of iron." The document
in question is a satire which seems to have been written in
or about 1886, though it did not see the light until 1890,
after he had sprung into sudden fame with the appearance,
under the pseudonym "Ahad Ha-Am," of his first article,
published in the spring of 1889. It derives a special interest
both from being markedly different from all his other published writings in character and manner, and from the
light it throws on his highly introspective and self-critical
habit of mind.

This satire, entitled *K'tavim balim,* which may be translated "A Discarded Old Manuscript," purports to be the
work of a Jewish shopkeeper (which is a euphemism for a
man whose wife keeps a shop while he himself studies or
goes about idle). It is a brief spiritual autobiography of one
who has been, but is no longer, a contributor to the Hebrew
press. Brought up as an observant hasid, he turned first
mithnagged and later maskil; but without entirely clearing
his system of either the hasid's religious yearnings or the
mithnagged's passion for rabbinic studies. Consequently,
when the itch to write seizes hold of him, he is at first restrained from taking up the pen by not knowing where he
really stands and to which party he belongs; but a book that
happens to come his way gives him the idea of dubbing himself "A lover of Israel," and so labeled he proceeds to write
articles for Hebrew papers on "The Solution of the Jewish
Problem." He is, however, compelled to change his ground

continually, because each of the solutions to which he successively pins his faith soon proves to be impracticable. He first advocates assimilation to non-Jewish manners and customs, and support of the recently established "Society for the Promotion of Agriculture among the Jews of Russia"; but the pogroms come and shatter that dream. His own shop is ransacked and his livelihood destroyed, and in his despair he becomes for a time an advocate of voluntary race-suicide, whether by the refusal of Jews to raise families, or by the less drastic method, which he afterwards prefers, of inter-marriage. But this solution too appears to be outside the realm of practical politics, and in any case the desire for Jewish survival reasserts itself. So our imaginary author swings round completely, and becomes a champion of the idea that the problem is to be solved by settlement on the land in Palestine.

He soon finds that this solution (which of course is that of Hibbath Zion) is in danger of breaking down in practice, because it lacks influential support; and he is reminded of a story told to him in his childhood. It is the story of Abraham the Fool, who was seen one day hurrying along with a stick in his hand, intending, as he told inquirers, to administer a thrashing to another man who had insulted him; but he desisted, and went back home, when a friend pointed out that the other man, being bigger and stronger, might thrash *him*. Certainly it is folly to plunge into an undertaking without giving any thought to the strength of the hostile forces which one may encounter. But in spite of all, the Palestine solution seems to be the only one left; and our author, despite his skepticism, tries to persuade himself that this may be a case in which the seemingly impossible can be attained. The people as a whole can do more than individuals. But suddenly the news comes that the Turkish Government will not permit Jewish settlement in Palestine. This is a crushing blow, not only because it makes the plan unworkable, but also because it suggests that the people

as a whole is no better than Abraham the Fool, seeing
that nobody took the trouble to clear up the most crucial
question before allowing so many hopes to be aroused and
so much enthusiasm to be worked up. So our author is reduced to despairing silence: and here the old manuscript
ends.

Ahad Ha-Am does not explicitly identify himself with
the imaginary author, and indeed often seems to be poking
fun at him; but there can be no doubt that the story told
in this satirical form is in substance that of his own early
development and of his wrestlings with the Jewish problem. (This is none the less true because it is possible to
regard the successive adoption and rejection of different
solutions of the problem as predicated of the Jews of Russia
as a body, or of the thinking element among them, rather
than of any individual.) Viewed in this light, the "discarded old manuscript" is a valuable supplement to the
little that we learn from his avowedly autobiographical
notes about his early life and growth. It graphically describes
the hasid-mithnagged-maskil progression through which,
as we know from the *Reminiscences,* he passed in his youth,
without ever completely discarding the old love when he
took up with the new. It adds point and meaning to the
bald statement in the *Reminiscences* that for some months
after the wave of pogroms in 1881 he was "like a man
stunned," that his "world began once more to totter," and
"once again a new theory began to take the place of one
that had been shattered." It suggests, what otherwise would
scarcely have been supposed, that in him too, as in Herzl
ten years later, the spark of Zionism was first kindled by
the sufferings of East-European Jewry, and that his discovery of the superior urgency of the spiritual problem, that
of the disintegration of the Jewish people and the atrophy
of Judaism, was subsequent to, and induced by, his realization that the economic problem could not be solved by mass

emigration from Europe to Palestine. It contains another surprise in the indication that among the solutions which he entertained at one time was that of voluntary race-suicide or wholesale intermarriage as possibly the only way out of an intolerable situation. Here again there is a parallel with Herzl, who, before his Zionist days, had conceived the idea of offering to lead a movement among the Jews for conversion to Christianity in return for a promise of the Pope's assistance in the fight against anti-Semitism.

When he published the satire (in a Hebrew annual called *The Beehive,* which he edited in 1890), Ahad Ha-Am provided it with a tail-piece which, alike in its irony and in its thinly-veiled self-criticism, is no less revealing than the satire itself. Times, he says in effect, have changed since this manuscript was composed, and its author has changed with the times. Among other things that experience has taught him, he has learned to regard Abraham the Fool in a different light. This Abraham is no longer for him a terrifying reminder of the hopeless folly of humanity; he has become the ideal figure of the practical man. Ahad Ha-Am's observation of life has led him, he tells us, to the conviction that so long as the fool is allowed to go his own way, and is not corrected by people wiser than himself, all is well. If Abraham had been permitted to go confidently forward, the probability is that his folly would have paid him, because his very self-confidence would have enabled him to achieve his object. And the conclusion is:

> We worship wisdom, but it is self-confidence that really matters. Wise men weigh the advantages of any course of action against its drawbacks, and move not an inch until they can see what the result of their action will be; but while they are deep in thought, the men with self-confidence "come and see and conquer."

Some time afterwards, when Ahad Ha-Am was widely known as the inflexible opponent of the happy-go-lucky

methods of the Hovevé Zion, and was always preaching the
folly of embarking on a practical undertaking without the
necessary knowledge and preparation, the passage just
quoted, with its virtual admission that faith may achieve
the apparently impossible, was thrown in his teeth by a
critic. His reply, to the effect that he had had in mind only
the confidence which springs from a determination to
overcome difficulties that are fully realized, is strangely un-
convincing, since the point of the apologue of Abraham
the Fool is that that worthy's faith was blind and unreflect-
ing. Ahad Ha-Am seems in fact to have hung his moral
on an inappropriate peg; but the moral itself was one in
which he thoroughly believed, and to which he attached
pivotal importance, notwithstanding his personal lack of the
robust optimism which may enable men to overcome the
most formidable obstacles.

❦ 3 ❦

Throughout the nineteenth century Odessa was one of
the most important centers of Jewish life in eastern Europe,
in the sense that its Jews were prominent in every movement designed to break down the barriers behind which
the Jewish masses maintained their distinctive type of life,
more or less completely unquickened and undistorted by
contact with European culture. From 1830 onwards it was
the home of many of the leading Haskalah writers; and
when the first Russian-language Jewish paper was founded,
in 1861, it was in Odessa that it was published. This paper,
the *Raszviet,* was assimilationist in tendency, but it had not
been long in existence before the first stirrings of Jewish
nationalism began to be felt, and again Odessa stood in the
van of the new movement of thought. It was for a few
years the home of Peretz Smolenskin, who became the first
great propagandist of the national idea in the columns of
his Hebrew monthly *Hashahar* ("The Dawn"), published

in Vienna; and it was in Odessa that Dr. Leo Pinsker, the
son of a Hebrew scholar and archaeologist of that city,
wrote in 1881, as already mentioned, the pamphlet in which
the plan of a Jewish State was sketched for the first time. It
was because the Jews of western Europe, to whom his plea
was addressed, showed no disposition to take up his revolutionary political idea that Pinsker threw himself into the
work of small-scale Palestinian colonization. The outbreak
of pogroms in Russia in 1881 having set in motion a wave
of emigration to Palestine (by the side of the much larger
one to America), and the numerous local emigration societies, which had sprung up all over Russia during the preceding decade, having decided to co-ordinate their activities
in a single organization, he became the first president of the
resulting Society of Hovevé Zion.

As an important Black Sea port, within comparatively
easy reach of Palestine, Odessa was ideally suited to be the
headquarters of this Society, and its Jews included a strong
nucleus of men who were capable of running the movement
under Pinsker's leadership. These men, who were to become Ahad Ha-Am's circle, were Jews of a type which
could not have come into existence except in such conditions as prevailed in the Russia of those days. They were
culturally assimilated to European standards, but, unlike the
contemporary Jews of western Europe and the United
States of America, they were not politically emancipated,
and the degree of their social integration into the non-
Jewish environment was small. Hence assimilation had not
seriously impaired the robust and spontaneous sense of
Jewishness implanted in them by their early upbringing and
education in wholly Jewish surroundings; and in so far as
they had opportunity and aptitude for public work, it was
natural for them to seek an outlet for their energies within
the ambit of Jewish life, which was not for them the life
of a confessional group. They varied widely in their individual attitudes to the religious tradition, but they had a

common interest in Zionist work, which for them included, as inseparable elements, both the organization of emigration to Palestine, and the promotion of Hebrew education and Hebrew literary activity in their own community.

For Asher Ginzberg the move from Gopitshitza to Odessa was the beginning of a new life. He had at last what he had so sorely missed during the long years of imprisonment in the village: unrestricted access to books, a congenial intellectual atmosphere, and associates with whom he could discuss the ideas and problems in which he was immersed. He continued his studies, with particular attention to English, French and Latin literature, and also renewed his active participation, begun during his brief stay in Odessa in 1884, in the work of the Central Committee of the Hovevé Zion. Though only an ordinary member of the Committee, with no official position, he made himself thoroughly conversant with all the details of its work, and for some years scarcely a day passed without his visiting its office. At the same time, he was laying the foundations of his future personal influence, not the less effectively because of the absence of design. His Hibbath Zion work brought him the friendship of a number of the more serious-minded adherents of the movement in Odessa, who were quick to recognize his exceptional gifts of mind and character; and he became the central figure and the inspirer of a group of young men who used to meet informally at his home for discussion of the affairs of Hibbath Zion. It was to the members of this group that he circulated the manuscript of his first article, when it came to be written, for comment and criticism before its publication, and from them were recruited the founding members of the Society of Sons of Moses, through which he and they made an unavailing attempt to lift the Hibbath Zion movement out of the slough of despond into which it had fallen for lack of vision and idealism.

These two crucial events in his career, his first appearance in print and the establishment of his Society, took
place, almost simultaneously, in the spring of 1889, nearly
three years after he had settled in Odessa; and neither was
due to his own initiative. In those early days he appears to
have had no sense of mission, and his shyness and lack of
self-confidence did not allow him to court public attention.
He seems to have remained unknown outside the circle of
his personal friends and colleagues, content to be a non-
entity, until an external stimulus forced him out of the
obscurity which, however congenial to his temperament,
was anomalous to the point of absurdity for a man of his
intellectual and moral stature and his burning zeal for his
beloved people.

✣ 4 ✣

His *Reminiscences* contain few references to his life after
he escaped from "the furnace of iron." One of them reads:

> We [*i.e.,* his father and himself] moved to Odessa in
> 1886, and there bought an oil plant and a distillery. We
> had also a wheat business in Odessa. But heaven did not
> prosper our affairs, and we went down and down. So
> things dragged on for some years, until the business went
> to pieces and we parted. My father moved to Kiev, where
> he had many business acquaintances, in search of a liveli-
> hood, and I turned to literature and went to Warsaw,
> where I became Director of Ahiasaf [a Hebrew publish-
> ing company].

The ill-success of the partnership in Odessa may well have
been partly due to the younger partner's lack of some of the
qualities that go to make a successful businessman. He had,
as we have seen, had some managerial experience on the
farm, and nobody could have been more precise and businesslike in his methods; but his very virtues were sometimes
a handicap. It is recorded that on one occasion a would-be

purchaser of a consignment of wheat, which was in some distant place, sought assurance that the wheat was dry, and he replied that he had not seen it himself, but was assured by those who had that it was in good condition. The intending customer, thinking that so lukewarm a testimonial from the vendor was suspicious, withdrew; and as there was a fall in the market price of wheat immediately afterwards, the Ginzbergs lost a considerable sum of money through Asher's scrupulous regard for the truth. Again, when their distillery was burnt down, in 1894, and Isaiah wanted to rebuild it with the insurance money, his son, who had never been happy at being engaged in an industry which promoted drunkenness, persuaded his father to invest the money in an oil refinery instead, the refining of oil being as clean and dignified an occupation as one could find, with honorable talmudic associations. Unfortunately this business did not go well; and when in 1895 the Ginzbergs faced ruin, Asher was less troubled by the prospect of poverty than by the fear that he might be unable to meet his debts. In course of time he succeeded in paying them all, and triumphantly announced to his father that he was free of debt. It mattered less to him that he had not a penny left.

There are indications in his published *Letters* that his lack of aptitude for trade was matched by his dislike for it; and he might have been expected to abandon commerce for a professional career at the earliest opportunity. With the appearance of his first published article in 1889, he was at once marked out as a Hebrew writer of quite exceptional quality; and obviously such a born student and thinker as he was would have been more usefully as well as more congenially occupied in writing and instructing public opinion than in buying and selling. In this matter, however, as in others, he was torn by conflicting inclinations, or inhibitions. The desire to escape from "the hateful world of business" was strong in him, but not strong enough to gain a decisive victory over his reluctance to degrade learning and the gift of writing by using them for the mundane object of earning a living. The talmudic injunction against "making the Torah a spade to dig with" had a very strong hold on him, for all his estrangement from religious orthodoxy; and writing was for him something in the nature of a sacred office, on no account to be undertaken except for the purpose of spreading the truth. When he took pen in hand he felt, as he wrote once to a correspondent, "like the High Priest ministering in the Holy of Holies." And to this quasi-religious attitude towards the writer's craft there was added a fiery independence of spirit, which could not brook the thought of being compelled to write when he had nothing in particular to say, or of having to trim the expression of his views to the taste of a Maecenas or of the reading public. Yet at times he felt the distaste for commerce so strongly as to be willing to contemplate the waiver of his objections to living by his pen instead of being merely (to use his own expression) "an occasional visitor to the shrine of literature"; and the result was a certain vacillation in his attitude, as now one and now the other of the two evils between which he had to choose was felt to be the less tolerable. But the evil of commerce had the advantage of being, so to speak, in possession; and he did not free himself from that thralldom until, after nearly ten years in Odessa, hard economic facts left him no alternative but to exchange it for the other.

3

THE
WRONG
WAY

The transmutation of Asher Ginzberg into Ahad Ha-Am came about through a chain of fortuitous events. In 1888 a Hebrew scholar and writer of great distinction in Vilna, Samuel Joseph Fuenn (1819-1891), celebrated the fiftieth year of his literary activity; and the maskilim of Odessa decided to send him a congratulatory address, of course in Hebrew. A number of the local littérateurs prepared drafts, and Ginzberg, who had not evinced any desire to write during his first two years in Odessa, was moved to try his hand. His draft was by common consent the best of those submitted. It was adopted, and was printed over his own name in *Hamélitz* ("The Advocate"), a Hebrew paper with Hibbath Zion sympathies, which was at that time appearing daily in St. Petersburg (now Leningrad), under the editorship of Alexander Zederbaum (1816-1893).

A short time afterwards he had another opportunity of using his literary gift. Zederbaum had fallen out with Judah Leib Gordon (1831-1892), the great poet and satirist of the pre-Zionist Haskalah, and the two were engaged in a highly undignified public exchange of personal abuse—a performance which unfortunately was not uncommon in Hebrew literary circles in those days. The Odessa maskilim decided to publish a protest against the two contestants for behaving in a manner so unworthy of themselves and of Hebrew literature; and they entrusted Ginzberg with its composition. It may be surmised that he had been among the most outspoken in condemnation of the erring writers, for discourtesy of any kind was abhorrent to him, and some years later another Hebrew writer, the well-known essayist and literary critic David Frischmann (1865-1922), sneeringly remarked of him that to hear an abusive expression made him "blush like a schoolgirl." His protest was duly published in the Hebrew monthly *Hamaggid,* over the signatures of a number of Odessa literary men, and was very well received by the reading public.

Not long after this, Zederbaum, on a visit to Odessa, was prompted by the local cognoscenti to approach the talented young writer for a contribution to his paper. His task cannot have been an easy one; but he persisted, and finally extracted a promise of an article from the reluctant Ginzberg. Two or three months later, in November, 1888, the promise was fulfilled by an article on Hibbath Zion policy under the title *Lo Zeh Haderekh,* "The Wrong Way,"[1] accompanied by a letter in which the author explained that he had almost despaired of being able to keep his word, because of business worries and lack of confidence, but in view of recent events in Palestine he could no longer withhold from the public certain views which he had long held, but had not had the courage to express hitherto. It might well be, he added, that Zederbaum and many others would disagree with these views; but he trusted nonetheless that the editor, aware of his genuine sympathy with the aims of Hibbath Zion, his great regard and respect for the leaders of the movement, and his close friendship with some of them, would publish his article at once.

The article did not have a smooth passage. It first ran into trouble with the Russian censor, who objected to certain expressions, and these had to be expunged or modified. Then part of it went astray in the censor's office, and there were other complications. Thus it was not till the spring of 1889 that the article actually appeared in *Hamélitz,* and

then, as a result of compliance with the requirements of
the censor, it was marred in parts by an obscurity which
was wholly uncharacteristic of its author even at that early
stage of his career. Before its appearance it had been shown
to and discussed with a number of its writer's closer associates in the movement. As already mentioned, it did not
bear his real name, but was signed "Ahad Ha-Am," to indicate, as he explains in his *Reminiscences,* that he was not
a regular writer, and had no intention of becoming one,
but was only expressing his views for once "as *one of the
people,* to whom the affairs of the people are a matter of
concern." The use of a pseudonym was also in accord with
his dislike of personal publicity and his desire to keep the
discussion of public affairs on an absolutely impersonal
plane. Under his assumed name he wrote for the rest of
his life, and it has become so completely identified with
him, not only as a writer but as a human being, that his real
name has fallen into disuse.

For a first attempt, *Lo Zeh Haderekh* reveals an extraordinary maturity and sureness of touch, and it contains in
germ the whole philosophy of Zionism which its author
was to develop in years to come. Its point of departure is the
failure of the Hibbath Zion movement to live up to the
promise of its early days. The enthusiasm aroused a few
years ago by the idea of the return to the ancestral home
has waned and given way to despondency. The movement
is not attracting new supporters, and, so far from expanding
its colonizing activities, is scarcely able to maintain the few
poor settlements that already exist. It is rent by internal dis-
sension, and stoops to practices unworthy of the great ideal
to which in theory its adherents are devoted. It is of no use
to look for scapegoats; to blame the old system of *halukah*
(the indiscriminate sending of alms to Palestine, which led
to much corruption and demoralization), or the faulty
methods of Baron Edmond de Rothschild, the princely

patron of the settlements, and his administrators, (who spoon-fed the settlers instead of encouraging them to become self-dependent). The real cause of the failure lies deeper, and must be sought in the policy of the movement itself.

There follows what appears at first sight to be a digression into general principles. The author analyzes the conditions necessary for the success of a movement which demands sustained effort, and concludes that, unless there is already a strong desire for the object to which the movement is devoted, the first thing that its leaders have to do is to create such a desire. This involves an appeal to the emotions in the first place, and for such an appeal action is more important than argument. When the right emotional attitude is sufficiently widespread, then, if the object to which the movement is directed does in fact meet a real need, the idea will take firm root, overcome opposition, capture people of influence, and finally reach the stage at which its champions can proceed with confidence to translate it into practice.

This doctrine is then applied to the question under discussion, that of the Hibbath Zion movement and its lack of success. The object of the movement is not a new one, but its attainment is extremely difficult, and nobody can demonstrate by rational argument that it is possible. What is necessary, therefore, is to use the existing desire for the object as a means to strengthen the will to work for its attainment and the readiness to believe that it can be attained. How is this to be done?

Next comes a brief excursus on the attitude of the individual to the community at different periods in Jewish history. In ancient times, argues the author, the happiness of the individual was entirely subordinated to that of the nation in Jewish life, or at any rate that was regarded as the ideal relation between the two; but after the destruction of the first Temple, when the national fortunes were

at a low ebb, and their restoration seemed hopeless, the
individual came to feel the need of a personal reward for
his labor and sacrifices. As there was little hope of this in
the present world, the idea of personal immortality, of
which there is little or no trace in the Pentateuch, found its
way into Judaism. Subsequent history tended still further
to weaken the sense of devotion to the nation, and to inten-
sify the need for the belief in the salvation of the individual
in the world to come; and so there developed among us
that individualism, that indifference to the national welfare,
which characterizes Jewish life today.

What, in these circumstances, ought the leaders of Hibbath Zion to have done? Clearly, they ought to have devoted their efforts first and foremost to the revival of the
national sentiment, and to have postponed the commence-
ment of actual colonization work in Palestine until, by
means of education and propaganda, they had trained up a
band of workers qualified to carry out that work efficiently.
Instead of this, they had abandoned the appeal to the national sentiment as soon as they found that it evoked little
or no response, and had endeavored to build up their movement on the appeal to self-interest. Hence the people attracted to Palestine were self-seekers, who were not prepared
for the sacrifices which settlement in an undeveloped land
involved; and when they found that they had been deceived
by information and calculations with no basis in reality,
they fled the country. Small wonder that the great ideal of
Hibbath Zion, presented in so unworthy a guise, no longer
wins adherents, and that a national edifice erected on the
basis of illusory figures and self-interest has become a heap
of ruins.

This, then, is not the way. Since the ruins are there, we
must indeed do what we can to repair and improve them;
but we must remember that our hope of success does not
rest on them. The regeneration of the Land must have its
foundation in the heart of the people; and the people is

fragmented, without any sense of unity or common purpose. Let us, then, return to the method with which we began: instead of adding yet more ruins, let us work for the broadening and deepening of the ideal, and then the day will at length come when we can effectively turn it into a reality.

This article, appearing at a time when the colonization movement was in the doldrums, and many of the disillusioned settlers were returning to Russia, created a tremendous stir in the ranks of the Hovevé Zion, and engendered much anger and bitterness. There seems to be nothing very new or shocking in the idea that a national object cannot be achieved unless individuals are prepared in some degree to sacrifice their personal interests and convenience for the general good. But in the light of the early history of Hibbath Zion it is not difficult to understand why Ahad Ha-Am's demand for the application of this truth to the particular case of the Jewish national movement provoked so violently hostile a reaction in Hibbath Zion circles.

The idea of the Return to Zion began to take shape in the seventies of the last century. We have seen that it was preached by Smolenskin in his monthly *Hashahar;* and before his death in 1885 Smolenskin was associated with Laurence Oliphant in the Englishman's abortive attempt to obtain from the Turkish Government permission for Jewish settlement on the land in Palestine. In 1878 another Russian Jew, Eliezer Ben-Yehuda (1858-1921), afterwards to become famous as the father of the revival of Hebrew as a spoken language, contributed to *Hashahar* an article (subsequently published as a pamphlet) in which he urged the re-establishment of the Jews as a nation in their ancient land, citing the example of Balkan countries which in recent decades had thrown off the Turkish yoke and gained their national independence. Other voices were heard to the same effect. Nor did the movement exist only on paper. In

the year in which Ben-Yehuda's pamphlet appeared, a group
of young Palestinian Jews, members of families subsisting on
the *halukah,* who were in revolt against the parasitic life
of their fathers, established the first Jewish agricultural settlement, at Petah Tikvah.

Initially the movement had grown, so far as it had grown
at all, without the stimulus of any external catastrophe, as
a result of the re-activation of the old messianic hope by the
success of national movements in Europe. On that basis no
popular movement worth the name could be built up; and
for some years there was only a trickle of emigration to
Palestine, promoted by small and unco-ordinated local
groups, with no central policy or direction. It was only
when the Russian pogroms of 1881 revealed the complete
insecurity of the Jewish position in eastern Europe, and sent
hundreds of thousands of Jewish fugitives to seek safety
and the possibility of a decent life in the United States of
America, that the scattered advocates of the return to Zion
joined forces in the Society of Hovevé Zion. During the
first ten years of its existence this Society failed to obtain
the recognition of the Russian Government, and had to
work underground; but there was at least some possibility
of organization and propagandist activity, and the pogroms
had created an atmosphere in which any plan to enable
Jews to escape from Russia was bound to have an appeal.
In these circumstances those who believed that the highest
interests of the Jewish people dictated emigration to the
deserts of Palestine rather than to the rich pastures of the
United States would scarcely have been human if they had
attempted to dissuade all except a few idealists from choos-
ing Palestine as their refuge. They conceived it to be their
duty to attract as many as possible to the land with which
Jews had always been linked by their hopes and prayers; it
was not for them to draw attention to the difficulties and
hardships which were sure to be encountered. But when
once they had adopted that policy, they were on a slippery

slope. They had to go on as they had begun, and found themselves compelled to suppress or distort the truth in order that the inevitable disillusionment should not cause a violent reaction against their movement, and against the ideal of a national restoration for which it stood.

It was not, however, to be expected that carefully chosen statistics and idealized pictures of life in Palestine could for long prevent knowledge of the real facts from spreading and producing their effect on public opinion. Enthusiasm for the movement rapidly waned, and the few agricultural settlements which it had established were saved from utter ruin only by the princely generosity of Baron Edmond de Rothschild of Paris, who spent millions on what was for him, at any rate at the outset, nothing more than a large-scale piece of philanthropy.

By 1889, when Ahad Ha-Am published his first critical article, Hibbath Zion in Russia was at a very low ebb, and whatever mass support it had had was reduced to exiguous dimensions; but the leaders of the movement appear to have lacked the courage to face facts, and to have clung to their old ideas and methods in the hope that somehow or other the impossible would be accomplished. Ahad Ha-Am's cold douche of reason and common sense was the first intimation to the general run of readers of *Hamélitz* that they had been living in a fool's paradise; and their reaction, as was only to be expected, was one of pained surprise and resentment.

Lo Zeh Haderekh provoked a reply in the columns of the same paper from Mosheh Leib Lilienblum (1843-1910), a controversial figure in the history of Russian Haskalah, who after a period of aggressive anti-religiousness became a stalwart of Hibbath Zion. Lilienblum was a "practical" Zionist in the narrowest sense of that term, of whom it used to be said that his heart rejoiced over every single goat and every single dunam of land added to the Jewish holding in

Palestine. He and Ahad Ha-Am were close friends, but Lilienblum had no understanding of the younger man's philosophical approach and his "spiritual" point of view. In his reply he not only challenged some of Ahad Ha-Am's more theoretical arguments, but contended, rather naïvely, that Hibbath Zion was compelled to speak to the Jewish masses in the language of self-interest because they understood no other. In a rejoinder printed in *Hamélitz* about three months after his first article, under the same title, Ahad Ha-Am pointed out that since, on his critic's own admission, the settlers in Palestine were living in abject poverty, the appeal to self-interest had clearly not been justified by results.

But if Ahad Ha-Am had the best of the exchange with Lilienblum, he had not scored a practical victory for his own policy. That was in the nature of things impossible. His criticism of Hibbath Zion policy was no doubt unanswerable, but that did not make its practical consequences any more palatable to the rank and file of the movement. The medicine he offered was altogether too strong. It was more comfortable to continue in the old way, hoping against hope that miracles would happen, than to embark on a campaign of national education which might not produce tangible results for generations, and meanwhile abandon hope of increasing the size of the Jewish settlement in Palestine, which for the ordinary Hovev Zion was the one thing that mattered. Ahad Ha-Am's policy, for all its theoretical attractiveness, was not, in the given conditions, a practicable alternative to the accepted one, as he was soon to discover through the experience of his own B'né Mosheh. But if it was beyond human power to bring about the complete change of heart which he in effect demanded, he had performed an inestimable service for the Hibbath Zion movement by bringing into the arena of public discussion a fundamental issue which had hitherto been ignored: the question of the underlying purpose and the true national value of what the Hovevé Zion, with their hopelessly inadequate resources, were trying to do. As a contribution to the solution of the practical problem of Hibbath Zion policy, *Lo Zeh Haderekh* was of no great value; as a challenge to accepted ideas and a call to serious thinking about the larger ideas of Jewish nationalism, it was epoch-making.

The appearance of the essay was also an event of note in the history of modern Hebrew literature. Whatever feelings might be evoked by the author's unconventional opinions, there was beyond doubt something new and arresting about the manner of their presentation. Readers of modern Hebrew had never before encountered such a combination of qualities in a single writer. Here were passionate sincerity and dignified restraint, wide learning and complete integrity, strong conviction and intellectual detachment. Here too was an unaccustomed impersonality of approach, and a tacit assumption that the writer and his readers were concerned solely with the merits or demerits of a policy, and not with the virtues and vices of its champions or opponents. The language and style of the article were not less distinctive. Though it had more of an old-world, biblical flavor than its author's more mature work, it was free from the worst faults of the early Haskalah writers, which Hebrew prose writers had not yet shaken off. Even this first effort of Ahad Ha-Am exhibited an economy of language and a concentration on essentials which were in marked contrast with the diffuseness and irrelevancies of so much of the Hebrew writing of the time; and the absolute clarity of his thought triumphed over the difficulties created by limitations of vocabulary—for modern Hebrew was then scarcely out of its swaddling-clothes—and aggravated by the attentions of the censor.

For its author himself the article turned out, somewhat unexpectedly, to be the beginning of a distinguished literary career instead of the first and last appearance in print of a plain man with no literary ambitions. Developments within the Hibbath Zion movement, particularly in connection with the Society of B'né Mosheh, provided further occasions for the expression of his views in print; and his pen soon became capable of moving into action without waiting for an external stimulus. The shyness which had so long kept him silent disappeared, and it became normal for him to contribute an article to *Hamélitz,* without any prodding from its editor, whenever the spirit moved him. In the result his contribution to the practical work of Hibbath Zion, though far from insignificant, has been completely overshadowed by his achievements as writer, critic and teacher. The literary and the practical aspects of his activity were, however, inseparably intertwined, and Hibbath Zion, in the sense which he himself gave to that expression, embraced the former no less than the latter.

4

FIRST
VISITS
TO PALESTINE

Dissatisfaction with the policy and methods of the Hibbath Zion leaders was not confined to the group of Ahad Ha-Am's friends and quasi-disciples in Odessa. It was felt not less acutely by some of the early settlers in Palestine, whose lives were spent amid the evidences of the movement's failure to realize even its modest possibilities; and during the time when Ahad Ha-Am was busy with his first article for *Hamélitz* they were contemplating the formation within the movement of a special group in which the advocates of reform were to be organized. The early stages of this revolt, which had its center in the port of Jaffa, are shrouded in obscurity, and it is not known whether it had been the subject of communication between Jaffa and Odessa before the arrival in the Black Sea port of Joshua Eisenstadt (afterwards Barzilai), an enthusiastic Hovev Zion, who was probably the originator of the proposal, and was charged by his Jaffa friends to get it carried into effect. Eisenstadt made contact with members of Ahad Ha-Am's little coterie and they agreed that the group should be organized, and that Ahad Ha-Am ought to be its leader. His friends, having no doubt a shrewd suspicion that he would refuse the leadership unless presented with a *fait accompli,* gave him no warning of their intentions. He received from one of his intimates, Abraham Lubarski, an invitation to attend an important meeting, and on arriving at the appointed place found to his surprise that those assembled had been led to suppose that the meeting had been called at his instance, and were looking to him to explain why they had been summoned.

When the conspirators disclosed the object of the meeting, Ahad Ha-Am found himself in general sympathy with their ideas, and, under pressure, agreed to accept the leadership of the movement. After further discussion it was decided to establish a society with the name of B'né Mosheh, "Sons of Moses." This name, linking the Society with the "lord of the Prophets," "whose image," as Ahad Ha-Am wrote years afterwards, "has been enshrined in the hearts of the Jewish people for centuries, and who has never ceased to influence our national life from the earliest times to the present day," was intended to stress the lofty ideals by which the founders were inspired; and as a symbolic act, the Society was formally brought into being on the seventh of Adar, which according to tradition is the date of the birth and death of Moses. (This was, incidentally, a few days before *Lo Zeh Haderekh* appeared in print.) In order not to prejudice its chances of success, Ahad Ha-Am did not at that time publicly contradict the prevalent belief that he was the originator of the idea. Of the fortunes, or misfortunes, of this experiment, more will be said in the next chapter.

Early in the following year, 1890, the persistent efforts of the Hovevé Zion to obtain official government recognition were at last rewarded by success. By dint of camouflaging their nationalist aims (which in any case, as we have seen, Pinsker was not anxious to proclaim from the housetops), they finally received permission to establish a "Society for the Support of Jewish Agriculturists and Workmen in Palestine and Syria"; and this philanthropic smoke-screen, which probably deceived nobody, enabled them thenceforth to carry on their work in the light of day.

The first business of the newly legitimized Society was

to elect a committee to conduct its affairs, and Ahad Ha-Am was urged by his associates in the B'né Mosheh to seek election to this body. Much as he disliked the rough-and-tumble of party politics, for which nobody could have been temperamentally less suited, he could not resist so reasonable a demand. In his *Reminiscences* he writes, in a tone of philosophical acquiescence:

> Thus I was drawn, reluctantly and in my own despite, into the thick of the battle of contending parties and individuals. All of a sudden I became a fighter and had, perhaps for the first time in my life, ill-wishers and enemies. . . . I was compelled to emerge from the obscurity in which I had lurked hitherto; I became a man of action, and took part in meetings and other public activities. A year or two earlier I should not have believed such a thing possible. This shows that one never knows oneself till one is put to the test.

To the end of his life he retained an intense dislike of publicity in every shape or form, a dislike only exceeded by his hatred of diplomacy. These two aversions combined to lend a keener edge to his later opposition to political Zionism.

It was in the following year, 1891, that he made his first visit to Palestine. Of this, as of his later visits, he wrote some fragmentary notes, which he incorporated in his *Reminiscences* when (in 1926) he sanctioned their publication. A footnote there explains that these are all the notes that remain in his hands, the bulk of his records having been handed over to the Central Committee of the Hovevé Zion in 1908, when he left Odessa for London, and having been subsequently destroyed in the Bolshevik revolution.

The notes on his first visit open as follows:

> The year 5651 will remain forever engraved on my memory as the year of my first visit to Palestine. I left home on Sabbath, the 6th of Adar (14th February 1891), and after a very hard and unpleasant journey, in which we

were in danger of shipwreck near Mount Carmel, I arrived safely at Jaffa on Thursday the 18th of Adar (26th
February). The first impression was not very favorable:
it was the rainy season, and the narrow and crooked
streets of the city were in a disgustingly filthy condition.

On the 26th Adar (6th March) I left Jaffa for a tour
of the neighboring Jewish settlements. I visited Rishon
le-Zion, Wady-el-Hanin [Petah Tikvah], Rehovoth,
Gedera and Kastinieh, and returned to Jaffa on Thursday
the second of Adar Sheni [12th March]. The impression
left on me by the settlements as a whole was a mixed one
—very depressing, yet at the same time heartening and
inspiring. One's first sight of Jews tilling the soil of our
ancestral land gladdens the heart, but the numerous and
fundamental shortcomings which an observant eye detects
cannot but cause disappointment, especially after the gross
exaggerations spread abroad by newspaper correspon-
dents in Palestine, which I brought with me from Russia.

There follows a very brief chronicle of his subsequent
travels, which covered the whole country, and at the end of
it a few lines in which for once he momentarily relaxes his
usually tight hold on his emotions:

On Tuesday the eleventh of Iyyar (17th of May), at 3
p.m., I left Jaffa and the beloved land, in which I had
spent eighty-two days, to return to my exile and my troubles in the midst of my exiled people. On Thursday we
reached Tripoli, the last place in Syria on our route. From
there I had my last view of the snow-capped Lebanon and
Hermon, and on the same day we sailed on, and Syria
and its mountains disappeared from sight.

Farewell, farewell to you, ancient land, land of my
longing and my waking dreams! Farewell to you, eternal
mountains, mountains of Judah and Ephraim, Carmel
and Lebanon! Shall I ever see you again?

His published reactions were less lyrical and more out-
spokenly critical. They appeared in the form of a lengthy
article called *Truth From Palestine,* which was published

in *Hamélitz* in several installments within a few weeks of
his return home at the end of May. This article aroused a
veritable storm of indignation and protest because of its
ruthless exposure of facts which those who were aware of
them had hitherto done their best to keep from the knowledge of the wider public.

The indignation was all the greater because the article
was published at a time when to outward appearance the
fortunes of the Hovevé Zion movement had taken a turn
for the better. The tardy government recognition of the
movement, which had enabled the so-called "Society for
the Support of Jewish Agriculturists and Workmen in Palestine and Syria" to work in the open, had given a fillip both
to the enrollment of members in Russia and to emigration
to Palestine. The membership had reached several thousands, all embraced in a single organization, and for the
first time there was some possibility of substituting orderly
and centrally-controlled activity for the haphazard and
unco-ordinated efforts of local groups. To a certain extent
settlers of independent means were being attracted to Palestine, as well as the larger number of the poor and needy.
The atmosphere was one of revived enthusiasm and hopefulness.

Ahad Ha-Am's bitter dose of truth was expressly designed to shatter the prevailing complacency. At the beginning of his article he says that he went to Palestine to find
answers to two questions: is the rebirth of Palestine possible,
and if so, is the Jewish people capable of bringing it about?
He has no difficulty in answering the first question in the
affirmative. It is the answer to the second question that he
finds difficult. He has returned from Palestine disillusioned
and dispirited, and he feels it necessary, by revealing the
worst features of the situation which he has now examined
at close quarters, to dispel the prevalent tendency to see
everything through rose-colored glasses.

He proceeds to say a word about the question which was
agitating the minds of all those East-European Jews who at
that time had, or hoped to have, a chance of escaping to
life and freedom: Palestine or America? A solution for the
economic aspect of the Jewish problem must, he says, be
sought in America; but the question also has another aspect,
which he defines as

> the need to create for ourselves a fixed center through
> the settlement of a great mass of our people in one terri-
> tory on an agricultural basis, so that both the Jews and
> their enemies may know that there is somewhere in the
> world a place where, though it may be too small to con-
> tain the whole people, a Jew can lift up his head like a
> man, can get his living from the soil by the sweat of his
> brow, and can create his own conditions of life in his
> own national spirit.

And "if there is any hope of a solution for that aspect of
the problem, it is to be found only in Palestine." Thus the
correct answer to the burning question is: both America and
Palestine.

This rather sobering preface, scarcely calculated to win
the applause of orthodox Hovevé Zion, is followed by a
detailed review of the weaknesses in the colonization work,
and the local difficulties by which it is confronted. The
amount of unoccupied good land is not large. The Arabs are
not "wild men of the desert," as is usually supposed, and "if
in course of time the Jewish holding in the country develops
to such an extent as to encroach in some degree on the
native population, the latter will not easily give up its position." This observation, expressed in guarded terms no
doubt for prudential reasons, is evidence of a truly remarkable prescience; and Political Zionism even more than Hibbath Zion might have been saved from serious errors had
it been taken to heart. Equally to the point is his warning

about the attitude of the Turkish Government, which, he points out, is alive to everything that happens in Palestine, and is already beginning to develop the country by building railways, so that we must expect "great changes in the condition of the country and its population, and an intensification of the difficulties in the way of our work." He proceeds to urge that the *yishuv* cannot be successfully built up exclusively on the basis of viticulture, which the settlers are rashly overdeveloping, without waiting, as they should, for the results of the first experiments. This criticism also was only too soon and too abundantly justified. Further, he points out that the blatant publicity which accompanies every purchase of land causes prices to soar, and also attracts the attention of the Turkish Government; and in these conditions "it will not be at all surprising if very soon it becomes impossible to find any land for sale, if the Turkish Government begins once more to put difficulties in our way, if our questionable proceedings [in land speculation] disgust all the best elements in our own people, and our great movement encounters a terrible reaction." Out of the ten existing settlements, there is not one that can stand on its own feet, and this is because the Hovevé Zion are not sufficiently equipped with knowledge of the facts and technical skill, and the settlers are lacking in the required ability and psychological qualities. Jewish workmen, too, who have recently begun to emigrate to Palestine, and "earn good wages in relation to the local conditions (the equivalent of 1½ francs a day), which enable them to save something," are not satisfied, and it is a mistake to endeavor to increase their number. In addition to all these troubles, the settlers do not treat the Arab inhabitants of the country as they should, and are too prone to indulge in quarrels and feuds among themselves and to fight about such trivialities as synagogue seats and the like.

Summing up, he says that "this is not the right way to achieve our purpose; and if we continue in it .... we may possibly succeed in course of time in settling some thousands of vine-growers and husbandmen on the land . . . . but it is almost certain that we shall never get near our real goal, and instead of finding a conclusive and final solution to the problem of Judaism, we shall simply create a 'problem of the Jews' in a country in which it has not hitherto existed—in our ancestral land." Here he draws clearly that sharp distinction between the spiritual and the material problems, between the "plight of Judaism" and the "plight of Jewry," which lies at the root of his prolonged controversy first with orthodox Hibbath Zion, and later with orthodox Zionism.

What is the way out of this apparently hopeless position? Salvation, he is clear, cannot come from individual philanthropy (a veiled reference to Baron Edmond), nor is much to be hoped from the Jews of eastern Europe, because "their material, moral and political condition precludes them from action on a large scale, and still more from taking the lead." There is only one other course open: "to turn to the Jews of the West, especially those of England, who have of late become much interested in the question of Palestine colonization" (a reference to the establishment of a Hibbath Zion organization in England under the leadership of Col. Albert Goldsmid). An attempt must be made to bring about the formation by western Jews of a National Society for Palestine settlement. Such a Society would begin by sending a commission of experts to Palestine to gather information and inaugurate experiments, and would afterwards buy land and prepare it for systematic and orderly settlement. A beginning might be made, he suggests, with Palestine east of the Jordan, which has so far been outside the ambit of the land-speculators and the propagandists.

The suggestion of a National Society for Palestine settlement under West-European leadership—an anticipation of part of the plan later outlined by Herzl in *Der Judenstaat* —aroused no echo at the time; nor does it seem that its author had fully weighed the difficulties in the way of its implementation. To begin with, he seems to have allowed himself to overestimate the hold of Hibbath Zion on the Jews of western countries, where whatever vitality it had was due to recent immigrants from eastern Europe, and it had not won a place among the recognized organizations of the established communities. But even had the soil been less stony, and had a Palestine Colonization Society under western leadership been established and well provided with funds, there is no reason to suppose that it would not have run at the outset into the political difficulties by which, as Ahad Ha-Am himself pointed out, the efforts of the Russian Hovevé Zion were frustrated. He had no right to assume that a western-led Jewish organization, carrying on its work "with great circumspection and without drums and trumpets," could dispense with a firm political basis for its work. No doubt the Hovevé Zion would have been better advised to avoid attracting the attention of the Turkish Government by unnecessary publicity; but the activities of the movement in Palestine were a political threat to Turkey's position as overlord, and no amount of circumspection in the conduct of its affairs could alter that basic fact. Ahad Ha-Am failed at that time to draw the conclusion, which followed inescapably from his own correct premises, that no real progress towards the realization of the Zionist idea was possible unless the Turkish Government could be either persuaded or coerced into acquiescence, or replaced by a régime likely to be more sympathetic.

Nor was it sufficient to realize, as he did even in those pre-Herzl days, that there was no future for a Jewish national effort unless its leadership could be transferred to the west. Had he been better acquainted with assimilated western Jewry at that time, he might have gone a step further, and have seen that a Jewish organization of East-European origin could not become all-Jewish by the simple expedient of placing itself under western control. The psychological relation between the assimilated and the unassimilated communities in those days was such that only an organization of western conception could hope to command the support of both sections. It was Herzl's western birth and upbringing that made it possible for him, given his vision, his idealism and the magic of his personality, to establish a Zionist organization which would be able not only to mobilize the nationalism of East-European Jewry, but also, after an initial period of distrust and indifference, to strike root in the western communities, instead of being doomed to remain forever, from their point of view, something "foreign" and not quite *comme il faut.*

Ahad Ha-Am himself may have realized at the back of his mind that the transfer of leadership to the west was not a practicable way out of the impasse which Hibbath Zion had reached: at any rate his article ends on a note of gloom not far removed from utter despair. He describes the scene at the Wailing Wall on the eve of the Passover, where he had watched "a large number of Jerusalem Jews standing and praying aloud," and adds:

> As I stand and look at them, a single thought fills my mind. These stones bear witness to the destruction of our land, and these men to the destruction of our people. Which of the two catastrophes is the worse? Which gives greater cause for mourning? If a land is laid waste, whilst its people is still full of life and strength, there may arise a Zerubbabel, an Ezra and a Nehemiah to lead the people back and rebuild it; but if the people is in ruins, what leader can arise for it, and whence can its salvation come?
>
> If at that moment I had had Jehudah Halevi's[1] inspiration, and had been able to lament the downfall of my people as he did, my threnody would have begun not with "Zion," but with "Israel"!

From the notes incorporated in his *Reminiscences,* it appears that shortly after his return from Palestine the Hovevé

Zion of Warsaw had the idea of sending a delegation abroad to endeavor to win over influential western Jews to the cause of Palestine settlement. Ahad Ha-Am was invited to be a member of the delegation, but he made conditions (not specified) as to its procedure which were not acceptable, and he did no more than take part in the discussions which preceded the departure of the delegation in August, 1891. On its return two or three weeks later he again consented with reluctance to go to Warsaw for a further meeting of several days, in which more than forty of the leading Hovevé Zion participated. We have no detailed account of the deliberations, but it appears that the French Alliance Israélite Universelle had promised to set up a Central Committee, presumably for colonization work, and that Ahad Ha-Am was to be one of the members of a body which was to visit Turkey and other countries in Asia in accordance with the wishes of Baron Hirsch, the millionaire founder of the Jewish agricultural settlements in the Argentine. It is not clear what this mission was supposed to accomplish; but evidently something was stirring, and there seems to have been some prospect of a strong reinforcement from the west of the wholly inadequate forces at the disposal of Hibbath Zion. However, Ahad Ha-Am himself was skeptical, as usual, and it seems that his skepticism was justified by the event, as it only too often was. At any rate, the negotiations and promises which he briefly mentions in his *Reminiscences* left no mark on the course of events. Meanwhile incautious land transactions in Palestine had involved the Hovevé Zion in a deficit of 75,000 francs, which was a very considerable sum (equivalent in those days to something like £8,500) by their financial standards. And a few months later, in December, 1891, came the death of their leader, Leo Pinsker, for whom Ahad Ha-Am had a great respect and admiration in spite of his being more of a "political" than a "spiritual" Zionist.

In May, 1893, he again visited Palestine, where he spent about six weeks. From the notes of this visit included in the *Reminiscences* it appears that, although he had an official entry permit from Constantinople, he was unable to land at Jaffa without the aid of underhand methods and baksheesh, and this made a most unfavorable impression on his sensitiveness. He also records that when he visited Jerusalem he was met at the railway station by a friend, who took him out of the station by a devious route, so as to save him from the cavalier treatment to which Jews were normally subjected by the Turkish police. Some of his friends from Russia who had already made Jerusalem their home urged him to follow their example, but in spite of all his efforts he did not succeed in obtaining the necessary permit, and he had to return to Russia. In his notes on the various settlements which he visited there are one or two expressions of satisfaction; but the general picture is no less gloomy than on the occasion of his first visit, and on the 1st of August, in Jaffa, he records: "I have sent *Truth from Palestine II* to *Hamélitz*. I wrote the article with my heart's blood. Ah, when will the occasion for writing such truths no longer exist?"

The second *Truth* is less detailed than the first had been, because, as Ahad Ha-Am points out at the beginning of the article, he found on this occasion that his views about the unsatisfactoriness of the position were broadly shared by the leading Hovevé Zion in Palestine. He confines himself for the most part to concrete suggestions for improvement. Whatever the Hovevé Zion do in Palestine must be done with the consent of the Turkish Government, and underhand methods must be abandoned. The emphasis must be shifted from viticulture to corn-growing. There must be an end to the system of subventions to the settlers and of assistance to individual merchants and craftsmen. Hebrew education must be improved. He repeats his previously expressed opinion that for the time being effort should be directed to improving the condition of the existing settlements, not to increasing their number; and he concludes, as before, with a reflection induced by a visit to the Wailing Wall, this time on the eve of the Ninth of Ab, when he had seen a congregation of old men and young sitting on the ground, some weeping, some studying and some engaged in talmudic discussions. But on this occasion what the melancholy scene suggests to him is the futility of this quietist attitude, and he is moved for once to give expression to a militant mood of revolt not unlike that of the "young men" with whom he was before long to cross swords in debate:

> It seemed to me as though we were surrounded by the shades of our heroic ancestors, who gave their lives on this spot and on this night for their country and their nationality, and that they were gazing in amazement on these their descendants, seated by their glorious graves with *books* in their hands.

The second *Truth* was no more palatable than its predecessor; but it aroused less animosity, because the temper of the movement had changed in the meantime, thanks partly to Ahad Ha-Am's influence, and realism was gaining ground. Some reforms in the colonization activity were stimulated by his criticisms, more particularly by his insistence on the danger of relying too exclusively on vine-growing before it had been shown to have a sound economic basis. In this very serious matter he held that Baron Edmond de Rothschild was much to blame. The baron's policy of buying at artificially inflated prices all the wine the settlers could produce, coupled with the insistence of his administrators that vine-growing must be the principal industry in all the settlements under their control, brought about a situation obviously not calculated to promote efficiency and enterprise. Ahad Ha-Am may or may not have been right in suspecting these officials of a deliberate attempt to prevent the settlers from achieving economic independence, but at any rate that was one result of the policy; and its unwisdom was amply demonstrated not much later, when there was an acute crisis in the wine industry, and thousands of vines had to be uprooted.

❦ 2 ❦

From Palestine Ahad Ha-Am did not return straight to Russia, but sailed early in August for Marseilles en route to London. He had reasons both public and private for visiting the British capital. On the one hand he wished to make a serious attempt to obtain Anglo-Jewish support for the colonization work, which in his opinion, as we have seen, vitally needed the backing of western Jewry. On the other hand, he wanted "to find some business in connection with Odessa"—presumably some commercial opening which would enable him to move to London—and also to obtain an adequate command of the English language, "in which I very much want to be able to write reasonably well." This latter design is evidence of an anglophile disposition which remained with him throughout his life; and it is also of interest as showing that at this early stage in his career he had not yet come to regard Hebrew as the only language in which he could properly write for publication. Some years later, in 1898, while he was still in Odessa, he made an abortive suggestion to the London *Jewish Chronicle* that he should act as its Odessa correspondent, on condition that he be allowed to write his dispatches in English, in spite of his imperfect command of that language; but a few years later still, when he took part in a controversy about the attitude of Jews to the Russian revolution in the columns of the assimilationist Russo-Jewish *Voschod,* he was careful always to put his contributions in the form of letters to the editor, and explained to a friend that he did so because he would have regarded writing full-blown articles in Russian as unfaithfulness to Hebrew.

After arriving in London in August, and finding everybody away on holiday, he crossed over to Paris and spent two or three weeks there. He met the few Hovevé Zion (of Russian origin), and the Chief Rabbi Zadoc Kahn, by whom he was greatly impressed. He also met the deputy manager of Baron Hirsch's philanthropies, who told him that the idea of settling Jews in Palestine was an admirable one, but the methods of the Hovevé Zion and their love of publicity made it impossible to co-operate with them in the work. Yet when he was later present by invitation at a meeting of a Committee over which Baron Edmond de Rothschild presided, he found that it had been making large purchases of land in Palestine on the assumption, which he knew from what he had recently learned in Palestine to be false, that the Turkish Government had decided to remove the restrictions on Jewish immigration: which suggests that those western Jews who showed some interest in Palestine were not necessarily less prone than the Russian Hovevé Zion to wishful thinking and precipitate action.

Returning to London, he found lodgings in the northern suburb of Canonbury, and spent the next two months in interviewing prominent Hovevé Zion and others, and to a lesser extent in sightseeing. His diary is very scrappy, but it records in an exceptionally lengthy entry of fifteen lines a talk with the then Chief Rabbi, Dr. Hermann Adler, who expressed sympathy with the idea of Palestine resettlement, but excused himself from active participation in public work of any kind on the ground that too much of his time was occupied in dealing with rabbinical matters such as *shechitah* and the like, the claims of which on his attention had greatly increased with the recent influx of Jews from Russia. The entry concludes with an ironical comment by the diarist on the sense of relative values thus revealed. His other interviews and discussions were with the leading Hovevé Zion in London, whom he found sympathetic and full of good intentions, but not well informed on the state of things in Palestine, and without much influence in their own community.

Among these scanty records of his fruitless efforts to serve the Hibbath Zion movement in England there appears, with startling irrelevance, this cryptic personal note:

> To-day I am not very well and cannot leave my room. It is not good to be unwell in a strange country.
>
> During these last few days my mind has been full of literary fancies and dreams, and letters from my wife and my friends encourage my dreams. Is there really a bright future in store for me? or is this only the last ray of light?

There is no known reason for the doubt and despondency indicated by these questions. To outward appearance he had no cause to fear for his future. His financial position, so far as is known, was not as yet bad. He had become a figure of importance in the Hibbath Zion movement, and was at the head of the Society of Sons of Moses, which included the fine flower of its adherents. Above all, though he had published little so far, he had won an undisputed place among the foremost living writers of Hebrew, and even at that early date his reputation had begun to spread beyond East-European Jewry. His forebodings point to some deep-seated *malaise,* which seems never to have left him entirely. It appears in a passage already quoted from his *Reminiscences,* and is hinted at now and then in his published *Letters,* as when he writes to Dr. Simon Bernfeld in 1897: "If you knew the story of my life, how I was educated and grew up, how all my ideals and highest ambitions have been shattered again and again, you would not be surprised at my tendency to gloom." And it was most distressingly evident in his last years, which were spent in Palestine, and should have been the happiest of his life. He seems never, except perhaps in fleeting moments, to have attained the inner harmony which one might expect to be enjoyed by a spiritual guide and teacher whose pen-name has become a symbol of clarity of thought and serenity of conviction.

The diary of his stay in London records only two experiences of the English way of life. One was a great Hyde Park demonstration of sympathy with striking miners, which naturally impressed a lover of freedom coming from Russia; the other was the Lord Mayor's Show, in which he saw "the strange spectacle of a great and practical people like the English, which has always so many important things to worry about, amusing itself with this sort of child's play," but at the same time was greatly impressed by the orderly behavior of the enormous crowd, which could be controlled by the wave of a single policeman's hand.

Before leaving London he concluded his diary with the following gloom-laden note:

What have I gained from my stay here? As regards business I don't yet know: perhaps something will come of it. But as for higher things, all I have gained is that I am rid of my great partiality for England. The English, I now see, have their virtues and their faults like any other people. The only difference is that we continentals, having the faults of the continental peoples, can understand those faults and get used to them, whereas the strange faults of the English are unintelligible to us, and we don't easily accustom ourselves to them. All the same, they are a very great people.

As to the English Jews, and the hopes I had that they would do something for the Jewish cause—I blush for shame and will say nothing.

Evidently the business propects also were unrealized, so that from every point of view his first visit to England was barren of results. Even a more effective propagandist than he was likely to be might well have failed to awaken the

Anglo-Jewish community of those days to a sense of the importance and urgency of providing the Jewish people with a foothold in Palestine, or to enlist the aid of its wealthier members for a project apparently so remote from reality. The only English Jew who might have been of any use, Sir Moses Montefiore, had died, a centenarian, eight years earlier. Colonel Goldsmid and the small band of English-born Jews who shared his interest in Palestine had little or no influence in the community; and such support as they had came almost entirely from the "foreign" element. So towards the end of 1893, after an absence of over half a year, Ahad Ha-Am returned to his home and his affairs in Odessa, which left him but little leisure. He had during that year been much attracted by the idea of assuming the editorship of *Hamélitz,* which had fallen vacant through the death of Zederbaum; but for reasons unknown the project came to nothing, like other plans of the same period for founding and editing a monthly of his own, and he continued to live by commerce for another year and more.

One of his published letters, written at the beginning of 1895, not long before the failure which put an end to his business career, shows him battling against indisposition as well as the triple burden of commerce, writing and committee work;

I now live out of town, and my business does not allow me in any circumstances to go into town more than three times a week for a few hours. These hours I have to divide among all sorts of different interests: the affairs of the *yishuv,* literature, family matters, business etc. As I must get back home by ten p.m., and the meetings of the Committee [of Hibbath Zion] now always commence at 8:30, I am often unable to attend them, and when I do attend, I nearly always have to leave before the end. Latterly things have become even more difficult: on my journey home from abroad I caught cold and fell ill, with the result that I am medically ordered to be very, very careful not to get hot or cold, not to do much work, and so on and so forth—the usual doctor's orders. Moreover, the matter of the Encyclopedia of Judaism is taking shape, and I absolutely must devote to it an appreciable part of the time I spend in town. And as though this were not enough, I have recently decided, for many reasons, to reissue in volume form all the articles I have written up to now, and of course their arrangement and revision will take much time.

5

SONS
OF
MOSES

Throughout the period of five or six years covered by the preceding chapter, and more especially during the first three years or so, the Society, or Order, of the B'né Mosheh claimed most of the time and effort that Ahad Ha-Am could find for the practical tasks of Hibbath Zion. The birth of this Society, coinciding in time with the publication of his first article, has already been mentioned. It was his one sustained attempt at Zionist leadership, and its somewhat melancholy history throws both his strength and his weakness into relief more than any other chapter in his career.

The originators of the idea insisted from the outset that the new body must have the character of a secret society; and Ahad Ha-Am, though temperamentally antagonistic to anything of the sort, bowed to the general will against his own better judgment, as was his wont where no fundamental question of principle was involved. The aim was to bring into being a *corps d'élite* of convinced and devoted Lovers of Zion to serve the national ideal with absolute unselfishness; and with that aim he was, of course, in complete sympathy. Membership of the order was not to be open to all and sundry, but was to be a privilege reserved for men of high moral character: the members must be prepared to shoulder serious duties and responsibilities, and must be united by close bonds of friendship and fraternal affection. For a society based on such principles, the Orders of Freemasons and the like, which were familiar in the western world, appeared to afford an appropriate model; and the Society of Sons of Moses followed their pattern in many details of its rules and regulations. There was provision for a thorough investigation of the moral character of each candidate for membership, a solemn ceremony of admission for those who passed this test, and an oath binding the new members to observe the rules of the Society and to keep its existence secret for all time. Great emphasis was thrown on the demand for moral integrity, unity, discipline, serious behavior, and the avoidance of time-wasting pursuits like card-playing. It was even the practice for the members to use fictitious names in their dealings with one another. The minimum age prescribed for membership was twenty (later raised to twenty-five), and every member was obliged to know the Hebrew language, and to contribute to the funds of the Society every year not less than two per cent (later reduced to one per cent) of the expenses of himself and his household. He was moreover required to be devoted heart and soul to the ideal of the national revival, and to be ready at all times to do everything in his power for its sake, without any thought of his personal interests.

At the outset the quasi-religious character of the Society was stressed, but in course of time a tendency to secularization asserted itself. Thus the oath sworn by new entrants originally began with the words "In the name of the God of Israel," but later the formula "With heartfelt conviction and in the name of all that I hold precious and sacred" was substituted.

The object of the Society, as defined in an authoritative statement of policy drafted by Ahad Ha-Am himself, did not differ from that of the Hibbath Zion movement; but it stood for a completely new approach to the question of methods of work, as is indicated in the following quotation from Ahad Ha-Am's introduction to its rules and regulations:

> The supreme object of our Society, like that of all earlier national organizations, is: the rebirth of our people in our ancestral land. But in our opinion there is no hope of salvation in isolated activities carried on in Palestine by individuals or groups with no bond of unity except the cash-box. The attainment of a national object demands a national effort carried out by a combination of the pick of the national resources both material and intellectual, and involving an inner moral unity. This effort must be a prolonged one, and there must be no indiscipline, no haste, no beating of drums, but circumspection, moderation and patience, guided always by good organization and settled rules of procedure. Such a national effort will attract to itself all the constructive elements in Jewish life, which are at present scattered and unorganized, and will gather momentum from generation to generation, growing quantitatively greater and qualitatively better, and progressing uninterruptedly towards its goal by steps that may be short, but will be secure.

The Society, in a word, was to be the embodiment of the idea of Hibbath Zion as Ahad Ha-Am conceived it, involving the willing self-dedication of men of high moral character to the national revival of the Jewish people, a sacred ideal not conceivably to be realized except after many generations of intensive and unceasing effort.

The rules of the Society were formally adopted at a meeting in Warsaw during the summer of 1890, in which representatives of fourteen centers took part, but at which, for some unknown reason, Ahad Ha-Am himself was not present. The most noteworthy provision in the rules is that regarding the management of the Society. Each local center (which must have a minimum of five members) was to be managed by a Leader and Advisers, chosen by the members, and the Leader alone was to have authority and responsibility for what the branch did, though he must not act without obtaining and considering the views of his Advisers. A President of the whole Society was provided for, but this office was never in fact filled. Ahad Ha-Am, who was elected Leader of the central branch, that of Odessa, was President *de facto* for the first two years, at the end of which, not being satisfied with the way in which the Society was developing, he resigned the position. Control of the Society then passed to the Warsaw branch, and subsequently to that of Jaffa, while Ahad Ha-Am retained a sort of moral leadership with the function (to use his own words) of "supervising the conduct of affairs and the proceedings of the Society generally, and influencing the course of events so far as [he] could." This vague function was certainly better suited to his temperament and gifts than the position of an autocratic Leader.

The establishment of the Society was greeted with enthusiasm by the select few who were admitted to membership, and especially by the idealistic youth, who were athirst for a satisfaction not to be found in the humdrum, uninspired, and uninspiring routine of Hibbath Zion work. Despite Ahad Ha-Am's skeptical outlook and distrust of enthusiasm, the Society of which he was the inspirer aroused in some at least of his followers the kind of fervor which might have rewarded the emotional appeal of a revivalist preacher. It was as though they responded to the warmth of the hasidic temperament which was his by inheritance, rather than to the cold intellectualism behind which it was concealed. We have a glimpse of what the Society meant to such men in the (Hebrew) memoirs of E. W. Lewin-Epstein, one of the earliest members:

> I remember the evening on which the two additional members necessary to make up the minimum of five were admitted to our Society. All five of us were gathered in one room, and the three documents were read in their order. The new members took the oath in the prescribed

form, with due solemnity. We were all in an exalted frame of mind. Of our own free will we had pledged our loyalty to the Society, the aim of which was to rebuild the Land of Israel in the spirit of true Judaism, and had devoted all our time to that task. That night I walked with the two new members until a late hour, discussing our new duties and the work that lay before us. When the time came to part and go home, they both exclaimed: "To-day we have been born anew! To-day we have come to know what our aim in life is." And these two members remained true to our ideal to their last day.

To Eisenstadt was entrusted the important task of traveling to all the Jewish centers in Russia and enrolling members in the B'né Mosheh. He met with a fair amount of success initially, and succeeded in bringing in even so determined an opponent of Ahad Ha-Am's distinctive ideas as Lilienblum. Of course, quality and not quantity was—or at least should have been—the criterion of success; and if, as seems probable, the society never numbered more than about two hundred members in its fourteen branches (all in Russia except that of Jaffa), this did not necessarily mean that it was a failure. Nor was the movement entirely confined to Russia and Palestine: there were a few isolated members, no doubt of East-European origin, in Germany, England, North America and other countries. Even Ahad Ha-Am was not dissatisfied with the results of the first few months of recruiting and organizational activity, all carried on, at least in theory, under the veil of strict secrecy.

It soon became apparent, however, that the Society was unlikely to live up to the high ideals and exacting demands of its Leader. Ahad Ha-Am, with his philosophical outlook and his ability to take the long view, insisted above all things on the postponement of concrete activity until everything had been properly planned and prepared, and until the necessary financial means were available. Until these conditions were fulfilled (and the latter of them, the financial, was one which in all the earlier experience of the Hovevé Zion had lain well beyond the possibility of fulfillment), the Society must stand at the ready and bide its time. "The Society," he wrote in answer to murmurs of discontent at the lack of action, "was not established to keep its members occupied all day and every day. If we have to let years go by without action, and only once in several years is our Society called upon to do something for the common purpose, that should be enough for us." His motto might have been Milton's "They also serve who only stand and wait." But even the best of the members were only flesh and blood; and the policy of doing nothing but keep their powder dry did not satisfy them. Why had they joined the Society except to do something? It is very likely that a widespread feeling was expressed by the Moscow member who opined that "a Society whose aim is not to do anything, but simply to exist, has no reality and no *raison d'être,*" and that "there is no need for a man to say to his friend: 'I'm an honest fellow, you're an honest fellow; come along, let's be two honest fellows!' "

Nor was the Society wholly composed, as according to the intention of its founders it should have been, of men who were single-minded in their devotion to the ideal of the national rebirth. Despite strict instructions, Eisenstadt on his apostolic tour had not consistently maintained the high standard of qualification which the rules demanded; and the original members included a not inconsiderable sprinkling of men who would not have been awarded high marks in a test for moral excellence. Such men were capable of lapses which tended to discredit the Society, whose existence of course became publicly known in spite of the efforts of its founders to shroud it and its proceedings in secrecy. Mutual tolerance between people of different opinions, which was a cardinal principle of the Society, came less easily to some members than to others; and the religious question in particular led to division and wrangling, not-

withstanding an express provision in the rules that the
Society was to be absolutely neutral in religous matters.
Ahad Ha-Am soon had to recognize, however reluctantly,
that the ideals of brotherly love and harmony, the lack of
which he regarded as one of the causes of the inability of
the Hibbath Zion movement as a whole to overcome its
difficulties, were little better served by his hand-picked élite
than by the rank and file of the movement. During his
first visit to Palestine, about two years after the establishment of the B'né Mosheh, he found the Jaffa branch torn
by internal quarrels; and there is evidence that this unhappy
condition of things was fairly general throughout the Society.

The stultifying effects of this inner weakness were intensified by the external opposition to which the Society was
exposed almost from the outset, and which compelled its
leaders to waste on polemics a great deal of effort that might
have been given to constructive work. There was, first of
all, opposition from within the Hibbath Zion movement.
Lilienblum, who according to his own principles ought
never to have joined the B'né Mosheh, showed no great
interest in the Society; and when in 1890 the Hovevé Zion
under their camouflaged title received Government recognition, he made this an excuse for leaving the Society and
joining its enemies. It so happened that about this time an
over-enthusiastic follower of Ahad Ha-Am named Ben-
Avigdor (previously Shalkovitz, 1866-1922), a Hebrew
novelist and publisher, who became in after years one of
Ahad Ha-Am's most virulent detractors, published an
extraordinary fantasy called *Moses, or the Three Prophets*,
in which he heaped almost divine honors on Ahad Ha-Am;
and this extravaganza furnished Lilienblum with the opportunity to write for *Hamélitz* a series of articles in which he
fiercely attacked Ahad Ha-Am and his associates. The general line of his attack is indicated by the title he chose for

his articles, which suggests that the most appropriate comment on the Ahad Ha-Am group and its leader is to be found in the verse of Ecclesiastes: "He that observeth the wind shall not sow; and he that regardeth the clouds shall not reap." It is the protest of the practical man against the visionaries, the men of the spirit (the Hebrew word for which, *ruah,* is also the word for "wind"). This attack naturally called forth replies from spokesmen of the B'né Mosheh, including Ahad Ha-Am himself, who, characteristically, did not include his article, called *Men of Conviction and Men of Action,* in the volume of his collected essays which he published a few years later because of its too polemical tone, but in the fulness of time incorporated it, with certain omissions, in his *Reminiscences* before releasing them for publication.

A different kind of attack, and one more difficult to meet, came from the religious wing of the Hovevé Zion; and even relatively liberal-minded rabbis accused Ahad Ha-Am of being an enemy of religion—an accusation which he of course strenuously denied, and in all sincerity; but his personal indifference to religion could not be denied, and that in itself was a rock of offense in the eyes of people who, even if they were not fanatical, could scarcely regard religious indifferentism with equanimity, or rid their minds of the notion that its professor, and any movement inspired by him, must somehow be dangerous to religion. Thus the Society of Sons of Moses, the whole intention of which was to serve the common cause in peace and quiet, became ironically a storm-center within Hibbath Zion.

As though this were not enough, the Society, itself an object of suspicion and hostility within the ranks of the Hovevé Zion, was sometimes singled out for attack by those whose real object was to discredit and damage the colonization movement itself, and particularly by the fanatics of the

halukah, to whom, for more reasons than one, Hibbath
Zion and all its works were anathema. In 1890 the Hoveve
Zion set up an Executive Committee, with its headquarters
in Jaffa, to manage its settlement work in Palestine, and it
so happened that three of the men appointed to this Executive were members of the B'né Mosheh, and one of the
three, Zeev (Vladimir) Temkin,[1] became its Chairman.
Temkin, a man of energy and ability, was rather remote
from Judaism and the Hebrew language, and the choice of
him as Chairman was resented by the other two, Pines and
Ben-Tovim,[2] who were fanatically religious. Serious trouble
arose when Temkin, acting on his own authority, made
some ill-judged land purchases, which involved the Hoveve
Zion in heavy financial loss, and naturally did the B'né
Mosheh no good. The affair was investigated by Ahad
Ha-Am during his first visit to Palestine, in 1891, and one
of the results was that Pines and Ben-Tovim were expelled
from the Society. They sought revenge by joining forces
with the *halukah* fanatics, and the result was a flood of
scurrilous pamphlets against the Society, in producing
which the zealots of Lithuanian Kovno joined hands with
their kindred spirits in the Holy City. The Society
was threatened with excommunication (*herem*—a weapon
which, whether under that designation or under its more
modern name "boycott," Ahad Ha-Am regarded as little
better than a survival from the ages of barbarism), and one
of the pamphleteers did not scruple to describe it as a "Jesuit
society." The veil of secrecy behind which the B'né Mosheh
had deliberately shrouded their activities played into the
hands of their less scrupulous enemies; and the attacks on
them from outside the ranks of the Hoveve Zion helped to
sharpen the internal conflict in which they were involved.
Ahad Ha-Am found himself in the unfortunate position of
a devotee of peace who is simultaneously attacked on two
fronts.

His experience of two years as head of the B'né Mosheh, into the work of which he had thrown himself with un-wonted optimism, had been one continuous series of dis-appointments, not the least among which was the realization of his personal lack of the qualities demanded of a Leader. In a letter to the Warsaw branch written towards the end of 1891 he makes this frank confession:

> It is true, as you say, that I always ask opinions instead of giving instructions. That is because I am not by nature the kind of person who gives instructions. I am far from believing myself infallible, and so my aim is always to give a reasoned opinion for others to examine and agree with. If they do not agree, I yield to the views of the ma-jority, even though it seems to me that I am in the right. That is my practice, or perhaps my weakness.

At about the same time he reproaches himself in a letter to a personal friend for the lack of firmness he had displayed in dealing with Temkin in connection with the affair men-tioned above. Temkin's rash and irresponsible action had caused a scandal and nearly ruined the Hibbath Zion move-ment, and it was clearly the duty of Ahad Ha-Am, as head of the B'né Mosheh, to administer a severe reprimand to the offender, if not to expel him from the Society. But Ahad Ha-Am, as he admits, knew himself incapable of taking the stern line, and resigned his leadership before interviewing Temkin, thus freeing himself of the respon-sibility and making it possible to talk to Temkin simply as one "brother" to another. In that capacity he contented him-self with a mild reproof; and though Temkin's attempts to exculpate himself did not convince him, they parted good friends. "Heaven knows," concludes Ahad Ha-Am, "that it was not in my nature to act otherwise. But is this how I *ought* to have acted, or how a man of strong will would have acted in my place?" One may admire the moral cour-age and the self-understanding revealed by his making these confessions, and even giving them to the world years later,

when he published a selection of his correspondence; but
there can be no question that he was right to resign a position in which only a man of a temperament diametrically
opposite to his own could have hoped to succeed. The wonder is that his close associates pressed him to accept such a
position, and that he allowed their insistence to overcome
his own reluctance.

His new position of spiritual guide to the Society no
doubt suited him very much better; but, as we have seen, the
Society suffered from weaknesses which were independent
of his own unsuitability for the position of a dictator, and
he was gradually and reluctantly driven to the conclusion
that he had been too optimistic in believing in the possibility
of finding among the Hovevé Zion the human material for
a *corps d'élite*—or, in his own idiom, *hever kohanim,*
"guild of priests"—of substantial size. Matters were brought
to a head early in 1895, when certain members of the Central Committee of the Hovevé Zion, on which the Sons of
Moses were represented by Ahad Ha-Am, Barzilai and
Lewin-Epstein, launched a frontal attack on the society
within the Committee, and adopted as their own the most
extravagant charges of the Jerusalem pamphleteers, including those of corruption and nepotism. There was a heated
discussion, and it was clear that a substantial body of opinion
in the Committee was adverse to the B'né Mosheh. The
secrecy which enveloped the Society was a powerful weapon
in the hands of its enemies, and in defending himself and
his colleagues Ahad Ha-Am felt compelled to disclose a
good deal about its rules and its activities that had not
hitherto been known except to its own members. It looked
at one stage as though his two associates might be expelled
from the Committee, and he himself, though safe against
so extreme a measure, had serious thoughts of resigning
from it. However, after investigation by a commission of
inquiry the baselessness of the charges was established, and
the leader of the attack tendered an apology. So the matter

ended without disaster; but this incident had confirmed a conviction which had for some time been taking shape in Ahad Ha-Am's mind, that if his cherished Society was to continue at all, its character and constitution must be radically changed. Before the commission of inquiry had made its report, he wrote a long letter to the Jaffa branch, in which the leadership of the Society was vested at that time, setting out his views and his ideas about its future.

He begins this letter by attacking the principle of secrecy and the paraphernalia associated with the conception of the Society as an Order like that of the Freemasons—the ritual prescribed for the enrollment of new members, the ceremonial laid down for the conduct of meetings, the concealment of the real names of members, the code of discipline and so forth. He had never been enamored of all this flummery—indeed, only his habit of subordinating his own views to those of his colleagues for the sake of the cause can explain why he ever acquiesced in a system so entirely foreign to his unromantic and anti-mystical temperament—and had suggested its abandonment on earlier occasions, but never with great insistence. Now he feels that the Society can no longer afford the luxury of carrying on its activities behind what he describes as a "Wall of China." There is some indication that his determination to get rid of this wall was sharpened by a fear that the documents and correspondence of the Society, with their elaborate system of false names or initials, were in danger of being seized and examined by some authority (presumably governmental), and that the system of false names in particular would be liable to misrepresentation. As for the ceremonial and the discipline, they had in practice meant little or nothing from the outset. He is convinced that the Society must henceforth be a public body, must proclaim its aims and objects to the world, and must open its membership to all who may be able to help in their realization. Only so can it hope to make effective use of the idealism and devotion to the national aim of those

of its members—for some such there are—who are really
imbued with its ideals, and do not need a ritual and a code
of discipline to persuade them to work together in unselfish
co-operation and harmony.

He then proceeds to a more far-reaching proposal. In
Russia, he says, the removal of the bogey of secrecy will ease
matters somewhat, inasmuch as the Society will be able to
carry on its work without exciting suspicion in the minds of
people like the members of the Central Committee; but
Russian conditions will still cripple its propagandist activities, and severely limit its potentialities. Consequently the
center of the movement must be transferred to the west of
Europe and America, where conditions are freer. And it is
the duty of the Jaffa branch to work for this transfer "without paying much attention for the present to our brothers
in the North"—*i.e.,* in Lithuania and Poland. No doubt he
feared that the idea of voluntarily surrendering the hegem-
ony would be strenuously resisted by the Russian Hovevé
Zion.

As a result of Ahad Ha-Am's appeal, the constitution of
the B'né Mosheh was made public, and the handicap of
secrecy was at length removed; but no serious action was
taken in the direction of internal reform or of moving the
seat of authority westwards. The various branches could
not agree on a new constitution. Ahad Ha-Am himself resigned from his position of moral leader in 1896, when he
left Russia for a time in connection with the launching of
his monthly *Hashiloah;* but instead of accepting his resignation, his colleagues asked him to take on additional functions, which he firmly declined to do. So matters dragged
on, with inconclusive discussions about reform of the constitution as more or less the sole activity of the Society, until
the meeting of the First Zionist Congress at Basle in August,
1897, when, as he afterwards put it, "the Society automatically went out of existence as the din of Basle rent the air."
Its effective life had ended at least two years earlier.

What had this "secret society" actually achieved during the few years of its somewhat hectic life?

Its achievements were neither spectacular nor large in scale, but they were nonetheless solid. It had taken a hand in establishing the first agricultural settlement in Palestine of which the founders were men of independent means, and were consequently in no need of the quasi-philanthropic assistance by which Baron Edmond de Rothschild and his administrators, with the best of intentions, were sapping the morale of the settlers as a whole, and turning what was meant to be a national enterprise into a costly piece of philanthropy. It had published in Jaffa a series of news-sheets giving accurate information about what was being done in Palestine, and these, distributed to perhaps a couple of hundred influential Hovevé Zion (not all of them necessarily members of the B'né Mosheh) had provided a useful corrective of the rose-colored accounts by which the propagandists of the movement were accustomed to angle for popular support. It had put forward a number of useful practical suggestions for the improvement of the colonization work, and had actually anticipated the later Zionist movement by establishing a National Fund, which on the dissolution of the Society handed over what little money it had amassed to the Jewish National Fund of the Zionist Organization. In the field of education, it had founded the first Hebrew-language school in Jaffa, a pioneer move of inestimable importance for the future, and had actually succeeded in inducing the French Alliance Israélite Universelle, a body with strong assimilationist leanings, to share the financial responsibility for this institution. It had also established and assisted Hebrew libraries in Palestine. In Russia, too, the Society had established a number of day schools in which Hebrew and other Jewish subjects formed a substantial part of the curriculum, and which blazed the trail for a significant development of modernized but not assimilationist Jewish education. It had also made a valuable contribu-

tion to Hebrew letters by establishing the Ahiasaf Publishing
Company, which published mainly books of a serious character, whether original or translated, and with which Ahad
Ha-Am was intimately connected for many years. Finally,
it had shown an awareness, which official Hibbath Zion
lacked, of the importance of political work as an element in
the Zionist program: it had representatives in Constantinople, from which Palestine was governed in those days,
and its efforts to win over the Jews of Egypt, Syria and
other eastern countries to the idea of Jewish nationalism
showed an appreciation of their potential importance which
was by no means common.

The Society had, then, a program which lacked none of
the essential elements—economic, cultural and political—of
a Jewish national movement; and in the practical sphere it
originated a number of "pilot projects" through which, if
they could have been reduplicated on a large scale, the
work of the Hovevé Zion could have been lifted on to an
altogether higher plane. That this did not in fact happen
was due only in part to Ahad Ha-Am's personal lack of the
qualities of leadership. A more stubborn obstacle lay in the
crippling disabilities under which Russian Jewry suffered—
its lack of any kind of security, its comparative poverty in
men of western education and political experience, and,
above all, the embargo placed by an autocratic and hostile
government on any kind of political organization or initiative.

When Herzl's Zionist Organization was born, and the
B'né Mosheh disappeared, many of the most active and influential adherents of the new movement whom Russian
Jewry provided were men who had been members of Ahad
Ha-Am's Society, or, if not formally members, had been
closely associated with its spiritual head in the work of
Hibbath Zion. Among them were Menahem Ussishkin (1863-
1943), who after Herzl's untimely death in 1904 played a
leading part in the switch to "practical" Zionism which

saved the Organization from collapse, and Chaim Weizmann (1874-1952), who led a revolt within the Organization against its neglect of Jewish culture while Herzl was
still alive, and to whom it fell later to become successively
the head of the Jewish Agency and the first President of the
State of Israel. When in later years Ahad Ha-Am described
the B'né Mosheh as "an unsuccessful experiment," he was
no doubt pronouncing a just verdict, in the sense that the
Society had achieved little, and had fallen far short of fulfilling his hopes (as, indeed, any organization was bound
to do); but he was being less than just to himself. The
Society was the principal channel through which the influence of his personal example of unwavering faith married
to sober realism, of personal integrity, and of devotion to the
moral values of Judaism as the vital element in Jewish nationalism was brought to bear on many of the most important figures in later Zionist history; and from that point of
view, if from no other, it has earned a place of honor in the
annals of Zionism.

To Ahad Ha-Am himself, as we have seen, the Society
brought little satisfaction, and much heartache, during its
brief existence. That was to some extent in the nature of
things. He was doomed to lament failures all his life, because it was impossible for any human institution to come
up to his exacting standards of conduct and achievement;
and where his own responsibility was so heavily involved
as in the case of the B'né Mosheh, the bitterness of an unrealized ideal was intensified by the sense of personal failure. But in this particular case he had, as it seems, unnecessarily laid up trouble for himself. The tribulations of the
Society were due in no small measure to its secret character
and romantic trappings; and these, as well as the principle
of autocratic leadership, were repugnant to his temperament
and convictions. He might have been spared much personal
unhappiness, and the Society's chances of success might have
stood higher, if he had refused from the outset to allow its

constitution to include important provisions of which he did
not personally approve. But, as he himself realized, he was
in practical affairs too ready to defer to the general consensus
against his own better judgment.

Twenty years later, when the Society itself had long been
dead and was scarcely remembered, it figured prominently
in a peculiarly vicious attack on its spiritual head by an erst-
while devotee, Ben-Avigdor, mentioned above as one of
Ahad Ha-Am's more extravagant admirers, who afterwards turned his enemy because of a quarrel between a publishing company which he founded and Ahiasaf. In 1913,
when Ahad Ha-Am, who had never carried out his intention of writing the history of B'né Mosheh, published
some of its documents at the end of the last volume of
his collected essays, Ben-Avigdor seized the opportunity
to deliver a vitriolic onslaught on his one-time hero in a
Hebrew miscellany. Not content with stigmatizing Ahad
Ha-Am as a purely destructive critic, and an unpractical and
narrow-minded fault-finder and skeptic, he accused him, on
the strength of the B'né Mosheh, of fancying himself a modern Moses, on whom the mantle of the ancient Hebrew
Prophets had descended, and whose ambition it was to be-
stow on the Jewish people, as Moses had done before him, a
new law and a new way of life. Ahad Ha-Am had once, as
we have seen, used a Hebrew expression which means "a
guild of priests" to describe the band of dedicated idealists
without which he saw no hope of success for the Hibbath
Zion movement; and in a different connection he had
drawn a distinction between the two types of Prophet and
Priest, representing the Prophet as the uncompromising
extremist, who insists on the full realization of his vision of
a better world in defiance of the facts of life and human
nature, and the Priest as the practical servant of the ideal,
who accepts the fact that perfection is unattainable, and
prefers the half-loaf to no bread at all. On the basis of evi-

dence such as this, Ben-Avigdor asserted that Ahad Ha-Am saw himself as a new Moses, and the B'né Mosheh as his "guild of priests."

This amazing onslaught on Ahad Ha-Am was not published until his reputation in the Jewish world was too firmly established to be hurt by it, but it has not been entirely without effect. In particular, the suggestion that he regarded himself as being in the line of the Hebrew Prophets has been taken seriously by some of his critics who belong to a younger generation, and had not the opportunity of knowing him personally. To those who had that advantage, the suggestion is manifestly absurd. Ahad Ha-Am regarded the Prophet as, at least in some respects, the ideal type of human being, and therefore as a type which ordinary men should take as a model for imitation within the limits of their capacity. But he was not less conscious of his own limitations than of his capabilities, and he had moreover a sense of humor. The idea that he regarded himself as a modern Moses or Isaiah is completely at variance with the known facts about his character and the way in which he comported himself throughout his life.

The secret society also figured prominently in another attack which was made on Ahad Ha-Am, from a very different source, in the last years of his life, after he had settled in Tel Aviv. In 1923 there was printed in Munich an anonymous twenty-page pamphlet bearing the title: *Achad Cham (Asher Hinzberg)*[sic], *der geheime Führer der Juden*. This German pamphlet professes to be translated from a French version of the Russian original, and did in fact appear also in Russian. It is a fantastic medley of factual statements and misstatements, childish absurdities and downright inventions. Its main object is to reveal that the notorious *Protocols of the Elders of Zion* were composed not by Herzl (!) but by Ahad Ha-Am, who was Herzl's great rival and succeeded him in the leadership of the Zionist movement, the aim of which is to bring the world under

Jewish domination; and it contains what purports to be a photograph of the Zionist Congress in secret session, with Ahad Ha-Am presiding and Herzl in a seat of honor. It was brought to Ahad Ha-Am's notice at the time of its appearance in print, and he had some thought of taking legal action against the publisher; but for various reasons, among them no doubt the state of his health and his absence from Europe, he abandoned the idea. His dislike of publicity was in any case so strong that he could scarcely have entertained the thought of going to law on such a matter unless he had been persuaded that the Jewish cause might be served by the sacrifice of his personal convenience. He did in fact authorize the Zionist Organization to bring an action against the German Count Reventlow, who had published the same statement about the authorship of the *Protocols;* and the court awarded nominal damages against the count.

6

AT

THE

CROSSROADS

Ahad Ha-Am entered on his literary career, as we have seen, under pressure, and with no idea that his first appearance in print would not be his last; but in this matter, as in so many others, his own inclinations and intentions were not permitted to determine the course of his life. He was drawn in his own despite into controversy on the policy of the Hibbath Zion movement, which he had criticized so incisively in his first article; and gradually his reluctance to write was overcome, and he came to be less dependent on the stimulus provided by current controversies. Though he wrote but rarely, his pen-name soon became familiar to the serious Hebrew-reading public as that of a critic and thinker of independent views and exceptional gifts. During the six years following the appearance of *Lo Zeh Haderekh* an average of five or six contributions a year from his pen appeared, mostly in *Hamélitz;* and at the end of that period most of what he had written was re-issued, after revision, in a volume of some 250 pages, bearing the title *At the Crossroads (Al Parashath Derachim)* and the subtitle *Kovetz Maamarim,* which means "a collection of articles" (but in the Hebrew of those days *maamar* had to do duty for both "article" and "essay"). Though published by the Ahiasaf Publishing Company, the book was printed in Berlin, and was also given the German title *Am Scheidewege,* with the subtitle, *Gesammelte Schriften.* The choice of name indi-

cated, as was explained in the preface, the author's conviction
that the Jewish people had reached a turning-point in its
history, and the time had come for it to decide whether it
wished to continue the struggle for existence.

Most of these thirty essays had been called forth by current events or controversies, and might have lost their relevance within weeks or months of their first appearance; but
his writing, though generally topical, was rarely if ever
ephemeral. If it was journalism, it was inspired journalism.
Any subject on which he wrote was invested by his style and
treatment with a certain weight and dignity, the reflection
of his high seriousness of purpose and his habit of seeing
even trifles in a wider context. It is not known how many
readers his "articles" had when they first appeared; but we
know from one of his letters that 1100 copies of his first
volume were published in 1895, that a second edition of
1500 copies issued in 1901 sold out quickly (there was a
third edition in 1904), and that in 1903 he suggested to his
publishers that they should print 2500 or 3000 copies of the
second volume, which was then ready for the press. These
are large figures for a serious Hebrew book, other than a
religious work, published at the beginning of this century.
And the enduring appeal of these occasional pieces is shown
by the fact that the four volumes of *At the Crossroads* which
had appeared by 1913 were re-issued in Berlin in 1921, while
their author was still alive, and their contents appeared
again in a one-volume edition in Tel Aviv in 1936, when
he was no more.

A survey of the principal articles and essays included in
the first volume (not all of which have appeared in English translation) will reveal the main lines of Ahad Ha-Am's
thinking on the problems of Jewish life and Judaism, and of
the general philosophy of life which underlay it. Though
later events, and in particular the emergence of the political
Zionist Organization in 1897, led to the elaboration of his

views in several important essays included in the later volumes, there is practically no aspect of his teaching which is not adumbrated, if no more, in the first.

Less than a year after the appearance of his first article in *Hamélitz,* a miscellany with the picturesque name of *The Beehive* was published under his (unavowed) editorship, and it contained, in addition to the *Discarded Old Manuscript* already mentioned, two contributions from his pen. One of these was named after a lately deceased rabbi, Mordecai Eliasberg, a Hovev Zion who had had the breadth of mind to recognize that non-religious Jews could be as sincere as the religious in their devotion to the national cause, and had upheld the principle of religious tolerance and co-operation for the common good. Ahad Ha-Am hailed this encouraging example of an attitude which was all too rare in the Russian rabbinate of his day. He hated intolerance in all its manifestations, and was particularly apprehensive of the danger that the Hibbath Zion movement might be wrecked by the inability of believers and unbelievers to work together. In his own B'né Mosheh, as we have seen, it was a cardinal principle that the harmony of the Society must not be disturbed by religious differences.

His other contribution to the *Beehive* is of special interest as being the first of his essays which can be described as philosophical rather than critical or polemical, though it is not without reference to a question of current controversy. This essay, *Many Inventions,*[1] is concerned primarily with the historical process by which the healthy naturalism of the "natural man," with his uninhibited desire for life and well-being, gives way, under stress of circumstances, to a disillusion which produces two antithetic philosophies: on the one hand the other-worldliness which seeks in the next life the fulfillment that is unattainable in this, on the other hand the sour-grapes attitude which decides that "all is vanity," and would crush out every desire in order to achieve Nirvana. The general thesis is then applied to the special

case of the Jewish people. After the destruction of the national life, and the loss of all hope of its restoration, the
prophetic promises of redemption were given a new, etherialized meaning, as though they had no relevance to life
on earth; but under the impact of modern thought many
of us have ceased to believe in the possibility of a supernatural restoration of our national life, and have sought
comfort in trying to prove that the grapes are sour, that we
do not need a national life at all, but have been endowed by
a beneficent Providence with a "Mission" different from
that of any other people, "a spiritual, intellectual mission,
which demands no practical service, but only preachers and
divines." In the case of the Jewish people as in that of
humanity at large, "these inventions, whether they assume
the guise of faith or of philosophy . . . are spiritual diseases,
with which the human race (or the nation) has become
infected as a result of certain historical causes"; and "both
alike prevent the human race (or the nation) from attending to this world, and lead it away from the plain, natural
course which lies before every living thing—to seek life in
life, and to defend its existence to the last gasp." The essay
is noteworthy alike for its marked positivist attitude and
for its insistence on the relatively unimportant part played
by pure reason—"cold reason, with its judgments and its
proofs, which promise so much and give so little"—in determining human conduct.

Meanwhile he had been busy with the Society of Sons
of Moses, and an article which he wrote for *Hamélitz* in
the autumn of 1890 under the title *Priests and People*
was in effect, though not avowedly, a defense of the idea
underlying that Society. The gist of it is that, notwithstanding a recent improvement in the condition of the Hibbath
Zion movement, due to its official recognition by the Russian Government and the accession to its ranks of people of
substance, its real object, which is national regeneration and

not individual betterment, will not be realized unless the
heart and mind of the people are penetrated by the Zionist
idea; and what is needed for this purpose is not an army of
fund-collectors, but a "guild of priests," a *corps d'élite* of
men devoted heart and soul to the idea and prepared to
sacrifice everything else for its sake. Of these men—

> those who can will settle in the Land and become the
> leaders and the guides of the rest of the settlers, whom
> they will inspire by their example to live and work in
> peace, mutual tolerance and harmony. Those whose cir-
> cumstances do not permit them to settle in the Land will
> find ample opportunities for work in the diaspora. It will
> be their task to win recruits for the ideal (and not merely
> members for the organization), to root out the habits of
> mind and conduct which have always militated against
> our success, and, above all, to educate the rising genera-
> tion in the right spirit, so that it may be better prepared
> than its predecessor for the great task that lies ahead. And
> all this they must do without drums and trumpets and
> battle-cries, quietly and modestly, as befits those who work
> for an ideal with no ulterior motive.

Shortly afterwards he contrasted the material and the
spiritual aspects of Zionism even more sharply in another
article, *A Friendly Attack*, written in reply to a critic of the
Hibbath Zion movement who claimed to be a well-wisher.
The critic, he says, confuses two different conceptions: that
of public needs which are really "public" in the sense of
being national, and that of public needs which are so called
only because they are common to a large number of individuals, each concerned with his own personal problem.
And he continues:

> If the critic had distinguished between these concepts, as
> he should have done, he would have understood that the
> Hovevé Zion, whose concern is only with the *national*
> need, are merely separate individuals, just like all other
> Jews, in regard to all the *personal* needs of the individual

members of the nation, their bread-and-butter needs. . . .
When he argues that only one per cent of the Jews will
settle in Palestine, he fails to realize that this one in a hundred is the one we want, and the one who provides us
with an answer to the problem of national survival—this
one, and not the ninety-nine individuals who will remain
in the diaspora. A circle has millions of points on its circumference, but the central point alone is the "soul" that
gives life to them all. . . . To the myriads of unfortunates
who look to Hibbath Zion to save them from a pauper's
grave we say: "Leave Hibbath Zion alone! It has nothing to
do with the troubles of the individual". . . . But there are
still many Jews whose material position is not so desperate,
and who nonetheless love their people and desire its survival; and they, seeing that our national unity is falling
to pieces for lack of a firm foundation, since religion has
ceased to be a sufficient cement, and the national sentiment is dwindling away, and will soon be extinct, as our
sons and daughters drift away from us one by one, to return no more—seeing all this, they ask in broken-hearted
anguish whether there is really no possibility of once
more turning these scattered atoms into a single whole, of
restoring to our people its lost *spirit,* or whether our disease is really incurable, because we are worn out by old
age, and the thread of our national life will grow weaker
and weaker until it breaks. To these, and *only* to these,
we reply—and there is no other reply—: Join the Hovevé
Zion!

Three points are here to be noted: first, the writer's conviction that without a revival of the national sentiment, such
as Hibbath Zion alone can produce, there is no possible
future for the Jewish people; secondly, his complete and
uncompromising refusal to regard Hibbath Zion as having
anything to do with the material problems of the suffering
Jewish masses; and thirdly, the adumbration, at this early
stage in his career, of the idea of the "national spiritual
center," which was to become his major contribution to the
philosophy of Zionism.

Early in the following year, 1891, he made another appearance in *Hamélitz,* this time in his most critical and pugnacious mood. A Jewish publishing house in Paris had recently celebrated its jubilee by the issue of a volume of essays by prominent French Jews under the title *La Gerbe,* and one of Ahad Ha-Am's close friends, the distinguished Russo-Jewish scholar and historian Simon Dubnow (1860-1941), had hailed this publication, in the Russian-language Jewish monthly *Voschod,* as proving how magnificently the Jews of France, in spite of anti-Semitism, were living up to the eternal ideals of Judaism. Ahad Ha-Am's impression was very different. He replied to Dubnow in a Hebrew article called *Slavery in Freedom,*[2] which, though much of it is topical only, ranks among the best of his less philosophical writings. His critical examination of some of the articles in *La Gerbe* reveals the desperate anxiety of its distinguished contributors to persuade their compatriots that their Judaism does not differentiate them from non-Jews in any significant way, and that they are thoroughly imbued with French ideals, to which they are convinced, in spite of the rumblings of Jew-hatred, that France, noble France, will always remain true. Moral and intellectual slavery is the price that the Jews of France have to pay for their much-prized emancipation; and in spite of their civil rights and their effusive French patriotism, they live always under the shadow of anti-Semitism. He concludes his onslaught with a proud assertion of the moral superiority of the rightless East-European Jew, who at least can call his soul his own:

> Terrible indeed are the backwardness, the degradation and the poverty that surround me here [*i.e.,* in Russian Jewry]; and well may I seek consolation by turning my gaze for a brief moment to that other land [France] in which we can find Jews who are professors and members of academies, generals and statesmen. But when behind all the grandeur and the glory I discern there also a two-fold slavery, moral and intellectual, I ask myself whether

I envy these Jews their civil rights; and in all sincerity I
answer, "No, a thousand times no!" I will have none of
them. I have no civil rights, but at least I have not sold
my soul for civil rights. I can proclaim my feeling of kin-
ship with my fellow-Jews, wherever they may be, without
having to defend it by far-fetched and unsatisfactory ex-
cuses. I can remember Jerusalem at other times than those
of prayer, and I can mourn its loss, in public or in private,
without being asked what Zion is to me, or I to Zion. I
have no need to idealize my people, and pretend that it is
superior to all others, in order to justify its existence. I
know why I remain a Jew; or rather, I can find no meaning in such a question, any more than if I were asked why
I remain my father's son. I can say exactly what I think
about traditional Jewish ideas and beliefs, without being
afraid that I may thereby cut myself adrift from my
people. I can even accept "the scientific heresy that bears
the name of Darwin" [this was a quotation from one of
the essays in *La Gerbe*] without any danger to my Judaism. In a word, I belong to myself, and my opinions and
feelings are my own. And this freedom of the spirit—
scoff who will—I would not exchange for all the civil
rights in the world.

Here is a complete reversal of the normal attitude of the
ghetto-bound East-European Jew towards his emancipated
brothers in the countries of the west. The superiority of the
western Jews was a dogma tacitly accepted by East and
West alike—so much so, that even a nationalist Jew like
Dubnow could be dazzled by the radiance of the spiritual
nobility of French Jewry as revealed by *La Gerbe*. Two
decades earlier Smolenskin had rebelled against the idoliza-
tion by the first maskilim of Moses Mendelssohn and the
assimilation to which he opened the gates; but it was reserved for Ahad Ha-Am to turn the tables on the assimilated
Jews by a proud assertion of the greater spiritual independence of those whom they were accustomed to pity and

patronize as their less fortunate and less enlightened co-
religionists.

Ahad Ha-Am's attitude to anti-Semitism, which is mentioned only incidentally in *Slavery in Freedom,* appears
more clearly in an essay called *Two Masters* (one of the
series of *Fragments*[3] to be mentioned below), which was
written a year later. In that essay he explains the apparently incongruous phenomenon of the survival of anti-
Semitism in civilized societies by an analogy from the Italian astronomer-priest Secchi, who, when asked how he
could reconcile his two occupations, replied: "When I study
astronomy I forget my priesthood, and when I perform my
priestly duties I forget astronomy." Experience has shown
that it is possible for civilized men and women to revert, in
their attitude towards the Jews, to the mentality of earlier
ages. And years later, in 1898, he wrote a bitter comment on
the Dreyfus affair,[4] the point of which was that since Ester-
hazy, the self-avowed traitor and Germanophile, had been
acclaimed by the people of Paris because he was the symbol
of Jew-hatred, clearly anti-Semitism was a more powerful
sentiment even than French chauvinism and hatred of Germany, which might have been supposed the strongest of
human passions. Unlike Herzl, he neither saw anti-Semitism
as the cause of Jewish nationalism, nor thought that it could
be ended by the establishment of a Jewish State. Like Smolenskin before him, he regarded it as a permanent feature of
human life, due basically to the unique character of the
Jewish problem, and not to be overcome by the advance of
liberal ideas.

At the end of 1891 the Hovevé Zion sustained a heavy
loss in the death of their President, Dr. Leo Pinsker, and
Ahad Ha-Am's next appearance in print was in a warm
tribute to the dead leader, for whom he had great respect.
In *Dr. Pinsker and his Pamphlet,* which was one of his contributions to the first volume of a Hebrew annual, *Pardess,*

edited by J. H. Ravnitzki (1860-1937), one of his closest
friends and associates, he describes how Pinsker, disappointed
by the failure of his pamphlet to attract support from the
Jews of the West for his project of a Jewish State, had become
a Lover of Zion—or rather a "Lover of the Lovers of Zion"—
and had accepted, and retained for eight years, the leadership of an organization whose activities were confined to
small colonization work in Palestine. There was no discernible relation between the work of the Hovevé Zion and the
large political scheme which Pinsker had propounded; and
he soon came to realize that they were not really inspired by
that strong national sentiment without which, as he himself
had stressed, no national object could be achieved. Yet he
had remained loyal to Palestine for the rest of his life,
and had declared in the presence of a number of his friends,
Ahad Ha-Am among them, that though it could not be
made a home of refuge for the Jews, he was no longer of
opinion, as once he had been, that it should be abandoned
in favor of some other territory still to be chosen. "In spite
of everything," he had said, "we must support the settlement
in Palestine and enlarge it as much as we possibly can. In
Palestine we can and must establish for ourselves a *national
spiritual center.*"

Ahad Ha-Am, who ten years later was to recur to this
subject of Pinsker's nationalism, and contrast it favorably
with the purely politico-economic approach to the Jewish
problem in Herzl's *Judenstaat,* was evidently much impressed by the discovery that Pinsker, like himself, assigned
to Palestine a function in Jewish life other than that of a
home of refuge for the victims of persecution and discrimination; and he ends his tribute by recounting an imaginary
"waking dream." He pictures a world entirely free from
anti-Semitism, in which there are nowhere any artificial
barriers between Jew and Gentile. As a result, the Jews
soon lose contact with their own tradition and culture, and

the Jewish people is on the verge of extinction. Most Jews view this prospect with equanimity; but there are here and there a few finer spirits who cannot but grieve to think that their nation, with its long history and its past glories, is about to disappear. These turn to the ancient home-land for salvation, and form a Society of "Philozionists," which in course of time succeeds, quietly and unobtrusively, in attracting a substantial following and obtaining the financial resources necessary to enable it to embark on the actual work of agricultural settlement in Palestine. As this work proceeds, carried on as it is with method and efficiency and with concurrent attention to educational and cultural needs, more and more Jews become interested in it, and the life and culture of Palestine Jewry exert an ever-growing influence on Jewish life elsewhere; until after several generations

the movement has achieved its aim: it has created in Palestine a national spiritual center *for Judaism;* a center which is held in esteem and affection by the whole people, and binds the whole people together in unity; a center of Torah and learning, of language and literature, of physical labor and spiritual purity; a true miniature of the Jewish people as it ought to be: so that a diaspora Jew thinks himself fortunate in being able for once to see with his own eyes the center of Judaism, and on returning home says to his friend: "Would you like to see the truly typical Jew, rabbi or scholar or writer, farmer or craftsman or businessman? Then go to Palestine, and you will find what you want."

So, Ahad Ha-Am concludes, the message of Pinsker is that Palestine cannot be a safe refuge for the Jews, but can and must be made a safe refuge for Judaism; and he adds, as his answer to the crucial question whether Jews or Judaism come first, that we must give pride of place to Judaism, and then, when the Jews have ceased to be merely so many disjointed atoms, the turn of the material problem will come:

for when Judaism is restored to its original home, and
when all the Jews of the dispersion, including those whose
condition is most secure, turn with genuine affection to
the Jerusalem of the present, and not merely to the Jerusalem of the past and the future, they will no longer need
wise men like Pinsker to convert them by rational argument to the idea of self-emancipation: the idea will arise
automatically as an inevitable result of their feeling of
affection for Judaism and for the country of Judaism. And
then, when the idea springs from the heart and is no
longer a child of reason and logic only, it will not be
deterred by external difficulties. It will look for means of
removing difficulties from its path, and will in due course
find them if it searches in the right way and with the
necessary patience.

Dr. Pinsker and his Pamphlet contains as clear and complete a statement as Ahad Ha-Am ever wrote of the essence
of Zionism as he saw it. We must look to Palestine here and
now, not to cure our material ills, but to restore our shattered
unity of sentiment and purpose; then in time the full realization of our national hopes will become possible. He never
deviated from this view. It is true that in the controversies
of the years that followed his tendency was to put the emphasis on the immediate need for a unifying force in Jewish
life, and to be silent on the prospect—vaguely hinted at in
the above quotation—of a fuller national redemption by
human means at some date in the more distant future; but
the suggestion that the establishment of a "national spiritual center" is only a first step, to be followed at a later stage
by a larger national effort, recurs now and then in his writings, and notably in the concluding sentences of his last
controversial Zionist essay, written in 1912. This notwithstanding, it was widely believed, first among Hovevé Zion
and later among Zionists, that for him the "spiritual center"
was the final goal and not merely a half-way house.

In another contribution to the first issue of *Pardess,* which took the form of a letter to the editor, he indicated his attitude on a question which was in dispute between the Zionist and the non-Zionist maskilim, and characteristically rejected the excesses of both sides. He called his letter *A Man in Private,* in allusion to the well-known maxim of J. L. Gordon "Be a Jew in private and a man in public." Gordon had given epigrammatic form to the ideal of the more moderate of the early maskilim, who did not preach root-and-branch opposition to traditional Judaism, but urged the masses of East-European Jews to adopt the language and culture of their neighbors, so as to be able to meet them on equal terms, while practicing Judaism in the privacy of their own lives. When the national idea began to spread, some of its devotees came to resent the implication of Gentile superiority, and by way of reaction developed a fashion of defending and even extolling every Jewish characteristic just because it was Jewish. Ahad Ha-Am, no less patriotic than the best of them, takes a different line. What the Jews of eastern Europe most urgently need, he thinks, is not to learn to behave like human beings—which means in practice like Russians or Poles or whatever it may be—in their dealings with non-Jews, but to rid their own Jewish life of those characteristics which prevent it from coming up to the highest human standards—the lack of unity and public spirit, the indiscipline, stubbornness and impatience of control, the excessive egoism and love of display, the boastfulness and the tendency to be too clever. When they have put their own house in order, they will be able to hold up their heads *as Jews* in the outside world.

But his most striking contribution to the first *Pardess* was a group of five essays under the title of *Fragments* (or more literally *Crumbs*), with the subtitle "Short Talks on Great Subjects." Three more *Fragments* appeared in the second *Pardess,* issued in 1894. He had already made a sort of trial flight in this *genre* a year or so earlier, with *Many Inven-*

tions; but the *Fragments* reveal a greater sureness of touch and a firmer control of his material. Moreover, though they do not stress the paramount importance of "the spirit" so much as his later work does, they are on the whole less nakedly positivist than the earlier essay: there is, for example, nothing in them to parallel the suggestion of *Many Inventions* that the "natural man" is in some sense an ideal, and the belief in immortality is a "spiritual disease."

The *Fragments* are philosophical essays dealing with religious and moral ideas, with the psychological forces that shape human behavior, and with the laws that govern the development of society. The title of the individual essay is in most cases an antithetic pair like *Sacred and Profane, Past and Future, Positive and Negative,* and this of itself indicates the author's general standpoint. He sees life as a struggle between opposing demands or ideas, which are ultimately compelled to come to terms because neither can obtain undivided sway. In the end some sort of equilibrium is reached, and ideas which are logically incompatible, and the modes of conduct based on them, live side by side in mutual tolerance and relative peace. This is the general theme on which most of the *Fragments* are variations. The exposition is masterly in its logic and lucidity, illuminated by flashes of insight, and without any parade of learning, though every now and then the author supports or illustrates his thesis by an appeal to history or literature, quoting now the Bible or the Talmud, now some modern thinker or philosopher, for the most part English, American, or French.

The *Fragments* reveal Ahad Ha-Am's thoroughgoing acceptance of the historical point of view, and his indifference to metaphysics. He assumes without question that the emergence and development of all human ideas, beliefs, institutions and customs is to be explained in terms of the reactions of man's desire for life and happiness to the challenges presented by constantly changing external circumstances; and this applies no less in the sphere of religion and morals than in that of the physical struggle for existence. Equally unquestioning is his assumption that a people or nation—which is for him primarily a race-cultural and not a political unit—has, like an individual human being, its own unique character and personality. The chief claim of these essays to originality lies in the emphasis thrown upon this last point, and in the concentration of attention on the psychology of the nation rather than on that of the individual. He often speaks of "the nation" where another sociologist would speak of "society," and makes the national history the framework in which the battle of antithetic forces is fought out. But the national history is for him a cultural or spiritual history, a history of the development of ideas, not one of the nation's economic and political life. Moreover, while the general propositions which he enunciates—about the difference between justice and mercy, the "hypnotic" influence of the environment on the mind and soul of the individual, or the tendency of a human group to become homogeneous through imitation of some outstanding member of the group by his fellows—are of universal application, it becomes obvious towards the end of each essay that he is thinking of the history and problems of one particular group, the Jewish people, and is not discussing abstract principles. The brief note called *Sacred and Profane* ends with a criticism of Reform Judaism for failing to recognize that in religious matters the external forms acquire a sanctity not inferior to that of the beliefs of which they are the shell. *Justice and Mercy,* which incidentally is unique among his essays in containing no reference, express or implied, to any current question of Jewish life, points to the Jewish conception of righteousness (though without explicit mention of Judaism) as the ideal mean between rigorous legalism and all-forgiving mercy. *Two Masters,* the theme of which is the puzzling co-existence of primitive prejudices with enlightened ideas, draws the moral that we cannot rely on progress to put an end to anti-Semitism. Of the five remaining *Fragments,* four end by advocating, with greater or less explicitness, the idea of Hibbath Zion, and the fifth, *Priest and Prophet,* proceeds from a consideration of these two types, representing broadly the compromising and the uncompromising idealist, to a condemnation of the "mission of Israel" theory beloved of assimilated Jews in those days.

Ahad Ha-Am seems to have been conscious that his pen was better occupied in writing philosophical essays like the *Fragments* than in Zionist polemics. In 1907 he wrote, in a letter to S. B. Maximovski (Maximon),[5] a younger friend and disciple who was then in London: "I remember that when I wrote the first *Fragments* I was certain that in future I should use only that form for the expression of my ideas, and should never again descend from that 'Olympus' to the battlefield of current events. But circumstances were too strong for me, and brought me down in my own despite." That circumstances were too strong for him in this case, as in so many others in the course of his life, is matter for regret; but the loss is not so serious as it might have been, because he brought down with him into the battlefield something of the Olympian breadth of vision.

For the time being the "battlefield of current events" was quiescent; and after the issue of the first *Pardess* he seems to have written nothing for some months. When next he addressed the public, in the autumn of 1892, it was with an article in *Hamélitz* occasioned by the notorious blood-libel —not by any particular example of this hoary slander, but by the puzzling phenomenon of its periodical recurrence even in the modern world. In *Some Consolation,*[6] as the article is called, the inveterate critic appears for once in the unaccustomed rôle of comforter, which perhaps helps to explain why the article has achieved a fame and a popularity which its intrinsic importance scarcely warrants. Its ingenious argument is that the blood-libel can help us retain our self-respect in the face of the indiscriminate abuse to which the Jews as a body are subjected because of the shortcomings of individual Jews. We are all apt to be influenced by such abuse, because of the difficulty of believing that "all the world" can be wrong; but we all know that in the particular case of the blood-libel we are as innocent as the babe unborn ("a Jew and blood—could there be a more glaring contradiction?"), and if "all the world" can be mistaken about that, there is no reason to assume that it must be right in accusing us collectively of lesser crimes or vices. He may have exaggerated the prevalence of the belief in the blood-libel; but the lesson was, and remains, much to the point.

The second *Pardess* includes, besides his tribute to Pinsker and the last three *Fragments,* a second letter to the editors,[7] in which he defines with greater precision than hitherto his views on the relation of Hibbath Zion to the religious tradition. Beginning with a defense of literature as a vehicle for the propagation of ideas, against critics who can see no use in anything but "practical work," he proceeds to argue that "the people of the Book" has become a slave to the book, and that Judaism has ceased to develop because the unchanging written word stands between the people and life, and renders impossible that healthy and spontaneous reaction which should keep religious law and practice abreast of human progress. He uses two telling illustrations from fiction, one from a poem of J. L. Gordon and the other from Zangwill's *Children of the Ghetto,* to drive home the point that needless suffering may be caused to individuals because the humaner instincts of the modern Jew are inhibited from asserting themselves against the harsh prescriptions of a code which was framed centuries ago in entirely different conditions. The remedy is Hibbath Zion: if worship of the written word can be replaced by allegiance to a

progressive ideal not imported from without, but derived
from the Jewish tradition itself, it will become possible to
modernize Jewish life and Judaism without obliterating
their distinctive character. In rabbinic times the law could
be adapted to changed ideas and standards, as for instance
when the biblical "an eye for an eye" was interpreted to
mean monetary compensation; and under the influence of
the national idea Judaism will cease once more to be bound
hand and foot by its past.

Here he comes very close to a demand for reform of
Judaism; but he treats the orthodox standpoint, as always,
very gently. He is at pains to make it clear that Hibbath
Zion (by which he means, of course, his own philosophy of
the movement) "neither excludes the written word, nor
seeks to modify it artificially by addition or subtraction."
No doubt in his own mind he emphasized the word "artificially," because he was, and always remained, hostile to
Reform Judaism as it had in fact developed, regarding it
not as a natural growth, but as a purely artificial response
to environmental pressures, the result of which would be
fatal to Judaism. He undoubtedly believed that Judaism in
its practical expressions would undergo far-reaching changes
when it was placed once again in conditions favorable to
spontaneous adaptation to modern conditions and needs.
But he refrained from offending orthodox sentiment by
being too explicit on so delicate a subject, not simply on
prudential grounds, but because of a genuine tenderness for
ideas and practices which, though they had lost their hold
on him personally, belonged to what he was in the habit of
calling "the holy things of the nation." Nor indeed was he
interested in religious reform in matters of detail so much
as in a shifting of the focal point of Judaism from observance to Hibbath Zion, of which he wrote, in the context of
the words just quoted, that "it is the whole of Judaism,"
and "stands for a Judaism which shall have as its focal point
the ideal of our nation's unity, its renascence, and its free

development through the expression of universal human values in the terms of its own distinctive spirit."

Ahad Ha-Am's contributions to the second *Pardess,* and particularly his letter to the editor, had the unintended effect of re-awakening the dormant flames of religious controversy. He was of course known to belong to the non-religious wing of the Hovevé Zion, and was always liable to attack on that score; but since the plea for mutual tolerance which he had made in his eulogy of R. Mordecai Eliasberg in 1890, the religious issue had not been in the forefront. Now, however, the relative outspokenness of the *Pardess* letter offered some of the fanatical opponents of the Hibbath Zion movement a chance which they could not forgo. There was an outcry against the annual, and in particular against Ahad Ha-Am, who was accused of being a heretic and an enemy of religion. Not only that, but he was falsely represented as being the head of the Hovevé Zion, all of whom accordingly shared his guilt. Not altogether unnaturally, some of the religious Hovevé Zion hastened to disown him and his associates; and thus the movement was threatened with a serious schism, which at best must weaken it, and at worst might destroy it altogether.

Ahad Ha-Am was in a quandary. Always willing to defend his views against reasoned criticism, he disdained to reply to mere calumny; yet the situation was so fraught with danger that it was difficult to keep silent. While he was still debating with himself whether to reply or not, he received a personal letter which put him out of his difficulty. The letter was from R. Jonathan Eliasberg, son of the R. Mordecai Eliasberg whose tolerance had won his admiration, and it challenged, in a moderate and friendly tone, what its writer not unreasonably regarded as Ahad Ha-Am's advocacy of religious reform. This gave Ahad Ha-Am the opportunity for which he was waiting, and he decided to make a public reply to the rabbi. In an elaborate article in *Hamélitz,* he again disclaimed, on behalf of himself and his associates, any intention of modifying the religious law, stressed the all-important distinction between spontaneous development and mechanical reform, and defended, with much learning and great dialectical skill, his contention that the adaptation of the religious law to the demands of the contemporary moral consciousness had been possible in rabbinic times. He reiterated his belief in the power of the ideal of Hibbath Zion to liberate the Jewish heart from its subservience to the petrified code, and ended with a plea for mutual tolerance and a warning against the machinations of those whose aim was to disrupt the national movement. This olive-branch (the Hebrew title of the article means "words of peace") is evidence of his constant anxiety to avoid alienating religious sentiment—an aim which was not rendered any easier of attainment by his rigorous intellectual honesty and complete candor.

In an essay in the Ahiasaf Yearbook for 1893-4 on *The Hebrew Language and its Literature* he broke new ground, or rather enforced a favorite thesis from a new angle. The theme of the essay is that the Hebrew language will not develop naturally, and its modern literature will not earn the respect and affection which Hebrew literature enjoyed in the Middle Ages, unless its practitioners cease to give pride of place to *belles-lettres,* and revert to the traditional Jewish attitude, for which knowledge and ideas were the real stuff of literature. This, he maintains, would accord with the character of the Jewish people, which goes to books primarily for instruction and not for aesthetic satisfaction. If the originators of the Hebrew revival a hundred years earlier had been true to the tradition, the expansion of the Hebrew vocabulary would have followed naturally in response to real needs. But in fact they had begun at the wrong end: they had made it their first object to restore the beauty of the Hebrew language by reverting to the poetical and colorful idiom and style of the Bible, which was not a suitable vehicle for the expression of modern thought. The literature of Haskalah had thus remained intellectually barren, and had not been able to win the respect of a reading public which esteems beauty and creative imagination less than learning and discussion of serious topics.

In this frontal attack on *belles-lettres* we have a striking example of the habit which Ahad Ha-Am developed, at an early stage in his literary career, of attributing his personal views and predilections to the Jewish people as a whole. His strictures on the Haskalah cult of imaginative literature clearly reflected his own intellectualist preference for learning and serious reading, and he had no apparent right to take it for granted that his was the attitude which was, and must forever remain, characteristically Jewish. It is true that there was backing for his assumption in the tradition in which he had been brought up. The traditional East-European Jew regards a book as primarily something to be studied. He does not speak of "reading" a book, but of "learning" it; what he wants from it is not diversion, but instruction or edification. But it does not follow that the traditional East-European Jew is typical in that respect, or in others, of what Jews always have been and always will be. As we shall see in due course, Ahad Ha-Am's insistence on the incompatibility of certain ideas to which he was unsympathetic with "the Jewish spirit" involved him later in much controversy, and his negative attitude to poetry and the literature of the imagination was in particular a target for attack. The issue remains, and must always remain, a controversial one; but it is not one on which Ahad Ha-Am's austere view can be lightly set aside, for all its apparent narrowness. Among his critics there was none with so sure an instinct for Jewishness as his.

A year later he contributed another essay in the linguistic field, called *The Hebrew Language and its Grammar,* to the next Ahiasaf Yearbook, and this time he showed his more radical side. His theme was the need for a reform of Hebrew grammar to meet the more recent developments of the language, which should no longer be strait-waistcoated by grammatical rules and principles formulated for the Hebrew of the Bible. He had evidently made a close study of the processes by which languages develop, and the essay contains some penetrating observations on the psychological aspect of that subject. His demand for a grammar of modern Hebrew, when the language was only beginning to emerge from the stage of a purely literary medium, was in advance of its time, and had to wait for its fulfillment until the development of spoken Hebrew and the establishment of the State of Israel transformed a revolutionary idea into a self-evident need.

It was during this same period that he propounded and defended in *Hamélitz* his ambitious scheme for a "Thesaurus (*Otzar*) of Judaism" in the Hebrew language. His statement of the arguments in favor of this project reveals his strong intellectualist bias. In an explanatory letter to Kalman Wissotzky, the Russo-Jewish philanthropist and patron of letters, which is reproduced in his first article on the subject, he writes that the best minds in Jewry "have recognized clearly that *knowledge* of Judaism is the most indispensable foundation of our survival as a scattered but not disunited people"; and after a glance at Jewish history he has no difficulty in showing that ignorance of Jews about Judaism was never more rife than now. The object of his projected thesaurus, he makes it clear, is educative and not scholarly. It is not to be primarily a work of reference for the specialist (though it may have its uses for him too); its chief aim will be to enable the general reader to acquire some knowledge of Judaism, that term being taken to include "everything that enables us to understand the Jewish people and its national spirit . . . . that is to say, the historical phenomena, both spiritual and material, both permanent and temporary, in which the spirit of the Jewish people has found expression from ancient times to the present day." It will be thoroughly abreast of modern scholarship both in content and in method, but it will be interested in the broad picture rather than in the minutiae of philology or archaeology, in synthesis more than in analysis. Its approach and its language and style will not be those of the dryasdust scholar. Though the alphabetical arrangement usual in encyclopedias will be adopted because of its practical convenience, the *Otzar* will be substantially a collection of monographs, each covering a wide field, and not a series of detached articles on individuals or points of detail. The language will be Hebrew—this was in Ahad Ha-Am's conception essential for a work so closely connected with the national revival—but the aim will be to make it intelligible to those whose Hebrew knowledge is not profound; and of course contributions will be translated into Hebrew from other languages in so far as qualified Hebrew writers are not available.

In his letter to Wissotzky he mentioned in passing a proposal which "Mr. Singer" had put forward in Paris some years earlier for a Jewish Encyclopedia in a European language, and which had been welcomed by Jewish scholars, but had fallen through, apparently because of financial difficulties. This is presumably the project realized a few years later in the *American Jewish Encyclopedia,* which appeared, under the editorship of Dr. Isidore Singer, in the years 1901-1906. Ahad Ha-Am's plan may have been stimulated by the early adumbration of the American proposal; but what he had in mind was something more akin to the great eighteenth-century French Encyclopedia of Diderot and his colleagues. His *Otzar* was to be a powerful instrument of the Jewish national revival.

Wissotzky promised to finance the project on condition that Ahad Ha-Am would accept the editorship of the thesaurus. This was a position of importance and dignity in

the literary world, for which Ahad Ha-Am was ideally
suited, and which would have afforded him an escape from
commerce; and his acceptance of Wissotzky's condition
would have contributed to the success of an undertaking to
which he attached the greatest possible importance from the
Jewish national point of view. Yet he did not accept. He
replied to Wissotzky that he could not find time to edit the
thesaurus without neglecting his business, and that if the
intention was that he should receive payment for the editorship, he would have to consider carefully how far he was
capable of combining "holy work" with material reward.
"Habit," he added, "is second nature; and I have never been
accustomed to make even a penny piece out of my public
work, which, on the contrary, has cost me a good deal."
His phraseology is very circumspect, but he probably knew
that a paid position was being offered to him, and was dis-
inclined to accept it. However, he refrained from giving a
definite reply until Wissotzky, who was abroad at the time,
returned home. He was sure, he wrote, that a question of
detail would not be allowed to interfere with a project of
such public importance; and he proceeded to publish details
of the scheme, mentioning Wissotzky's promise of financial
support, but not the question of the editorship, as though
the matter were settled.

The scheme, however, did not reach the stage of fruition.
The promulgation of the idea aroused a good deal of opposition, not only from obscurantists in Russian Jewry, who
were opposed in principle to anything that smacked of
modernism, but from some (not all) of the Jewish scholars
of the West, who could not grasp the idea of a sort of
encyclopedia designed not to help to furnish specialists with
the tools of their trade, but to give the average intelligent
Jew some knowledge of his own culture and history. Opponents of the latter type were to some extent misled, as
Ahad Ha-Am soon realized, by his choice of the alphabetical
arrangement for a thesaurus which had so little in common

with the scholarly type of encyclopedia; and he obtained
Wissotzky's agreement to a modification of the scheme,
under which, for an experimental period, the alphabetical
arrangement would be discarded, and a volume of monographs on some of the most important subjects would be
issued once or twice a year. This change of plan, however,
was of no avail. Wissotzky appears to have withdrawn his
promise of support, discouraged by the opposition with
which the project had met; and the scheme made no headway, though in a sense it remained alive for some years. A
letter of Ahad Ha-Am (quoted on page 148 below) suggests that in 1902 Hebrew readers were being asked to subscribe to the *Otzar;* and four years later still a slender
specimen volume, containing half-a-dozen monographs by
various writers (not including Ahad Ha-Am) and edited by
Dr. Joseph Klausner, was published by Ahiasaf. But there
the matter ended. Once more, as in the case of the B'né
Mosheh, the stern realist had allowed himself the luxury of
optimism and had met with disappointment.

❧ 2 ❧

In 1895, when he re-issued in the first volume of *At the
Crossroads* most of what he had written for publication
during the past six years, Ahad Ha-Am provided the volume
with a preface, to which he prefixed a quotation from Mon-
tesquieu to the effect that there are some truths which men
must not merely be persuaded to accept, but must be
made to *feel*. His own advocacy of Hibbath Zion, to which,
as he avowed in the preface, the whole volume was devoted,
was based on that principle. The appeal must be primarily
to the heart, and only afterwards to the head. His strong intellectualist bent did not preclude recognition of the sterility
of reason where the propelling force of emotion is lacking.

In summarizing his views on Hibbath Zion, the preface
stresses the need for "spiritual concentration" in the Love of

Zion before the physical concentration of the Jewish people in Palestine can become possible. It also repeats his familiar insistence on the importance of aiming at quality rather than quantity, and puts this point pithily in a sentence which earned him much obloquy: "A single flourishing settlement, capable of arousing our love for Palestine, would be better than a dozen tumbledown settlements which nothing but our love for Palestine can excuse." By this time he was already used to being attacked for his unpalatable views, and, as the following passage from the preface shows, was disheartened by an opposition which he suspected of being largely due to willful misunderstanding:

Whoever sets out to persuade men to accept a new idea, or one which seems to be new, not just as an idea, but as a truth which is *felt*, should know beforehand that the human mind is not a blank sheet, on which one can write with ease, and should not therefore grieve or despair when he finds that people do not pay attention to him. But when one sees that the public does not understand him, that is to say, does not wish to understand him aright, and that the more he exerts himself to make his meaning perfectly clear, the more others continue, some willfully and some mistakenly, to attribute to him opinions which he has not expressed, or even opinions directly contrary to those he has expressed, and to pester him with entirely irrelevant questions and criticisms— when one sees this, and sees the reasons for it, and those reasons are none too creditable, it is not surprising if at last he begins to feel weary and discouraged.

Feeling latterly that I am indeed weary and getting discouraged, I conceived the idea of collecting together some of the articles I have written so far: it may be that in their collected form they will achieve their purpose more successfully than they have done as scattered units, in course of time if not at once, and that at any rate they will provide material for any future inquiry into the theory and practice of Hibbath Zion in our generation.

The contents of the volume fully bear out the author's description of it as "devoted entirely to the idea of Hibbath Zion *in the broad sense.*" These essays and articles, many of them quasi-philosophical in form and approach, deal with a great variety of subjects, and reveal an astonishing range of knowledge and wealth of ideas; but there is not one of them that is concerned solely with abstract truth or theory. The author constantly invokes general principles, but he writes always with a single object in view: to influence the opinions and the feelings of his readers in a way which will contribute to the success of the Jewish national movement, which is his first and his last concern.

Throughout his career he was wont to complain of deliberate distortion and misrepresentation of his views by those who did not wish to accept them, in spite of his ceaseless efforts to make his meaning perfectly clear. It is true that his Zionist policy was and still is extensively misunderstood; but it seems probable that his own passionate conviction of the truth of his philosophy, and of the imperative necessity of its acceptance for the salvation of the Jewish people and Judaism, led him to suspect malevolence where the real reason for his failure to convince lay rather in the novelty of his approach and the remoteness of his scale of values from that of the ordinary man. The "man of the spirit," even though he may be a master of lucid and logical argument and exposition, is apt to miss the mark because those whom he would persuade have unconscious assumptions and presuppositions which are different from his own; and Ahad Ha-Am was none the less a man of the spirit for being at the same time a man of affairs, with more practical sense than many of his less unworldly colleagues possessed.

But if the unwillingness or inability of the Hovevé Zion to understand him and to adopt his ideas as the basis of their policy induced a mood of despondency, he can scarcely have failed to be aware, even at that early stage, that he was

widely appreciated as a thinker and teacher with a message
for his generation. There was, indeed, already in his occasional articles and essays something of an *ex-cathedra* air,
as of one who is laying down the law while in the act of defending a thesis. He had by now developed that sense of
mission which he seems not to have had six years earlier,
when the leadership of the Sons of Moses was thrust upon
him. As he says in his Preface, his desire to see the Hibbath
Zion movement working on what he considered the right
lines had overcome his original diffidence, and he had come
to feel entitled, and later in duty bound, to address the
reading public whenever he seemed to himself to have something to say that might help towards a better understanding
of the movement on which in his conviction the future of
the Jewish people depended.

The revolutionary nature of his message is indicated in
the statement, thrown off almost casually in the Preface,
that his volume of essays is "devoted entirely to the idea of
Hibbath Zion in the broad sense." No other writer would
have so described a book in which he had expressed his
views on almost every problem of contemporary Jewish life,
as well as adumbrating a philosophy of Judaism and Jewish
history. For the general run of Hebrew readers and writers,
"Hibbath Zion" meant nothing more than an organization
engaged in an attempt to re-establish Jewish national life
in Palestine by small-scale agricultural settlement, accompanied by such educational and cultural activity as might be
necessary to achieve that practical purpose. It had nothing to
do with the everyday concerns of Jewish life, with the Jew's
heritage of belief and practice, or with his intellectual interests and moral standards. Ahad Ha-Am placed the Love
of Zion at the center of Jewish life and thought, and used
it as the touchstone for a re-appraisal of both. For him, Hibbath Zion was intimately concerned with the religious and
moral ideals of the Jewish people, and held the key to the
solution of the problem of Judaism in the modern world

in its two aspects, that of the dejudaization of the assimilated Jews of the West, and that of the tyranny of the ritual code in the ghetto. He saw in the ideal of the Return to Zion, and in the practical effort necessary for its realization, a force which could breathe new life into a people harassed by enemies without and threatened by internal divisions, could restore its spiritual harmony and prepare it for a new era of creative self-expression. As a Hovev Zion he was concerned not only with the transfer of Jews from Europe to Palestine, but with all the spiritual values and excellences that went to the making of the ideal Jew, whose most precious heritage was in his view the moral law of the Hebrew Prophets. In a word, his Hibbath Zion was nothing less than "the whole of Judaism, but with a different focal point."

This novel presentation of Hibbath Zion was in fact a restatement of Judaism rather than a restatement of the program of the national movement, and as such it had an appeal to all Jews as such, Zionists and non-Zionists alike. By its insistence on the paramountcy of the national sentiment, it even transcended the difference between the religious and the non-religious, offering a basis of ideological— and not merely organizational—unity which had its roots in the Jewish tradition, and yet was independent of religious conviction or sentiment. Most of all it appealed to the *yeshivah*-trained intelligentsia, many of whom were no longer satisfied either by the stereotyped Jewish tradition or by the assimilationist Haskalah. To thousands of young men of that type Ahad Ha-Am's teaching came as a new revelation, and its author was invested by them with something of the sanctity which the hasidim attribute to their Tsaddik—as though Hasidism had taken its revenge on its recalcitrant son by making him the object of the kind of hero-worship against which he had revolted in principle. His noted personal integrity, and the strong emphasis which he placed on moral and spiritual values, fitted him for this rôle, and his outstanding intellectual gifts and dialectical skill reinforced the appeal of his moral personality. Thus, at the very time when his criticism of Hibbath Zion, and later of political Zionism, caused widespread resentment among the organized Zionists, he attained a unique position as the guide and teacher of his generation on the fundamental issues of Judaism and Jewish life. Nor did his preaching and teaching remain entirely without effect in the more limited sphere of practical Zionist policy, although his demands were too exacting for his advice to be often accepted against that of the recognized leaders. When, in 1901, his volume of articles and essays appeared in a second edition, he noted with some satisfaction in the Preface that since the date of the first edition certain of his ideas had passed into the currency of Zionist thought, though the opposition to him had become stronger than ever because of his hostility to political Zionism.

His style and technique as a Hebrew writer were no less distinctive and influential than his thought and his personal example as a Lover of Zion. His achievement in this field was to complete the emancipation of modern Hebrew prose from the artificiality and sentimentality which had been its besetting sins.

The prose writers of the earlier Haskalah period saw no virtue in saying a plain thing in a plain way; they luxuriated in archaisms and ornamental flourishes (*melitsoth*), designed rather to demonstrate the author's familiarity with the more difficult books of the Bible than to make his meaning clear to his readers. In a healthy reaction against the unaesthetic medieval habit of treating the language of the Gemara as though it had been Hebrew, they went to the length of refusing to accept as Hebrew any word which could not be found in the Scriptures; and this restricted them to writing what could be expressed in the pure biblical idiom, and led to the use of cumbrous and often absurd circumlocutions for the expression of simple ideas.

A revolt against the tyranny of the *melitsah* and the biblical vocabulary had begun some years before Ahad Ha-Am's first appearance in print, but it had not gone far enough to develop a Hebrew prose style completely suitable for the discussion of modern topics by modern men. Carrying to its logical conclusion the idea of emancipation from the pure biblical style, he took as his model the Hebrew of the Mishnah, which deals with the problems of everyday life in plain, workmanlike prose, and, as compared with the Bible, gains in precision what it loses in aesthetic and emotional appeal. He did not, however, go to the extreme of renouncing even occasional recourse to the earlier model. In the result, after a short period of somewhat less than complete emancipation from the *melitsah,* he produced a Hebrew of great lucidity and precision, lacking neither warmth nor color, but not overburdened with either, in which the reader's attention is never distracted from the argument by superfluous ornamentation or linguistic tricks, but he is every now and then reminded, by some felicitous use of a phrase familiar to him from his knowledge of the Hebrew classics, that what he is now reading is genuine Hebrew, and not a translation into Hebrew words of modes of expression indigenous to some other language. He used neologisms and borrowings from modern languages but sparingly: his aesthetic sense forbade frequent recourse to obviously non-Hebraic words from European vocabularies, and he was sufficiently conservative to be prejudiced against the new coinages from the Hebrew mint which were already gaining currency in his day. Yet despite the inadequacy of his vocabulary, he was able to make intelligible to Hebrew readers a wide range of ideas which had not so far found their way into Hebrew literature, and often had little affinity with its stock conceptions. And whatever he wrote was distinguished by economy of words and scrupulous care in their choice.

At the same time he developed a technique of essay-writing that was new in Hebrew literature. His strong sense of form and design enabled him to make of each essay a work of architecture, in which every paragraph appears in its appropriate place, and makes its due contribution to the effect of the whole well-knit and well-proportioned structure. Language, style and design combined to impart to his essays a truly classical dignity and weightiness, which were appropriate to the character of his mind and thought.

His far-reaching influence on the development of Hebrew literature was exercised both positively through the qualities of his own Hebrew writing, and negatively through his self-sacrificing work as editor of *Hashiloah,* the famous Hebrew monthly which he established in 1896. This influence must be reckoned as one of his major services to the Jewish renaissance of our day, in which the revival of the national language is a factor of such crucial importance.

7

THE
EDITORIAL
CHAIR

The publication of *At the Crossroads* was followed within a year or so by the collapse of the business in which Ahad Ha-Am was his father's partner. There is no contemporary record of what happened, but a few years later he included the following laconic statement in a brief autobiographical note written at the request of a correspondent in New York: "In 1895 I lost my money through a business misfortune (but did not, thank Heaven, involve others in loss)."

With a wife and three children to support, and with no other resource open to him, he was compelled to pocket his dislike of depending on Hebrew literature for his livelihood; and he accepted a paid position as Director of the Ahiasaf Publishing Company, which had been founded some years earlier on the initiative of the B'né Mosheh, and of which he had been from the outset the unpaid literary adviser. This involved his temporary transfer to Warsaw, which was the company's headquarters. Our information about this important change in his circumstances is woefully scanty, particularly as regards dates: but it appears from his published letters that it must have been early in 1896 that he became director of the company (which had only just been legally constituted), and that his acceptance of the post followed a period of acute anxiety and strain from the effects of which he did not immediately recover. He had to edit the Ahiasaf *Almanac*—a literary miscellany

—for 5656, which appeared in August, 1896; but his state
of mind was such that he did not feel equal to writing anything for it himself, or to contributing to the new *Pardess*
which Ravnitzki was then preparing to bring out in Odessa.

When he accepted the position of Director of Ahiasaf,
the members of the company's Board of Management hoped
that he would take up permanent residence in Warsaw;
and, the wish being father to the thought, they not only
co-opted him on the Board, but without his knowledge
styled the company "A. Ginzberg and Company" in its articles of association. This precipitancy was characteristic of the
happy-go-lucky mentality, so repellent to a man of his almost abnormal scrupulousness, which was a fruitful source
of trouble in his relations with the company during the ensuing years. In fact he left Warsaw after only a few months,
but his colleagues insisted on his retaining his membership
of the Board, with the result that he was made to share
the responsibility for policies of which he did not approve,
and on which he had sometimes not even been consulted.

His unexpectedly early departure from Warsaw, which
took place even before the Ahiasaf *Almanac* for 5656 appeared in print, was due to the new and alluring prospect
opened out before him by the public spirit of Kalman Wissotzky, who had undertaken to finance, for the first year
at any rate, a Hebrew monthly which Ahad Ha-Am was to
edit. Here was a chance to fulfill one of his most cherished
ambitions; for he had ideas of his own on the subject of the
Hebrew periodical press, and had long desired an opportunity of giving them practical expression by becoming an
editor himself.

During the latter half of the nineteenth century an extensive periodical literature in the Hebrew language had
come into existence in the East-European centers of dense
Jewish settlement. Dozens of Hebrew monthlies, bi-weeklies,
weeklies and even dailies testified to, and in a measure satis-

fied, the ambition of the maskilim, that numerically small but important section of the vast ghetto population, for contact with the culture of Europe. Many of these periodicals, probably most of them, were mushroom growths, which vanished after a few issues; but they all helped in some degree to break down the cultural isolation of the ghetto, and a few of them achieved some degree of stability and a lasting influence on opinion. The Warsaw *Hatsefirah,* first a weekly and later a daily paper, provided— under the editorship of Nahum Sokolow, the distinguished Hebrew writer who in his later years became second only to Weizmann in the leadership of the Zionist Organization— a veritable west-looking window for the Hebrew reader. Smolenskin's monthly *Hashahar,* published in Vienna, with intermissions, for fifteen years from 1869 onward, was one of the major influences in the swing of ideas away from the assimilationist aims of the earlier Haskalah towards the nationalist Haskalah which inspired the Hibbath Zion movement. This trend was also represented and fostered by the St. Petersburg *Hamélitz,* to which, as we have seen, Ahad Ha-Am contributed several articles in the early years of his literary career.

There were other periodicals of importance; but there was not, in 1896, a single Hebrew monthly of any note in existence. No very clear line was drawn in the Hebrew press of those days between journalism and literature, and apparently it struck nobody as anomalous that, for example, Ahad Ha-Am's reply to the younger Rabbi Eliasberg, replete as it was with talmudic learning, appeared in the daily *Hamélitz.* None the less, a serious publicist and scholar could scarcely regard a weekly or daily paper, necessarily giving much of its attention to day-by-day happenings, and precluded by considerations of space from publishing an article of any length except in installments, as a satisfactory platform for the sustained discussion of ideas and views on Judaism and the future of the Jewish people. There was, then, a gap which he felt himself qualified to fill. If three years earlier he had been eager to succeed Zederbaum as editor of *Hamélitz,* the prospect of editing a monthly journal, which he would be able to fashion from the outset in accordance with his own ideas and standards, and which would have no concern with the trivialities of the daily press, must have appeared even more attractive.

As permission to issue the journal in Russia was not forthcoming, he decided to have it published in Berlin, and himself moved to that city so as to avoid the inconveniences of lack of direct contact with the printer. In Berlin he became acquainted with a group of young Hebraists whose radical tendencies had earned the half-patronizing sobriquet of "the young men"—nowadays the adjective "angry" would probably be added—and with whom he was soon to cross swords in a debate about the conflict between Judaism and modern culture. With one or two of these, and especially with Micah J. Berdichevsky,[1] who became a Hebrew writer of note and his most redoubtable critic, he formed lasting friendships. Their personal intercourse, however, was of comparatively brief duration, for after nine months in Berlin, he returned to his home and thenceforth did his editorial work in Odessa. Meanwhile *Hashiloah* had been successfully launched.

As early as May, 1896, while he was still in Warsaw and engaged on the Ahiasaf *Almanac,* he had set about approaching possible contributors and collecting material for his first issue. The initial results were to some extent disappointing, and he expressed his pained surprise at the lack of eagerness to help him on the part of friends who took it as a matter of course that it was his duty to help them in their own literary projects whenever he was asked. His sense of injury led to a certain coolness between him and many of his Odessa friends; and in September he wrote to Ravnitzki, who had expressed regret at the impairment of their friendship, that he felt this so keenly as to be almost reluctant to return to Odessa. However, the ruffled calm of his personal relationships was soon restored; and he overcame his initial editorial difficulties in time to bring out the first issue of his monthly in October. He gave it the name of *Hashiloah,* the biblical river whose "waters go softly," thereby indicating his conviction of the need for deliberateness both in the pursuit of practical ends and in the expression of opinions, and his belief in slow and steady progress as against precipitate revolutionary change.

It was not part of his intention to use his opportunity, as another man might have felt entitled to do, for the propagation of his own views on the problem of the Jewish future. Probably his fastidious sense of fair play precluded any idea of taking partisan advantage of the advent of a Maecenas. He was firmly convinced of the correctness of his own views, but no less firmly convinced that public opinion must be formed by free and frank expression and discussion of ideas; and it would have been contrary to his principles to discriminate, as editor of a paper, against opinions that did not coincide with his own. Thus the object of *Hashiloah* was not propaganda, but the clarification of ideas. Its readers were to be given the opportunity of deciding for themselves between conflicting views honestly and reasonably expressed. The editor might of course express his personal opinions in signed articles, which would have no editorial authority; and he would be at liberty, when he thought it necessary or desirable, to append a dissenting note to any contribution with which he was not in agreement. It was probably in order to emphasize his editorial neutrality that from the outset the name of the editor shown on the cover was Asher Ginzberg, and not the pen-name under which exclusively he expressed his own views in print.

Editorial neutrality extended, however, only to the substance of the views expressed by contributors. As regards the mode of their expression, the position was entirely different. Here the editor must be the sole authority, and his

criteria of logic and grammatical correctness, of good taste
and good manners, must be binding. This was a requirement
to which Ahad Ha-Am attached the greatest possible importance, and which in the result, as we shall see, made the
burden of editorship extremely onerous.

An editorial introduction to the first issue of *Hashiloah*
sets forth the editor's intentions regarding the scope and
objects of the monthly, as well as his conception of his own
functions. The program makes it clear that *Hashiloah* is
intended for the general reader, not for the scholar, and indicates the kind of literary fare with which it will provide
him. The bill of fare conforms broadly, so far as its ingredi-
ents are concerned, to the customary pattern. There are to
be articles dealing with Judaism in the broadest sense of that
term; articles on current affairs; critical articles, in which
not only books, but the whole field of man's intellectual,
moral, and aesthetic life will come under review; and, finally, *belles-lettres*. It is in the way in which the dishes are
to be dressed up and served that the highly individual point
of view of the editor is revealed.

In spite of the headway made by the national idea during
the preceding quarter of a century, the fundamentally assimilationist philosophy of the earlier pre-nationalist Haskalah had not been abandoned by the modernizers. They
still saw the primary function of Haskalah as one of Euro-
peanization. Ahad Ha-Am in his program explicitly rejects
that idea. Our most urgent need at the present time, he insists, is to study *ourselves,* to understand our own history,
our own literature and distinctive ideas, our own problems,
in order to come to an intelligent decision about our own
future. Hence his program throws the principal emphasis
on subjects of specifically Jewish interest, and treats humanist culture in the broader sense as relevant only insofar
as it has a bearing on Judaism or Jewish life. His standpoint is thoroughly Judaeocentric. He is out to produce a
monthly which will not merely be Hebrew in its language,

but will reflect the specific character, outlook, and needs of the Jewish people.

Not less challenging to accepted ideas is the precedence he gives to learning and scholarship over current affairs and *belles-lettres*. He does not accept the tacit assumption that *Jüdische Wissenschaft* is or should be the preserve of dryasdust specialists, who bury themselves in the past and do not recognize any obligation to make themselves intelligible and interesting to ordinary folk. In the course of his actual editorship he was to make attempts, not all of which were successful, to obtain the co-operation of certain western Jewish scholars of note in what was for him the all-important task of presenting the fruits of scholarly research into the Jewish past in a form in which they could enlighten and guide the intelligent layman in dealing with the problems of the present and the future. For him that function of a Hebrew monthly was even more important than the provision of an informed commentary on current affairs. Regarded from this point of view, *Hashiloah* was another attempt, less comprehensive but more immediately practicable, to achieve the object with which he had planned the abortive thesaurus of Judaism.

There is yet another challenge in the announcement of his intentions regarding *belles-lettres*. He promises his readers "well-written stories of Jewish life, past and present, which will faithfully depict our mode of living at different times and in different places, or will throw light on some unfamiliar aspect of our internal life"—thus ruling out any excursion into the outside world, and subordinating entertainment to instruction. As regards poetry his austerity is even more unyielding. Poems are to be few in number and didactic in character. "Most of our contemporary poets," he says by way of justification, "do not make their poetry, as J. L. Gordon made his, the vehicle of ideas about Jewish life and its multifarious needs; and poetry pure and simple,

lyrical rhapsodies over the beauties of nature, the joys of
love and so forth—whoever wants these will find enough
of them in other languages." Here speaks his personal lack
of interest in imaginative literature, of which he had already given evidence in a published article. It may well be
that he would have liked to exclude *belles-lettres* entirely
from his program; but that would not have been tolerated,
even from Ahad Ha-Am, by a reading public which had
been taught to look upon *belles-lettres* as synonymous with
literature. So he did not place an absolute bar on poetry and
short stories, but severely limited the space allotted to them,
and restricted their writers to subjects drawn from Jewish
life. In practice he went even further than the program suggests in the matter of poetry, for, though he welcomed
poems from Bialik,[2] who was his disciple, and whose poetic
gift he had been among the first to recognize, he rejected,
with one solitary exception, all the poems submitted by the
rebel Tchernichowsky,[3] whose genius he appreciated, but
whose outspoken Hellenism seemed to him the negation of
the spirit of Judaism.

His program for *Hashiloah* let loose a storm of protest
reminiscent of that which had followed the first *Truth
from Palestine*. The "angry young men," and not they alone,
were outraged by what they regarded as the narrowness of
his conception of the subjects appropriate for treatment in
a Hebrew monthly, and the rigidity of his canons of what
was consistent with the Jewish spirit. His ill-concealed dislike of *belles-lettres* was a further rock of offense. The second issue of *Hashiloah* contained vigorous protests against
the program announced in the first; and, as we shall see,
the question of the extent to which Jews were at liberty to
adopt ideas seemingly at variance with the old Jewish tradition involved him in much controversy in the ensuing years.
He was not, however, the man to be deflected by opposition
from the course dictated by his convictions; and so long as

he continued to edit *Hashiloah,* it remained faithful to his principles.

The doors of *Hashiloah* were not, of course, closed to the advocates of ideas or policies opposed to those of its editor. Some of his most persistent critics, men like Berditchevsky, Ehrenpreis[4] and Thon,[5] were men for whom he had a great liking, and with whose general forward-looking attitude he was in close sympathy—so much so that he was even accused by opponents more conservative than himself of siding with them in their revolt against the traditional outlook. Even if this had not been so, his invariable refusal to allow personal feelings to influence or to be affected by differences of opinion on matters of public interest would have insured their receiving just treatment at his editorial hands; and this applied equally to all the other contributors. What gave him endless trouble as editor of *Hashiloah* was not the inevitable clash of opinions on questions of Judaism and Zionism and the like, but his insistence on imposing his own canons of form and taste on all his contributors. Those canons had been derived mainly from his extensive reading in European literature; and his ambition was to produce a Hebrew monthly which would measure up to European standards and be worthy of mention in the same breath with journals like the English *Nineteenth Century* and the French *Revue des Deux Mondes.* Referring at the end of his programmatic article to the duties of the editor, he wrote: "He must be the watch-dog of good taste and manners; he must reject anything that runs counter to ethical canons or the rules of good behavior; he must give to the organ which he edits a homogeneous character so far as concerns the subjects with which it deals and the manner in which they are presented." One of his main objects as editor—he even speaks of it in one of his letters as his principal object—was to teach the Hebrew-reading public the elements of European taste and literary manners, to lead them to appreciate and imitate the restraint, the tolerance, the sense of responsibility, and the regard for order and logic, with which cultivated Europeans were wont to expound their ideas and conduct their controversies in print.

There was certainly need for education of this kind, even if it was not quite so great as it was represented to be by Ahad Ha-Am, who was prone to sweeping judgments in such matters. The modernist Hebrew writers and readers of eastern Europe at that time were largely self-educated as far as non-Jewish culture was concerned. Most of them had not gone through the discipline of a modern school and university, and had had no opportunity of developing a tradition of approach and method parallel to that which is taken for granted among literate people in the European community. They carried with them into the new world of Haskalah characteristics and habits of thought and behavior which belonged to the very different intellectual climate of the world in which they had been brought up: they tended to be happy-go-lucky, inaccurate, imprecise, loquacious, lacking in the sense of measure and fitness. These and similar characteristics were an abomination to the aristocratic temperament and the sternly logical and orderly mind of Ahad Ha-Am, who by some miracle had himself escaped the half-bakedness of the typical autodidact; and they are summed up in the expressive but untranslatable Hebrew word *batlanuth.* The name *batlan,* meaning "unoccupied," was originally a title of honor, given to a man who devoted the whole of his time to the service of the community. While most people were too busy to attend synagogue except on the Sabbath, *batlanim* would be available even on weekdays to make up the *minyan,* or complement of ten required for a full service; and when in more degenerate times it became necessary to hire mendicants or near-mendicants to perform that sacred duty, the name *batlan* came to be applied to a paid *minyan*-man. Hence *batlanuth* has lost its once distinguished associations, and connotes characteristics such as those just mentioned. So it was against *batlanuth* in Hebrew literature and journalism that *Hashiloah* declared a kind of holy war.

After two or three numbers of *Hashiloah* had appeared, Wissotzky's son-in-law, Zeitlin, expressed his opinion of the paper in a private letter to the editor, and received a reply which runs in part as follows:

> The editor's duty is not to write articles himself, but to see to it that the contributors write as they should; and that duty I am fulfilling. I am aware of the deficiencies of *Hashiloah* in comparison with the *best* European periodicals; but when you compare it with *Hashahar,* and express the hope that in time it may reach that level, you must allow me to differ. If I knew that *Hashiloah* would be like *Hashahar,* I should not have the heart to put so much work into it. Whether the articles in *Hashiloah* are good or only average—that is a matter on which everybody may judge according to his own taste. But this I guarantee, that a European reader will not find in a thousand pages of *Hashiloah* as much *batlanuth* and pointless drivel as he will find in every issue of *Hashahar.* For me the main object is to educate the *taste* of the Hebrew reading public to the point at which they will cease to derive any satisfaction from the insipid and ill-mannered articles which at present they devour with gusto, and the like of which is not to be found in any other literature. I always say that the real influence of *Hashiloah* on its readers will be exerted not through what it prints, but through what it does not print. That is why it is far more highly appreciated by western readers than by those in our own country. Every Jewish paper in Germany, France and England which has mentioned *Hashiloah* has warmly welcomed it, and I have received private letters in the same sense. . . . The western reader . . . is pleased to see a Hebrew journal in which the articles are written in European style, and give him no cause to smile or raise his eyebrows. . . .

A month later he writes to Ravnitzki:

> We have scarcely any literature, or any writers, or even
> any decent people who can write two or three pages
> properly—I mean what would pass for "properly" in any
> other language than Hebrew. When by the grace of God
> I send to the printer the first article which I have not cut
> and corrected, it will be a red-letter day. What is worse,
> the less their ability, the greater their conceit. . . .

Similar uncomplimentary remarks about the quality of the
Hebrew writers on whom he had to depend for contributions to *Hashiloah* abound in his letters of this period, and
they show that he was not long left in any doubt about
the formidable nature of the task he had undertaken. The
asperity of his strictures suggests the impatience of a perfectionist, and he would have been bound to admit under
cross-examination that his condemnation was too wholesale.
But it is true that several contributors on whose promises
he had relied disappointed him, and that many of the
articles sent to him fell very far short of satisfying even less
exacting requirements than his. Many of the would-be contributors had not the slightest idea how to write a serious
article, and one at least had to be told that *ouvrage cité* was
not the title of a book. Ignorance of grammar and spelling
were as common as businesslike habits were rare. Manuscripts were carelessly written, illegible, or without space for
editorial corrections. Much of what was submitted had to
be rejected outright; and the hapless editor, who hated
hurting anybody's feelings, had to spend precious hours in
thinking out comparatively inoffensive ways of rebuking
the inconsiderate and slovenly, enlightening the ignorant,
and intimating to ungifted aspirants to literary fame that
they were engaged in a hopeless quest.

But though it was tiresome enough to have to waste so
much time and effort on rejected articles, his worst trouble
was with the residue that survived the first critical examina-

tion and were judged worth printing. There ought at that stage to have been little or nothing further for the editor to do; but in fact this was, in a great many cases, only the beginning of his labors. He rarely found himself able to pass an article for publication precisely as it had reached him. Besides careless or ignorant verbal errors, there would be obscurities, redundancies, unnecessary verbiage, mistakes of fact, above all personalities, lapses of taste, sins against good manners. All these things the conscientious editor felt it his duty to remove, without of course cutting out anything that was essential, or saddling a contributor with opinions that he had not expressed, or effacing the distinctive qualities of his Hebrew style. This was back-breaking work, and demanded the sacrifice of an enormous amount of time which might have gone into original writing, or study, or public work; but he submitted to it all, not cheerfully, but with resignation, because his ideal of producing a Hebrew monthly of European quality came first, and his personal convenience a long way behind.

In 1899, before leaving for Palestine on a mission which would occupy several months, he had to find somebody to fill the editorial chair during his absence from Odessa. His choice fell on Dr. Simon Bernfeld, of Berlin, an old friend and a man of wide knowledge, whom he felt he could trust better than anyone else to maintain his standards. In a letter to Bernfeld written a few weeks before his departure, he thus describes his way of dealing with articles sent to him for publication:

> Besides corrections of a purely literary character—corrections of language and style to conform with the rules of grammar and logic, to which many of our writers pay no regard—I try to get rid of all *batlanuth* and tasteless twaddle, all personal recriminations, and all showing-off and extravagant laudation of the writer himself or of others, and so forth. I hope that you will do the same.

Most of the articles I print in *Hashiloah* I treat as though they were my own, cutting and altering as required (but of course I never put into a writer's mouth ideas or opinions which he has not propounded himself), and I am sometimes compelled to omit *whole pages*. The authors have got used to this, and send me their articles on that understanding. So you too will sometimes have to make a whole out of bits and pieces. There is no other way of producing a decent Hebrew journal, because as yet we have not a great number of writers capable of turning out an article that will pass muster from the point of view of taste and manners.

None of his contributors, not even the most experienced, was in principle exempt from this cavalier treatment; and some of them not unnaturally resented it, and refused to write for *Hashiloah*. Ahad Ha-Am was quite inflexible. Whoever was not prepared to contribute to his paper on his terms; could go elsewhere. He incurred a great deal of enmity, but he won and retained the loyal cooperation of a substantial body of writers, including both veterans and tyros, who submitted to his high-handed treatment because they realized that he was entirely disinterested, and because generally they had to admit that he did not alter their manuscripts without improving them. Writers of note, like Berdichevsky and Klausner,[6] were restive under the treatment; but when either of them had occasion to re-issue in a volume of essays an article which had appeared in *Hashiloah,* he did not attempt to undo the editor's handiwork.

Ahad Ha-Am's dictatorial behavior as editor of *Hashiloah* is in strong contrast to his lack of self-assertiveness as head of the B'né Mosheh. In this latter capacity he had admitted the justice of the reproach that he always asked opinions instead of giving orders; as editor he laid down the law as to whether and in what form an article should appear in his journal, and refused to argue with discontented contributors about the reasons for his rejection or drastic alteration of their manuscripts. No doubt he was conscious of being as well qualified for the editorial position as he was unsuited for one which called for the exercise of arbitrary authority in the direction of practical affairs.

His qualifications were in the first place intellectual. A born student, with a phenomenal memory and a rare capacity for synthesis, he had absorbed and assimilated an enormous amount of knowledge in a wide variety of subjects. To begin with, he had superimposed Jewish scholarship of the modern type on the biblical and talmudic erudition and the profound knowledge of medieval Jewish philosophy which he had derived from his early studies both within and without the bounds set by orthodox tradition. Over and above this, his "external" studies, his reading in history, philosophy, psychology and sociology had been much more extensive than that of the general run of Jewish scholars, who tend towards specialization rather than broad culture; and he had achieved a rare, probably a unique, combination of Hebrew and Jewish knowledge with European humanism—a combination in which, though the humanistic element was no less integral than the Jewish, the latter remained the basic component. Many of his contributors could write with greater authority than he on this or that particular subject, but none was at home in so many different fields.

His many-sided erudition was matched by the sanity and objectivity of his judgment. He had strong views—his detractors might have called them prejudices—on many subjects, but he belonged to no party and had no personal axe to grind. He disdained to flatter or to be flattered, and he had an almost disconcerting regard for the truth. Whoever submitted an article for his judgment could be confident that its merits would be assessed without fear or favor after scrupulously careful consideration, and that if it was accepted, any alterations of substance made or suggested by

the editor would be based on grounds more solid than mere
personal preference. Even the poets and the story-writers,
whose work was intrinsically of little or no interest to the
unromantic editor, could derive benefit from his advice, for
he could show Bialik how a weak line could be strengthened, and Brainin[7] how the plot of a story could be made
less implausible. And his freedom from bias was apparent
in the impartiality with which he encouraged younger
writers in whom he detected exceptional promise. His
protégés included not only Bialik, who was in the closest
sympathy with his outlook, but also Berdichevsky, his most
forthright critic.

In the result he won for his monthly a prestige such as
no other Hebrew periodical has ever enjoyed or deserved.
To write for *Hashiloah* was in itself a distinction, and other
journals were glad to print its rejected manuscripts. And
its editor enjoyed a position in the world of Hebrew letters
not unlike that of Samuel Johnson in eighteenth-century
English literature. Before embarking on his editorial career,
as merely "an occasional visitor to the shrine of literature,"
he had become one of the foremost living writers of Hebrew,
and the extent of his influence on the younger writers had
been out of all proportion to the quantity of his literary output. Now, as editor of the premier Hebrew monthly, he
was at the center of the intellectual life of East-European
Jewry, and was in frequent contact with its leading figures,
who felt the impact of his combination of uncompromising
idealism with practical sense, and of intense Jewishness with
unquestioning acceptance of European canons of taste and
style. Not only the ten half-yearly volumes of *Hashiloah*
which he produced, but the whole of contemporary Hebrew
literature, bore witness to the tonic and cathartic effects of
his war against *batlanuth* in all its aspects, of his dictatorial
treatment of aspirants to literary honors, and of his incul-
cation, by precept and blue pencil alike, of the virtues of
simplicity and intelligibility. In the adventure of editorship

he achieved a greater measure of success than was granted to him in any of his other undertakings in the field of Jewish national endeavor.

The success was not achieved without a vast amount of labor, much of it distasteful. His extreme conscientiousness, and his determination not to allow anything to appear in the paper without his personal approval, made delegation of work impossible. He felt it necessary to read every contribution carefully himself, because even experienced and reliable contributors could make slips which must not go uncorrected, and as for the inexperienced, "it goes without saying that it is my duty, as editor, to teach them how to write, which I cannot do unless I read all their manuscripts carefully and revise them in detail." Then he must read the proofs also, because he always found that, in spite of all his care, he had failed to make all the necessary corrections in the manuscript. When Frischmann asked to be given charge of a section of the paper (presumably the *belles-lettres* section), he found the request "merely amusing," and added: "Even if Herbert Spencer were to ask me to place a section of the paper entirely at his disposal, I should refuse." He insisted on seeing even the green-paper cover of the journal in proof, for fear the publishers might word some literary advertisement in a way of which he did not approve. Small wonder that he was often on the point of throwing in the sponge. But he had found a vocation for which he knew himself qualified, and he held on until he found his position untenable for reasons not connected with the excessive labor involved in the attempt to discharge its duties as he understood them.

⁂ 2 ⁂

His editorial tribulations might have been less difficult to bear if the financial position of *Hashiloah* had been rea-

sonably secure; but that turned out to be an unattainable
ideal. Readers and critics gave the first number a mixed reception, and from the sales point of view the journal was
far from being an unqualified success. It was not, however,
in the editor's nature to trim his sails to the wind, and he
went his way without troubling about other people's opinions or about circulation. It is characteristic of his independent attitude that during the first year, when he himself
was responsible for the circulation of the paper outside
Russia, he indignantly rejected a suggestion that he should
send copies of the first issue to a number of possible subscribers unasked and free of charge. He would not for anything in the world adopt a procedure which he regarded
as an insult to Hebrew literature. But it is equally characteristic that in the following year, when the responsibility
for foreign as well as internal distribution was in the hands
of the Ahiasaf Company, to which Wissotzky had handed
over the paper after its first year, he replied to a correspondent who made the same suggestion that he personally was
against it, but the matter was no longer in his hands, and
if his correspondent cared to put the proposal to Ahiasaf,
they might adopt it. This is only one of many instances in
which, by acquiescing in a course of action of which he did
not approve, but for which he had no personal responsibility, he made co-operation possible between himself and
men who were not in thrall to his own almost frightening
standards of behavior.

Wissotzky, who had provided the capital with which
Hashiloah was started, seems to have been disheartened by
the failure of the paper in its early stages to attract a large
public. He did not relish the prospect of having to meet a
considerable deficit for an indefinite time; and there was a
danger that the journal would not outlive its first year.
However, Ahiasaf, of whose Board Ahad Ha-Am was still
a member, with responsibility, at least in theory, for its

publishing policy, stepped into the breach, and took over
the financial burden. In the following years the paper was
more than once on the brink of death from financial inani-
tion, and there were gaps in its appearance, so that only
ten half-yearly volumes, instead of twelve, had been completed when Ahad Ha-Am retired at the end of 1902. His
salary of 2,000 roubles a year, equivalent to just over £200,
was a miserable pittance even in terms of the monetary
values of sixty years ago, and apparently had to be supplemented by non-literary activities of some unspecified
kind; and the death of his father in 1899, leaving him with
his mother and two sisters to support—"a father of two
families," as he put it—added materially to his financial
burdens. He did not complain of his inadequate salary; but
indirectly it was finance that led to the final breach with his
publishers, with whom, no less than with his contributors,
he was always having differences of opinion.

Despite his kindly nature and his readiness to stretch
points so far as his overmastering conscience allowed, he
must have been a somewhat "difficult" person. Ordinary
flesh and blood cannot work easily with a man who is so
intensely critical, so sensitive, so exacting in his standards—
even though he demands less of others than of himself—so
scrupulous and punctilious, so apt to exaggerate the importance of minor failures in the performance of obligations.
His letters to Ahiasaf, and still more his personal letters to
the Chairman of the Board, his close friend A. Kaplan, are
full of reproaches for unbusinesslike methods, for not keeping him informed of what is going on, and for failing to
consult him before taking decisions for which he must
share responsibility. The reproaches were no doubt justified,
and his plain speaking and occasional asperity were accepted
as part of the price that had to be paid for having him as a
colleague. It was no doubt realized that he acted as he did
because he "could no other." But if he could answer those
who complained of his stubbornness in matters of principle,

as he sometimes did, with "I am as God made me," his colleagues might have entered the same plea when he complained of their failure to conform to his standards; and, moreover, it was they who had to find the money.

It was here that the real difficulty lay. The number of subscriptions to the paper, never large, tended to diminish as the years went by, and the other members of the board put the blame on the editor's lofty standards and his inflexible refusal to compromise with them. How unbending he was is indicated in a letter he wrote to Berdichevsky in the middle of 1897:

> As regards *Hashiloah,* the outlook is very gloomy. . . There is a great difference between myself and other editors who have successfully struggled through. They were willing to accept subsidies, to beg help from institutions, to make lavish promises to their contributors and readers without worrying about their ability to fulfill them. I could not do these things even if I thought it legitimate to do them for the sake of Hebrew literature.

Similarly he returned a blank refusal to all suggestions that he should make the paper more "popular" in order to attract a wider public. As a way out of the impasse, his fellow-directors decided in 1900, against his protests, to start a less serious paper, the weekly *Hador,* under Frischmann's editorship, in the hope that it would make a profit sufficient to cover the loss on *Hashiloah.* This hope soon proved illusory, and Ahad Ha-Am was again pressed to liven up his own paper; but he was unmoved, and wrote to Ahiasaf:

> I value *Hashiloah* as it is, and I cannot change it into a light magazine suitable for reading in bed. If you find that there is no public for the paper, the best thing to do is to discontinue it and to go on with *Hador,* which in your opinion is the kind of paper the Hebrew public wants. Please do not suspect me of sarcasm. I assure you that I really mean what I say. *Hashiloah* must either retain its original character or cease to exist. To compromise,

to change its form and contents, or, in a word, to publish *Hador* under the name of *Hashiloah*—that I cannot agree to. You can of course decide to do it without my agreement, but I will have no part or lot in it, either as editor or as contributor. Better that I and my family should go hungry than that I should help with my own hands to drag in the dust the standard which has been sacred to me so far.

On the day following this outburst he wrote another letter in calmer mood, with the eminently practical suggestion that *Hashiloah* should become a quarterly, should be restricted to literary and scholarly contributions, such as are not appropriate to a weekly, and should be available to subscribers to *Hador* at a reduced price. Nothing came of this suggestion; *Hador* expired not long afterwards, and *Hashiloah* continued as before. But the financial position did not improve, and in May, 1902, the general meeting of Ahiasaf decided that the position would have to be seriously considered if the deficit rose above a thousand roubles a year. Ahad Ha-Am was hurt by the implication that his paper was not worth more than that trifling sum; and in a letter to Mordechai ben-Hillel Hacohen,[8] in which he said that he would like to find another occupation, he referred to the bickerings between rival Hebrew publishers in Warsaw, and added with his usual forthrightness: "I would gladly be a crossing-sweeper if I could escape having anything to do with Hebrew literature on its business side." Later in the year the financial position of *Hashiloah* reached the danger-point, and Ahiasaf decided that the paper must close down unless its editor would consent to a reduction of his already exiguous salary. Thereupon, in October, he formally resigned the editorship as from the end of the year. He had at that time no prospect whatever of any other means of livelihood; but his indifference to prudential considerations did not in fact expose him and his family to the risk of

starvation, for within the next few weeks he was offered,
and accepted, a position in the Wissotzky firm.

The mingled feelings of relief and disgust with which he
left the editorial chair are reflected in his published letters.
To Hacohen he wrote, when his resignation was imminent:
"So henceforth I shall be just a plain man, and a literary
amateur, as I used to be; and the 'lovers of Hebrew literature'
will no longer be under obligation to subscribe to *Hashiloah*
or to the Thesaurus of Judaism in order to provide Ahad
Ha-Am with a living. Thank God, who hath delivered me
from the charity of my fellow-Jews!" And to Ahiasaf he
wrote at the same time, with more restraint and less bitterness:

> I have written at great length, but I have not told you one
> hundredth part of what is in my mind, and perhaps not
> one thousandth part of what the future historian will
> feel—if, as we hope, there is a brighter future in store for
> our people—when he has to tell his readers that in this
> age of ours, this age of the much-vaunted "revival," one
> of the foremost Hebrew writers, after editing for six years
> the only Hebrew monthly of any literary value, was
> compelled to give up the editorship and accept a position
> in a business house, so as not to have to eat the bread of
> beggary and humiliation.

So ended his only experience of Hebrew letters as a pro-
fession. It was at best a precarious and poorly-paid profes-
sion, and many another Hebrew writer had found himself
under economic compulsion to transfer his allegiance to
Yiddish or some other language. For Ahad Ha-Am that
way was not open: it would have involved treachery to his
own principles. Fortunately his business experience and his
connections provided him with an alternative which was not
within the reach of the general run of Hebrew writers; but
he cannot have relished the prospect of a return to commerce, and in the capacity of an employee at that. Even

more galling was the realization that there was so little genuine demand for the *Hashiloah* that he had made, and that there was an element of disguised charity even in the meager financial support which the paper had attracted. His sense of personal humiliation was sharpened by a growing doubt whether, if such a thing could happen, the idea of a Jewish cultural revival could be more than a mirage.

In fact the position was not so desperate as he allowed himself to believe under the shock of disappointment. *His* monthly could not exist without him; but the event proved that *Hashiloah* could survive his departure without falling too far below his standards. On his retirement, the editorship was entrusted, with his unenthusiastic consent—for he did not think that anybody else would carry on his tradition, and he would have preferred the paper to die rather than to lose its distinctive character—to Joseph Klausner, still a young man under thirty and a recent graduate of the University of Heidelberg. Klausner was broadly a follower of Ahad Ha-Am, but temperamentally less austere and more optimistic. He united a genuine and immensely productive devotion to scholarship with a taste for imaginative literature and a touch of the radicalism of the "young men"; and he was not prepared to accept the view of his predecessor that the Hebrew writers of the day were not capable of dealing with the broader aspects of humanistic culture. He modified the policy of the paper in accordance with his own views, especially in the department of *belles-lettres,* in which Bialik was for a time his co-editor, and succeeded in carrying it on, with some intermissions, for twenty-five years, taking it with him when he left Odessa for Palestine in 1919. The last number of *Hashiloah* appeared in Jerusalem in 1927—a few months after the death of its founder and first editor in Tel Aviv.

8

MISSION

TO

PARIS

Within a year of the first appearance of *Hashiloah,* the launching of Herzl's Zionist Organization provided a new target for Ahad Ha-Am's criticism, and thenceforth his campaign against political Zionism—another holy war— became his major preoccupation, though not to the complete exclusion of an important controversy with the "young men" about humanism and occasional skirmishes on other issues. We shall be concerned in later chapters with his activities as critic and controversialist during the *Hashiloah* period. For the moment his work as a member of the Odessa Committee of the Hovevé Zion once more claims our attention for a brief space.

The vast majority of the Russian Hovevé Zion, far from scenting a dangerous rival in Herzl's new movement, greeted it with enthusiasm, and enrolled in the Zionist Organization almost as a matter of course. They were not, however, prepared to abandon the agricultural settlements already established in Palestine, or indeed to give up entirely the attempt to increase their number, although Herzl was in principle opposed to petty colonization. Thus the birth of the new movement did not bring about the demise of the old. Hibbath Zion lived on, as an organization for the settlement of Jews on the land in Palestine, with its headquarters in Odessa, until after World War I, and in its later years became for practical purposes a part of the Zionist Organization. And Ahad Ha-Am found time, in spite of the exacting demands of editorship, to remain a member of the Odessa Committee, and continued to take an active interest in its colonization work so long as he lived in Russia.

Since his second visit to Palestine, in 1893, there had been no substantial improvement in the condition of the agricultural settlements. Most of them were dependent on the generous help of Baron Edmond de Rothschild, and his administrators, largely assimilated French Jews, had no understanding of Jewish nationalism and no personal interest in Palestine. The baron's paternalist methods sapped the intiative of the settlers, who, if they lost money, could rely on the administration to make good their losses; and he insisted on the concentration of effort on viticulture, with the result that there was excessive producion of wine, for which the administration paid the settlers an uneconomic price in order to save them from ruin. No Jewish peasantry was being built up: the number of Jews actually working on the land was small, and most of the settlers employed, and preferred to employ, Arab labor. The cultural picture of the *yishuv* was little more encouraging than the economic one. Hebrew was beginning to take root as a spoken language, thanks mainly to the idealism of workmen and schoolteachers; but as a medium of elementary and secondary education it was severely handicapped by inadequate terminology and lack of text-books. The colonization movement seemed to be losing whatever vitality it might once have possessed, and its prospects looked bleak indeed when the Zionist Organization appeared on the scene. The new movement, as already mentioned, looked askance at petty colonization, and its rise must have had the effect of reducing still further, by the appeal of its large promises and wide horizons, the amount of effort and leadership that East-European Jewry had so far been contributing to the work of Hibbath Zion.

The Odessa Committee was growing increasingly uneasy about the situation, and at the end of 1897 asked Ahad Ha-Am to go out to Palestine as its emissary for three or four months in order to make an investigation on the spot and bring back the exact facts. Though he would have welcomed an opportunity of seeing the beloved land again, he felt unable to accept the invitation at that time because of his editorial duties; but when it was renewed a year later, the future of *Hashiloah* being then somewhat uncertain, he agreed in principle. However, he was prevented from leaving Odessa by the illness of his father, and the plan again fell through. His father died in the following April. (It is of some interest that, in spite of his long estrangement from the synagogue, he apparently attended service and recited the *ḳaddish* daily during the year following his bereavement.) Then in the summer of 1899 he had some nerve trouble, and was ordered by the doctors to take a complete rest—an injunction which he obeyed only in a very limited sense. Not till the end of 1899 did he set out on his mission, accompanied by an agronomist named Zussman. No private notes on this journey, which occupied in all about six months, appear in his *Reminiscences;* but his expense account was unearthed and published long after his death. It shows that he repaid to the Committee after his return over a fifth of the sum that he had received in advance, and that his subsistence costs amounted to about twenty dollars a month (equivalent to perhaps 120 at today's prices). We know from another source that he spent nearly 100 dollars on incidentals which he did not feel that he ought to charge to the Committee, that he was in straitened circumstances at the time, and that the fatigue of the journey more or less incapacitated him from writing for six months after his return home.

Back in Russia in the middle of 1900, he reported orally to the Committee, and because of the wide public interest in his mission, a summary of his report was published both in Russian and in Hebrew. He was not satisfied with this, and resolved to deal with the current problems of the *yishuv* more fully in a series of articles in his own monthly *Hashiloah,* but was unable to carry out this intention for a considerable time, during which the position in Palestine worsened to an alarming degree. At last, in 1901 and 1902, he produced two long articles—the longest he ever wrote— each of which was published in *Hashiloah* in installments over a number of months. The first, *The Jaffa Schools,* dealt with the problem of the two Hebrew schools, for boys and girls, in Jaffa, which had been the pride of the Hovevé Zion, but in which his critical eye and his exacting standards could find little cause for satisfaction, whether from the point of view of general or of specifically Jewish education. The second article, which was called *The Yishuv and its Patrons,* dealt in considerable detail with the practical and economic aspects of the colonization effort, and was in essence a full-scale attack, supported by a wealth of detailed evidence, on the system of spoon-feeding which he had con- demned six years earlier as one of the main causes of the ill-success of the settlements, and which had not been modi- fied in the interim.

As before, he held Baron Edmond de Rothschild respon- sible for this pernicious system, which had also to some extent infected even the few independent settlements; and he suggested that the Hovevé Zion should send a delegation to Paris to draw the Baron's attention to the harm that his well-meant philanthropy was doing, and to demand a thoroughgoing reform of the administration. This sugges- tion was taken up, and Ahad Ha-Am was appointed a mem- ber of the delegation, the leader of which was his close friend Meir Dizengoff (1861-1936), later to become the first mayor of Tel Aviv. Another of its members was Mena- hem Ussishkin. In its original conception the delegation was intended to be representative of the Hovevé Zion of Russia, or of Russian Jewry generally; and Ahad Ha-Am was greatly disappointed when most of the men of light and leading who were appointed members found themselves unable or unwilling to make the journey to Paris.

Later it was decided to give the delegation a still wider character, and to include members from Palestine and other countries, among them some prominent representatives of Herzl's Zionist Organization, which at that time had its headquarters in Vienna. It appears that Max Nordau at one time intended to join the delegation, and that the Zionist Executive wished the members to hold their preliminary meeting, which was necessary to enable them to iron out differences of approach and formulate a common policy, in Vienna rather than in Warsaw or elsewhere in Russia. Ahad Ha-Am was indignant at what he regarded as an attempt on the part of the Zionist Organization to control or influence the policy of the delegation, and threatened to withdraw from it. His indignation was increased when not only did Nordau withdraw on the ground that the delegation would carry no weight and could achieve nothing, but the Vienna Executive compelled another of its members, Dr. Kokesch, to cancel his agreement to participate in "a begging mission to the Jewish Colonization Association" (to which the baron had recently handed over the management of his settlements). Ahad Ha-Am's view was that in the dire extremity of the *yishuv* those who cared about it could not allow considerations of their own dignity to stand in the way of any action that might prove helpful. He was, however, under no illusions as to the prospects of a successful outcome.

In the end he was one of a delegation of only five or six that went to Paris and had an interview with the baron. The result justified his worst forebodings. He was for taking the strong line which he considered appropriate to the representatives of a national movement, and telling the great philanthropist in plain terms that he had no right to treat the Palestine settlements as a rich man's plaything; but his advice was not taken. At the meeting of the delegation which took place on the evening before the interview with the baron, it was decided, with two dissentient voices of which presumably his was one, to adopt a conciliatory attitude and avoid saying anything that might offend the great man and possibly lead him to withdraw his financial support. This line was duly followed at the interview; and when in reply the baron, speaking deliberately and with great emphasis, said that *he* had made the settlements, that nobody, no farmer and no organization, had a right to meddle in his affairs or express an opinion on his policy, and that he objected *"complètement, catégoriquement, énergiquement"* to any such interference, they submitted tamely to this rebuff, and went away with their tails between their legs.

Ahad Ha-Am was furious. He resigned from the delegation, and in a stinging article in *Hashiloah,* with the title *Delegates of a Penniless People,* castigated both the autocratic philanthropist and the spineless representatives of the national movement, who in his opinion ought to have been ready to sacrifice the immediate interests of the *yishuv,* if necessary, rather than acquiesce in its degradation. There was some support for his views on the Hovevé Zion Committee; but the majority not unnaturally approved the less heroic course that the delegation had taken. The pretense was for a time maintained that the delegation was still in being and would continue its efforts to secure a reform of the administration of the settlements; but in fact the pass had been sold with its submission to Baron Edmond's dictatorial attitude. It should be added, in fairness to the baron,— who may or may not have seen or heard of Ahad Ha-Am's strictures—that in later years that attitude was considerably modified, and that when he visited Palestine in 1925, and was received by the *yishuv* with almost royal honors, his critic of old, then living in retirement in Tel-Aviv, was treated by him with marked deference.

The affair of the delegation illustrates Ahad Ha-Am's moral courage, but also reveals his limitations as a man of action. He stood up boldly for the principle that the *yishuv,* as the spearhead of the national revival, had an importance which transcended even that of a Rothschild; and there was something magnificent in his indifference to prudential considerations when the choice lay between them and the national dignity. But his strong sense of discipline forbade him to defy the majority resolution against plain speaking; nor was he ruthless enough to risk jeopardizing the colonization work—though probably the risk was not large in practice—by taking a strong line. A man less scrupulous and of stronger will might well have ignored protocol and spoken his mind to the baron, instead of holding his peace at the crucial moment and expressing his disgust afterwards.

9

JEWISH
HUMANISM

One of the complaints leveled against Ahad Ha-Am as editor of *Hashiloah* was that his own contributions to the paper were too few. He replied that the editor of a European monthly rarely contributed to his own paper, and that in any case the task of correcting other people's articles was too exacting and time-consuming to allow him to write much himself. In point of fact, his literary output during these six years was, for so unprolific a writer, quite considerable in quantity, and it included much of his most important work.

Throughout the years of his editorship it was his practice to contribute to *Hashiloah,* at irregular intervals, notes and comments, some short and some longer, on all sorts of questions of current interest. He gave this series from the start a general title, which may be freely translated *A Little Miscellany*,[1] and later he included the whole of it in his collected works, because, as he wrote, "many readers have always liked the *Miscellany* both for its contents and for its language and style, and many expressions which appeared in it for the first time have passed into general currency, and are used by people who do not know their origin."

There was more justification than might appear at first sight for treating this collection of disconnected notes and comments as a single work. The strongly-marked individuality and the independent standpoint of the writer lent a kind of unity even to so mixed a bag of disquisitions on a bewildering variety of subjects of different degrees of importance and unimportance; and the *Little Miscellany* played its part, no less than the *Fragments* and other quasi-philosophical essays of that kind, in establishing their author's position of leadership in the world of Hebrew letters. Here was an exceptionally alert and acute mind ranging over the whole field of contemporary Jewish life, and an exceptionally gifted pen recording observations on the most diverse phenomena from the point of view of a coherent philosophy of Judaism and Jewish history, and displaying both dialectical mastery and intense but disciplined emotion. The occasions of his comments included, to take a bunch at random: the beginnings of the liberal Jewish movement in England; an article on manure in a Jerusalem Hebrew paper; the overdone custom of celebrating literary anniversaries; locusts in the Hirsch colonies in the Argentine; A Hebrew translation of Goldsmith's *Vicar of Wakefield;* journalistic ethics in the Hebrew press; the *halukah;* the Dreyfus affair; a pamphlet in which a leading French Jew, Salomon Reinach, advised the Jewish masses to emancipate themselves from the ceremonial law of Judaism[2]; and Max Nordau's views on the weekly rest-day. The sharply critical notes on the anti-orthodox opinions of Reinach and Nordau are both caustic expressions of Ahad Ha-Am's instinctive resentment of the attitude of superiority sometimes adopted by assimilated Jews towards the tradition hallowed by centuries of Jewish history and suffering; and the one about Nordau includes an epigrammatic phrase which has become famous—"The Jews have not so much observed the Sabbath as been preserved by it."

A few of the notes in the *Miscellany* deal, like some of the longer articles written during his editorship, with the then new-born political Zionist movement, which will claim our attention in the next chapter; and one of them[3] recurs to the question of the adaptation of the ceremonial law of Judaism to modern ideas, which he had already discussed

in *The People of the Book,* and reveals more boldly than
the earlier essay, though still in guarded terms, his conviction that a great deal of that law will not survive the creation of conditions in which Judaism can develop freely and
naturally.

Some of the longer essays of this period belong to his
argument with the "young men" on the then burning question of finding a synthesis between Judaism and modern
thought (which latter was habitually dignified, in the controversies of those days, with the question-begging name of
"humanity"). It was, as his controversies were wont to be,
conducted strictly on the plane of ideas, and was free of
personal rancor. He was in fact, as we have seen, on terms
of friendship with some of the most prominent spokesmen
of the view opposed to his own, especially Berdichevsky. He
was in full sympathy with their desire to get away from
the narrowness of the petrified Jewish tradition of the
ghetto, and to let some of the light and air of modern
thought and culture into Jewish life; and they, unlike David
Frischmann, another great "westernizer," were at one with
him in being nationalists. Berdichevsky and Marcus Ehrenpreis, another of the "young men," were frequent contributors to *Hashiloah;* the latter was even commissioned at the
outset to write its monthly review of current affairs. When
they planned to issue a journal of their own, which would
of course have been the spearhead of the opposition to his
views, he showed great interest in the project, and he would
no doubt have kept his promise to help if it had matured.
In Berdichevsky, who was a struggling young writer in
straitened circumstances, he took an almost paternal interest,
which survived many years of polemic about "Judaism and
humanity" (and of sometimes heated argument about Ahad
Ha-Am's correction of the younger man's defective Hebrew).

The conflict of opinion between the two turned on the
question how the antithesis between the Jewish and the

"human" was to be resolved. Berdichevsky and the others complained bitterly that they had to suffer from a sort of split personality—what they called "a cleavage in the soul." As Jews, they were heirs to a system of beliefs and a culture which had remained static and circumscribed for centuries, while the field of human interests and the range of human knowledge and ideas had expanded enormously. They found it intolerable that a human being, just because he was a Jew, should be precluded from participating in all the fruits of human progress, and from adopting and advocating any *Weltanschauung* that might appeal to his individual taste. They demanded the "extension of the bounds" of Jewish culture to include every manifestation of the human spirit. They refused to accept Ahad Ha-Am's thesis that the survival of the Jewish people as a distinct human group demanded its continued faithfulness to certain fundamental ideas which he regarded as characteristic of its attitude to life. They saw an infringement of the individual's right to freedom of thought in what was for him a self-evident corollary of Jewish nationalism. In their view the distinctiveness of Hebrew culture would be preserved, like that of any other national culture, by its language, independently of the ideas of which that language might be made the vehicle.

A concrete example of what was involved, and one not without its practical aspect, was provided by the philosophy of Nietzsche, which at that time had not yet lost its novelty. Some of the "young men," including Berdichevsky, were dazzled by the brilliant paradoxes of the German philosopher, who taught that Judaeo-Christian morality was entirely in error in standing up for the weak against the strong, and sought to replace it by the ideal of the Superman, the ruthless "blond beast," the destined lord of creation, whose will should be law. This appealed to them as a vigorous and virile gospel, beside which the Jewish belief in justice, mercy and loving-kindness was pale and anaemic, and it seemed to have a bearing on the present situation of the Jewish people, which for centuries had suffered in spineless passivity at the hands of those who did not scruple to use their superior might in defiance of moral considerations. Why, because they were Jews, must they be precluded from being Nietzscheists? Why, in terms of the fashionable antithesis, must they champion the Book against the Sword? "Extend the bounds" was their cry; remove any inhibition which restricts the range of the Jew's permitted interests and convictions.

Ahad Ha-Am agreed that somehow the "cleavage" must be healed. He had no doubt felt it himself during his years of lonely study and thinking in the "benighted village," where he had been in close touch with the intellectual life of Europe through books, though not through actual human contacts. But he held that the cause of the cleavage did not lie in any basic opposition between Judaism and "humanity," but in the failure of the unhappy young men to understand Judaism aright. For him Judaism, which he identified with the creativity of the Jewish people, was not an old-fashioned system of beliefs and practices, antithetic by its very nature to modern thought and progress. It was itself a part of humanistic culture; it was the Jewish people's distinctive way of expressing universal human ideas, which other nations expressed each in its own distinctive way.

True, the circumstances of Jewish history, the destruction long ago of the corporate national existence, the enforced substitution of learning and prayer and ritual for the normal foundations of a nation's life, the havoc wrought by centuries of hatred, segregation and persecution—all these had stunted and distorted the spiritual development of the Jewish people, and robbed it of the opportunity which a normal nation has, of continuously renewing its youth through the process of attacking and solving in its own individual man-

ner the new problems thrown up by the progress and the increasing complexity of material civilization. But that disability was not to be remedied by simply overthrowing the
dykes behind which Judaism had sheltered and stagnated,
and allowing the ocean of western culture to come flooding
in. The first requirement was for those who thirsted after
western culture, instead of starting with the assumption that
historic Judaism had no place for it, to delve into the past of
their own people, to rediscover and revivify the human or
humanist elements in the Jewish tradition itself, to rehabili-
tate Judaism as a civilizaton. That once accomplished, it
would again become possible for a living Judaism, developing in accordance with the law of its own being, to meet
other cultures on equal terms, and to give as well as receive
in the commerce of ideas and ideals. The problem of the
"cleavage" would ultimately find its solution in the restoration to the Jewish people of the possibility of a free, creative
life.

Meanwhile, however, the paucity of Hebrew writers com-
petent to contribute anything original to the discussion of
general human problems pointed, in his opinion, to the
wisdom of limiting a Hebrew monthly with a high standard to the field of Jewish life and thought. No less than his
critics, he wanted Hebrew literature to become universal in
its scope; but that was a goal to be reached by a process of
gradual evolution, not by a headlong plunge. For the time
being, to open the doors of *Hashiloah* to essays on subjects
entirely unrelated to Jewish life or thought would be to
invite inferior Hebrew imitations of what was written in
other languages. It hardly seems that it was necessary on his
own principles to press this point of view to the extent of
insisting that even stories and poems, not intended to incul-
cate or influence ideas, must have a Jewish content; but
here, as has been suggested, his personal bias was probably
the determining factor.

What he meant by "the Jewish people's distinctive way of expressing universal human ideas" is illustrated by a brilliant essay called *The Transvaluation of Values,*[4] in which he deals faithfully with Berdichevsky's Nietzscheism. He tells the Jewish would-be disciples of Nietzsche that they would have done better if, instead of swallowing the German philosopher's ideal of the Superman holus-bolus, they had first inquired what relation it bore to Jewish ethical principles. Nietzsche's ideal, he points out, combines two distinct and separable elements. There is in the first place the notion that society exists only for the purpose of producing and serving the highest human type, and the masses of men are of no account except insofar as they minister to that purpose; there is in the second place the notion that the highest type is a "blond beast." There is, he points out, no necessary connection between these two elements. It is possible to accept the general conception of the Superman as the aim and object of society without also accepting Nietzsche's Aryan idea as to what are the distinguishing qualities of the Superman. The general idea of the production of a supreme human type as the aim of society is not strange to Judaism, as witness the importance attached to the Righteous Man, the Tsaddik, in Jewish ethical literature. That idea is, indeed, as he pointed out in a later essay, an integral feature of the philosophy of Maimonides. But the Aryan worship of physical force and ruthlessness symbolized by the "blond beast" is and must always be anathema to Judaism, for which the ideal human type is the embodiment of the virtues of the scholar and the saint. Thus Judaism has no difficulty in coming to terms with the universal element in Nietzscheism; but the conclusion it draws from the general conception of the Superman will differ *toto coelo* from Nietzsche's, as the Jewish national spirit differs from the German. And, not content with thus convicting the Jewish Nietzscheists of having unnecessarily gone abroad to discover what they might have found at home, he goes on to remind them of an idea already thrown out centuries ago by Jehudah Halevi, that the Jewish nation is, ideally, a sort of "supernation" in the sphere of morality.

The controversy over "the extension of the bounds" with Berdichevsky and his colleagues spent itself in course of time, as is the way of such controversies, without giving either side a decisive victory. The modified Ahad Ha-Amism of Klausner's *Hashiloah* was a synthesis in which the more conservative and the more radical view could live together. But some years later Ahad Ha-Am was stung into angry protest by a demand for a degree of latitude which went far beyond anything that a Nietzscheist like Berdichevsky or a Hellenist like Tchernichowsky had claimed.

In 1911 a socialist Hebrew paper published in Tel Aviv, *Hapoel Hatzair* ("The Young Workman"), printed an article which claimed that Hebrew nationalism was in no sense tied to Judaism, that the young Hebrews did not share the reverence of their ancestors for "some sort of heavenly father," that they were emancipated from the "hypnosis of the Scriptures," and that they held it possible "to be a good Jew and at the same time to be thrilled with religious emotion by the Christian legend of the son of God who was sent to mankind and atoned with his life for the sins of all the ages." The author of the article was Joseph Haim Brenner (1881-1921), one of the most gifted among the younger Hebrew writers of his day. Ahad Ha-Am fell upon this extravagant expression of freedom of thought in an article in *Hashiloah* under the sarcastic title *The Law out of Zion,* in the course of which he wrote:

> Even a man who does not believe in the existence of the Deity *as a literal fact* cannot deny its existence as *a real factor in history;* and a national Jew, even if he is an unbeliever, cannot say that he has no part or lot in the God of Israel, in that historical factor which has kept our people alive and influenced its character and life for thou-

sands of years. Anybody who really has no part or lot in the God of Israel, who does not feel in his own soul any spiritual affinity with that "higher world" in which our ancestors were intellectually and emotionally absorbed through the ages, and from which they drew their moral strength—such a one may be a worthy human being, but he cannot be a national Jew, even if he lives in Palestine and speaks the holy tongue.

Not content with printed protest, he persuaded the Odessa Committee (he was then living in London) to withdraw its subsidy from the offending paper, on the ground that it could not reasonably be expected, and had indeed no right, to use the Society's money for the support of a paper which had moved so far from its outlook and that of the Society it represented. He was strongly criticized for this action, but that did not perturb him. His published letters show how deeply his feelings were stirred, and how firm was his conviction of being in the right.

The Brenner article is indeed a *reductio ad absurdum* of the claim for "extension of the bounds" if pushed to its logical conclusion. There have been isolated instances of nationalist Jews who have professed the Christian faith, or have been avowed atheists, and there may be more in the future; but no Jew, religious or not, can seriously contemplate the possibility of a Christian or avowedly atheistic Jewish State or Jewish people. History has made it impossible for Jewish survival to be entirely independent of Judaism, and Ahad Ha-Am's insistence on that fact did not justify the charge of narrowness and intolerance which was leveled against him. For him, passionately devoted as he was to freedom of thought, there could be no question of an enforced conformity. It was a cardinal principle of his own conduct in life that he must be free to hold and express whatever opinions commended themselves to his reason; and he would not withhold from others the privilege he claimed for himself. He had a hatred of excommunication and boycott in all their forms, and it would have been absurd for him of all men to demand of any individual Jew that he must either hold this or that religious or philosophical belief, or cease to be accepted as a Jew. But he thought in terms of the nation, and it was his conviction that the survival of the Jewish people as a distinct human group was conditional on its holding fast to a certain (not precisely definable) outlook on life. It seems to be implied in his position—though he did not himself develop the argument—that individual Jews who are actively unsympathetic to the Jewish outlook will sooner or later dissociate themselves from their people; and thus, without any use of compulsion, the carrying on of the torch of Judaism from generation to generation will be left in the hands of those who remain, if only passively, true in essentials to the "national spirit" as manifested in Jewish history. So long as there are men of that type, even though their number be small and their influence in the world inconsiderable, the Jewish people will continue to exist. Its survival will be secured not by the use of bell, book and candle, but by what might be called a process of natural selection.

Ahad Ha-Am's view of the essential connection between the Jewish religious tradition and the survival of the Jewish people was based on his belief—essentially a metaphysical belief—in "the spirit" as the abiding reality behind the phenomena of human history, and in particular of Jewish history. He saw the continuous working of the "national spirit" as the guarantee of the national existence. It is of course possible to disagree with him, and to hold that "the spirit" is an unreal abstraction, and a nation exists so long as, and no longer than, it can maintain itself against external forces on a particular piece of the earth's surface; but they are mistaken who accuse him of having put forward a theory which in its very nature denied the individual Jew's right to freedom of thought.

Two other essays of the *Hashiloah* period may be mentioned here as bearing in different ways on this question of what is and what is not compatible with the cultural revival of the Jewish people.

In one of these, called *National Morality,* after asserting, contrary to the accepted idea, that the refinement of the moral sense is the cause and not the consequence of the development of religion in a given society, he argues that nationalists ought to be no less solicitous for the national code of ethics than for the national language, to which they attach so much importance; and from this point of view he criticizes a recent drama by Max Nordau called *Dr. Kohn.* In this play Nordau makes his Jewish hero insist on fighting a duel on the ground that his refusal to fight would be regarded as cowardly, and would bring dishonor on the Jewish people; but Ahad Ha-Am points out that from the point of view of Jewish ethics dueling is an act of criminal folly, and suggests that it is by refusing a challenge to fight that a Jew would really do his people honor. He is here dealing summarily with a very complicated problem, and he admits that the whole concept of "national morality" needs elucidation. It is unfortunate that he was never able to carry out his cherished idea of writing a book on Jewish ethics, the more so as in his belief it was in the field of morality, individual and social, that the Jewish people was destined in future to make its most distinctive contribution to human thought and progress.

The other essay, which is better known, was originally an address on "the question of culture" delivered before the general meeting of the Russian Zionists in the summer of 1902, and later published in *Hashiloah* under the title *The Spiritual Revival.*[5] This, one of his longest essays, is both a reasoned and powerful plea for greater attention to "cultural work" on the part of the Zionist Organization, and a criticism of the assimilationist tendencies still prevalent in the literature of Haskalah, which he roundly condemns as being "almost all translation or imitation, and badly done at that: the translation being too far from the original, and the imitation too close to it." The essay deals with a number of points connected with the cultural problem, including that of the place of Yiddish in Jewish culture. In a section which touches on the question of Judaism and humanism, he condemns the widespread tendency of Jewish writers and artists to turn their backs on Jewish life when they are in search of subjects, and by way of illustration quotes very appositely the case of the Russo-Jewish sculptor Marc Antokolsky, who had recently died. Instead of taking the Russian, Ivan the Terrible, for the model of a brutal tyrant, as he did, Antokolsky might equally well have gone to Jewish history, which he knew before he learnt Russian history, and have chosen Herod; and similarly there was no need for him to dig into the Russian past for the type of scholar-recluse, and produce a statue of a well-known monkish chronicler of the eleventh century, seeing that in his own birthplace, Vilna, he must have been familiar with the Jewish "perpetual student," and must have heard stories of the great scholar-recluse Elijah Gaon, who had spent a lifetime of ceaseless study and writing in that city only a century before the sculptor's own day. In this case it is the assimilated Jew, not the ghetto-bred youth in quest of "humanity," who comes under the lash; but in both cases the point of view is the same. The paramount need of the Jewish people is to modernize itself without impairment of its spiritual independence and originality, and for that purpose it must cultivate its own neglected vineyard, with modern implements, before it can with safety drink freely of strange vintages.

10

POLITICAL
ZIONISM

Theodor Herzl's *Der Judenstaat* burst upon the world in February, 1896, about eight months before the first number of *Hashiloah* appeared. Ahad Ha-Am must have read the pamphlet soon after its publication; but we have no means of knowing what his first reactions to it were. None of his extant writings bears a date between February and October, 1896; and there is no mention of *Der Judenstaat* in the programmatic introduction to *Hashiloah,* or in any of his contributions to that journal before the date of the first Zionist Congress (August 1897). The first sign we have of an interest on his part in the new movement is found in a letter[1] to his friend Menahem Ussishkin, dated June 3, 1897. By that time preparations were in hand for the first Congress, which it was intended to hold in Munich, and Ussishkin had evidently asked for Ahad Ha-Am's views. The reply betrays no enthusiasm:

> I too hope that good will come of the Munich meeting, although not for the same reason as you. I do not believe that it will impress public opinion in Europe, apart from Turkey, whose opposition to Palestine colonization will certainly be sharpened. But I believe that this meeting, which they call a "Congress," will to some extent help to raise the prestige of the movement among the Jews here in Russia, who have hitherto feared that it might be beneath their dignity to take an interest in a movement of *batlanim*. It seems to me idle to hope for any "diplomatic" achievement so long as we have not at least a hundred thousand Jews working on the land in Palestine.

If so, you may ask, what can we hope for? Only a "practical" man like you can be disheartened by that question. For my part, I hold fast to my belief that one day we shall understand what Palestine means for us and our spiritual life; and then we shall cease to squander our halfpence on things of no substance, and instead shall collect them together and use them to do small things well, thus creating something to which Jews can look as a model. Then the Jews will turn their eyes again to Palestine, and thousands will settle there and live in comfort, without needing the stimulus of réclame and advertisement. And then—no matter whether in the twentieth century or in the twenty-first—then the time will come for diplomatic action as well. . . .

The event proved him right on the uselessness of diplomacy with nothing behind it: for Herzl's premature diplomatic activity ended in smoke, and the Zionist movement had to revert to small colonization before it had any basis on which to proceed in the political field. He failed, however, to do justice to the practical importance of an all-Jewish forum which could make Zionism an international issue, and to realize the impossibility, in our imperfect world, of achieving even the worthiest public object without any of the display and the réclame which he elsewhere dismissed as "noisy demonstrations." Nor was it to be expected that many would share with him the perspective in which a trifle of a century or so was of no account.

Other letters to his friends indicate his dissatisfaction with what he regarded as the tactless treatment of the Russian Hovevé Zion by the inexperienced organizers of the Congress, and mention his decision to write nothing about the new movement until after the Congress is over. The general impression is of a somewhat suspicious attitude towards the movement, which does not, however, prevent him from hoping that it may be of some use to the national cause.

Towards the end of July, he replied to a personal invitation to attend the Congress, now to be held at Basle, from
Herzl himself, who had apparently been misled into sup-
posing that he had taken offense at not having received one
earlier. His reply was that he realized the great importance
of the Congress, and did not need a special invitation to it,
but was not yet certain whether he would be able to be
present.

In the end he did find it possible to go to Basle—as a
visitor, not as a delegate, to the Congress—and the result
was disastrous. Throughout the sittings, which were marked
by ebullitions of almost hysterical joy and enthusiasm, he
alone sat in gloom, "like a mourner at a wedding-feast," as
he afterwards wrote. On the morrow of the close of the
Congress he wrote to Ravnitzki:

> Last night the meeting ended. My head still aches, my
> nerves are on edge, and I do not allow myself to say what
> I think, because I cannot yet control my feelings. I hate
> to say it, but one could see how low we have fallen. The
> vast majority of those present were young people, espe-
> cially from Russia, and ninety-nine per cent of the rest
> were blind, and followed the leader like sheep. We have
> destroyed much more than we have built. After the meet-
> ing I had a short talk with Herzl, and came to the conclu-
> sion that his hints about what he has achieved in Constan-
> tinople are worth nothing at all. He got no promise, and
> there is no doubt that henceforth the Turkish Govern-
> ment will be much stricter with us than it has been. Who
> knows whether this was not the last cry of the nation's
> death-agony!

From a letter[2] written a year later to another friend, Yehiel
Tchlenow (1864-1918), who afterwards shared with Ussishkin the leadership of Russian Zionism, it appears that he had
two conversations with Herzl, one before and one after the
Congress. In the second of these he asked Herzl on what
he based his hopes of success in his approach to the Turkish

Government, and received a reply which convinced him
that there was nothing whatever behind the hints of pending diplomatic successes with which the fires of Congress
enthusiasm had been stoked.

His public reaction to the Congress was no less hostile. In
a short note[3] in *Hashiloah* he acknowledged the value of the
Congress as a proclamation to the whole world, without
parallel since the dispersion, of the *national* answer to the
Jewish problem, and paid tribute to Max Nordau, whose
great address on the Jewish position was the highlight of
the Congress, for having spoken like one of the prophets
of old. But for the rest of the proceedings of the Congress
he had not a good word. He uttered a solemn warning that
the exaggerated expectations aroused by the Zionist leaders
would be followed by a disillusionment even more disastrous than that which had mocked the extravagant hopes of
the Hovevé Zion some years earlier. He stigmatized the
Congress delegates as "a rabble of youngsters—in years or
in knowledge," treated the practical results of the Congress
with contempt, and belittled the ambition for a petty Jewish
State as a poor substitute for the true aim of Jewish nationalism, which was nothing less than the universalistic ideal of
the ancient Hebrew Prophets of Righteousness. He reiterated his conviction that Palestine could solve only the *moral*
problem of the Jewish people; and he ended with one of
those inspired flashes which every now and then in his writings reveal the white heat of the sacred fire that burned
within him: "The salvation of Israel will be achieved by
prophets, not by diplomats."

Four months later, in another and longer article called
Jewish State and Jewish Problem[4] he admitted that he
had written his note on the Congress in anger, and, contrary
to his wont, had used harsh expressions, which he now re-
gretted; but he withdrew nothing, either then or later. The
new Zionism seemed, indeed, almost expressly designed to

wound all his susceptibilities. To begin with, it was not, what in his view a Jewish national movement must be, a natural development of the native Jewish tradition: it had been created and was led by assimilated Jews of the West, who were both geographically and spiritually out of contact with their people. It vetoed practical colonization work in Palestine, which for him was a vital necessity. It pinned all its hopes on diplomacy, which in his vocabulary was synonymous with lying. Its leaders made extravagant and baseless promises, exaggerated their successes, and covered up their failures; whereas he could be satisfied with nothing less than complete candor and the unvarnished truth. They tried to attract the masses by the methods of noisy propaganda; he abominated publicity in every shape and form. His deep sense of responsibility was outraged by the offhand and superficial manner in which, as it seemed to him, they dealt with questions of importance. They appeared also to be using every effort to prevent discussion within their movement of the fundamental problems of Zionist theory, for fear of bringing into the open the conflict between the "western" and the "eastern" approaches; but in his view there could be no co-operation without full and frank elucidation of underlying ideas. And, perhaps worst of all, the new movement showed no interest in the Hebrew language and culture, which were for him the very breath of life of Jewish nationalism.

It hurt him particularly that so many of his friends and associates in Hibbath Zion shared in the enthusiasm aroused by the new movement, and found no difficulty in pledging their allegiance to an organization which in his view was based on principles fundamentally opposed to those of true Zionism. They seemed to him to have deserted overnight the ideals for which he and they had fought and worked together in Hibbath Zion and in the closer intimacy of the Sons of Moses. And while tried and trusted colleagues like Ussishkin and many others succumbed to the lure of political Zionism, he saw the new movement bringing into prominence a "rabble of youngsters," men with no roots in Jewish life and no regard for Jewish learning, ignorant upstarts whose sole qualification for participation in the national movement was blind devotion to the new messiah who was its leader. This long remained a sore point with him, imbued as he was with the traditional Jewish reverence for the dignity that belongs of right to age and learning, and the conviction that youth and ignorance must be kept in their place. Messiah-worship was his *bête noire,* and ten years later he used the talmudic aphorism "When the Messiah comes, impudence will be rife" as the text for a homily[5] on the effrontery habitually displayed by the ignorant and uneducated devotees of a Messiah, whether early Christians, or hasidim, or political Zionists, or the German Social Democrats of his own day, towards those whom they ought to have respected as their elders and betters.

He did not, of course, quarrel with old friends on the Zionist issue, though it gave rise to many a fierce argument between him and them, in which his ample resources of indignation and sarcasm were fully deployed. He himself preferred to remain outside the ranks of Herzl's organization (though it was his practice not to decline to buy the Zionist shekel when it was offered to him), so as not to be subject to its discipline and therefore less free to criticize its policy. He was convinced that the new movement was a negation of the values by which the Jewish people had been preserved for centuries, that the Hovevé Zion were being misled into forsaking their true goal for the pursuit of a will-o'-the-wisp, and that the inevitable failure and disillusionment would leave them bereft of their old ideals and with nothing to take their place. He felt it his duty to do everything in his power to avert this calamity while there was still time; and he had the moral courage to embark almost single-handed on a crusade which made him before long the most dreaded and best hated critic of the Zionist

Organization. Years later, in 1903, he defended his decision to remain outside the Organization on the ground that if he had joined it, he would soon have been expelled. The little opposition that there was within the movement was tolerated, he felt sure, only because the leaders knew that it would do them no harm, and it enabled them to boast of their tolerance. He presumably realized that, so long as the congresses were dominated by Herzl, there could be no hope of creating within the movement an opposition that would have to be taken seriously.

❧ 2 ☙

The war of ideas did not, at first, preclude attempts at practical co-operation. During the two or three years immediately following the Congress, although he was writing articles severely critical of the principles and policy of the Zionist Organization under its western leaders, he showed a certain willingness to help it. He also made some attempt to establish contact with Max Nordau by sending him, a fortnight after the Congress, a copy of *At the Crossroads,* and a polite German letter,[6] which reads in translation as follows:

> I am taking the liberty of sending you a small Hebrew book of mine which was published some years ago (*Al Parashath Derachim*). Your unforgettable speech at Basle is my excuse for doing so. In that speech you lent the great weight of your authority to some of the views expressed in my book, which at the time were regarded as paradoxes. You may imagine how much pleasure it gave me when these same views, so admirably expressed by you, gained unanimous and enthusiastic acceptance. I wanted to thank you while I was still at Basle, and at the same time to consult you on some points of detail; but unfortunately you were so busy that I could not venture to intrude upon you. I am therefore writing what I could not say in per-

son; and in sending you my book I hope (as I am told that you read Hebrew with ease) that at your leisure you will read at any rate the articles which I have marked in red in the table of contents. These are the articles which are most clearly related to the subject of your address. The others touch on kindred subjects, but are not so directly relevant.

He had greater respect for Nordau, who was a thinker with a European reputation, than for Herzl, the dramatist and feuilletonist. Herzl's *Judenstaat* seemed to him journalistic and superficial, and in an essay called *Theory and Practice,*[7] written at the end of 1901 on the occasion of the tenth anniversary of Pinsker's death, he compared it, much to its disadvantage, with Pinsker's *Auto-Emanzipation*. He took Nordau much more seriously, and once went so far as to extend to him an invitation, of which Nordau availed himself, to reply in *Hashiloah* to an "open letter" to him which had appeared in the journal from the pen of one of the younger Hebrew writers. This was shortly after the second Congress, which met in August, 1898, and in his letter to Nordau he expressed his regret at not having been present, and said that he had hoped to be able to attend the Congress primarily in order to meet Nordau and discuss Zionist problems with him. Nordau's article in *Hashiloah* revealed little understanding of the point of view of his critics, and any hopes that Ahad Ha-Am might have entertained of bridging the gap were disappointed.

He had exhibited a lively interest in the program of the second Congress during the months of preparatory work, and in a correspondence with Dr. J. Bernstein-Kohan (or Kohan-Bernstein), another old Hovev Zion, who had been elected a member of the Zionist Executive, had made suggestions for the agenda, in particular one for discussion of "the attitude of the Zionist Organization to activities in the fields of national culture and colonization at the present time and in the near future." He was unable to attend either a preparatory meeting in Vienna, to which Herzl sent him a personal invitation, or the Congress itself; but he was present (not as a delegate) at a great meeting of Russian Zionists held in Warsaw just before the Congress, and came away with the impression that many of the old Hovevé Zion were still faithful to their ideal, and had been glad to hear it reaffirmed by himself, but had not themselves the courage to stand up for it in opposition to the western leaders. His assessment of the situation turned out to be correct, and the second Congress did nothing to repair the omissions of the first. Some years were in fact to elapse before there were any signs of serious challenge to Herzl's policy within his Organization.

Before the Warsaw meeting Ahad Ha-Am had accepted an invitation from the Zionist Executive in Vienna to become a member of an international Hebrew Committee, whose function it was to advise the Executive on cultural questions; but there is no evidence that his membership on this Committee ever meant anything in practice. Later, in 1901, the fifth Congress appointed him a member of a Cultural Committee, along with two of his old friends, Ravnitzki and Bernstein-Kohan, and the three of them explored the possibilities of using the authority and the machinery of the Zionist Organization for serious cultural activities. They resigned when it became clear that the Zionist leaders had nothing in mind beyond the preparation of a report for the next Congress on the cultural position, and the supervision of the propagandist literature of the Organization. In September of the following year, the Russian Zionists held a general meeting in Minsk, at which Ahad Ha-Am delivered the address already mentioned on the question of Jewish culture (*The Spiritual Revival*). This address was loudly applauded; but in the subsequent discussion it was severely criticized, and there were even cries of "anti-Zionist." This may be explained not only by what

was known of Ahad Ha-Am's general attitude towards the
Zionist Organization, but perhaps more particularly by his
having suggested at the end of his address that since a single
organization cannot be expected to be capable of coping
with both political and cultural work, the latter should be
entrusted to a new organization to be specially established
for the purpose, which would be entirely independent of,
but would work in close co-operation with, the Zionist Organization. This far-reaching proposal suggests that he had
by that time abandoned all hope that the political Zionist
leaders might be persuaded to take cultural work seriously.
Nonetheless, he consented to serve on a second Cultural
Committee which was appointed at Minsk, and on which
his colleagues were Bialik, Klausner and Idelsohn, and
attended its first two or three meetings; but this Committee
also beat its ineffectual wings against the void.

No further attempt was made during Herzl's lifetime to
find a place in Zionist work for the great critic of political
Zionism; but in 1906, somewhat surprisingly, his old friend
Judah Grazowsky,[8] who was then serving the Zionist Organization in Palestine, offered him a position in its service
in that country. Ahad Ha-Am declined the offer, in spite
of his strong desire to settle in Palestine. "I cannot," he
wrote, "subordinate myself to the Zionist leaders headed by
Wolffsohn"; and he reminded Grazowsky that some years
earlier he had not accepted an invitation from the Jewish
Colonization Association to manage its affairs in Palestine
for a similar reason, adding: "in this matter the Zionist leaders are no better from my point of view than those of the
ICA—I am not in agreement with either." What precisely
was the post offered to him by Grazowsky we do not know,
for he had forgotten the details when he came to prepare
his letters for publication nearly twenty years later; but the
terms in which he refused the offer suggest that even in

1906 he had not altogether shaken off his old distrust of the leaders of the new Zionism.

❧ 3 ❧

Much heat was engendered in the bitter controversies in which Ahad Ha-Am became involved in the course of his protracted war against political Zionism, and his enemies were none too scrupulous in their choice of weapons. One of the charges leveled against him, and one that he found particularly offensive, was that of being actuated by personal jealousy of Herzl. Examination of the available evidence lends no color to such a suspicion. He was scrupulously careful for his part to confine the argument to the merits of the case, and to steer clear of personalities. It is known from his letters that he refused to print in *Hashiloah* anything derogatory to Herzl as a man, and rebuked another opponent of Herzl, Dr. Aaron Kaminka, who conducted an agitation against the new movement before the second Congress, for stooping to personal attacks on the Zionist leader, which could only serve to deflect attention from the weaknesses of his policy. He himself was willing after Herzl's death to deliver an address on him in the principal synagogue of St. Petersburg (where he happened to be at the time), and was prevented from doing so only by the decision of the communal authorities that none but their rabbi should perform this office. The third volume of his collected essays, which contained some trenchant criticisms of Herzl and his organization, appeared not long after Herzl's death in 1904, and he wrote for it a preface in which, while showing no appreciation of the lasting importance of Herzl's achievements, and suggesting a doubt whether the organization would survive its creator, he foretold that the figure of the dead leader would in course of time be invested by the Jewish people with all the attributes of a national hero embodying its highest ideals, and would become a source of inspiration and vigor in its struggle for survival. It is scarcely reasonable to suppose that the author of this tribute was jealous of its subject. Ahad Ha-Am's crusade against Herzl and political Zionism is sufficiently explained, without the attribution of unworthy motives, by his deep conviction that Jewish national aims could not be expressed in purely political terms, coupled with his almost violent dislike of the methods of mass leadership and persuasion.

The war of words was not only an affair of pitched battles. The new movement became for him a sort of obsession, apt to crop up incidentally in whatever he might write on any subject. But his main criticisms were developed in three set pieces, which were written during the first two years of the movement and afterwards reprinted in the second volume of *At the Crossroads* (published at the end of 1903); and a specially noteworthy broadside was delivered in 1902, in a scathing review of Herzl's *Altneuland*.

The first of the three early articles, *Jewish State and Jewish Problem,* has already been mentioned. It was Ahad Ha-Am's reply to the storm of indignation aroused by his angry note on the first Congress, and is the widest in scope of the three. It exposes the baselessness of the idea that the material problem of the Jewish masses in eastern Europe could be solved by emigration to Palestine, even if the necessary political conditions could be created, and proceeds to contrast the unattainable aims of political Zionism with the more modest objects of Hibbath Zion, which expects no more from Palestine than "a home of refuge for Judaism and a cultural bond of national unity," knowing that a Jewish State cannot solve the problems of Jewish poverty, insecurity and national degradation until "universal justice is enthroned and holds sway in the lives of nations and states." The best that he can find to say of the new Zionism is that it has value for the Jews of the western world, whose dormant national consciousness it may awaken, and some of whom, when they find that the Jewish State is not attainable in the near future, will examine the whole problem more thoroughly and find their way to true Hibbath Zion. What drives him almost to despair is the danger to the Jews of eastern Europe, who, if the ideal of the State entices them away from the moral ideal by which they have been inspired hitherto, will never recover what they have lost.

The second of the three articles, *Political Zionism and Palestine Colonization,* is in the main a protest against the diplomacy by which the Zionist leaders tried to avoid a split in the movement over the question of their attitude towards immediate colonization work in Palestine. Their own view was that such work must be postponed until guarantees for the Jewish State had been obtained; but it would have been impolitic to make this too clear to the Hovevé Zion, who formed a large part of the membership of the new movement, and for whom Zionism without practical colonization activity was unintelligible. Ahad Ha-Am pillories the official lack of candor on this issue, particularly in connection with the plans then being considered for a Zionist Bank. He demands a clear answer to the question whether the funds of the bank will be available for colonization work if it proves possible to obtain legal guarantees for work of that kind, though not for sovereignty over Palestine.

The bank is the theme of the third article in the series, *Political Zionism and the Jewish Colonial Trust,* written after the issue of the prospectus of the Zionist bank, the establishment of which had been approved at the second Congress. Although the Congress had explicitly laid it down that the activities of the bank must be limited to Palestine and the neighboring countries, the prospectus was in fact drafted in very wide terms, which would permit the bank to carry on colonizing and other activities in any part of the world Ahad Ha-Am saw in this a deliberate attempt on the part of the western leaders to set at naught the clearly expressed views of their followers, and an indication that they would be prepared to use the resources of the bank for the foundation of a State elsewhere if Palestine proved unobtainable. For once he was not in a minority of one: there was widespread criticism of the prospectus within the Zionist movement itself, and at length, after much controversy and litigation, the seventh Congress decided in 1905 (after the death of Herzl and the catastrophe of East Africa) that the articles of association of the bank must be so altered as to restrict its activities to Palestine and Syria.

Ahad Ha-Am's letters show how deeply he felt on this question. He was of course at one with the political Zionists in recognizing the importance of a legal basis for colonization activities in Palestine; but he shrank in horror from the possibility that the Zionist movement might turn its back on Palestine altogether. Palestine was, so to speak, in his blood, and to look elsewhere for the accomplishment of Jewish national aims was treason in his eyes.

A few years later he was again stung into vigorous protest on another issue which was equally vital: that of Hebrew culture. The occasion was the appearance in 1902 of Herzl's Zionist Utopia, *Altneuland*. This romance assumes that the charter which was the political objective of the Zionist Organization has been obtained, describes the ensuing process of Jewish mass emigration to Palestine, and pictures life as it will be in the Jewish State of the future. It paints an idyllic picture of a progressive and prosperous modern country, equipped with the latest technical devices and inspired by the most liberal ideals—an example to all mankind of progress and tolerance, advanced culture, and freedom from racial and religious descrimination. The whole Zionist world was thrilled to ecstasy by this forecast of how Zionism would not only solve the Jewish problem in twenty years—for in Herzl's vision of "the old-new land" most of the Jews have settled in the Jewish State, and anti-Semitism has ceased to exist, within that time—but would

also demonstrate the enlightened and progressive character
of the Jewish people.

It was left for Ahad Ha-Am to ask the awkward questions. In an extended review of the book he not only allowed
his gentle sarcasm to play on the many absurdities in
Herzl's story of how millions of penniless Jews are settled
in a barren land and achieve prosperity in the twinkling of
an eye. He also inquired, as nobody else had done: wherein
is the Jewishness of this cosmopolitan society of Herzl's
imagining? And he found no satisfactory answer. Theaters
there are in "Altneuland," where plays can be heard in several European languages; there are an opera house and an
academy modeled on those of France, and in Jerusalem a
temple of the best German-Jewish type; there are news-
papers in several languages, museums, concerts, and all the
other signs of a highly civilized life. But there is no sign of
the Hebrew language except in the synagogue service and
in a song of welcome sung by school-children to admiring
visitors; there is no single trace of Hebrew literature or
Hebrew culture, of a recognizably Hebraic pattern of life
and thought, of anything whatever to differentiate this
"Jewish" society from one which might be created by
negroes if they had the means and set about to build themselves a new life modeled on the latest ideas and inventions
of western civilization. In fact Herzl's Utopia, with its repeated insistence on the absence of any kind of originality in
the Zionist haven of refuge, is a glaring example of the
assimilationist mentality which Ahad Ha-Am had pilloried
years earlier in *Slavery in Freedom*.

This criticism, the acidity of which was not tempered by
any acknowledgement of the merits of Herzl's romance as
a work of imagination, was unanswerable from the point of
view of a Zionism rooted in the Jewish past; and it should
have appealed to many members of Herzl's Organization
who had been reared in the older tradition. But they were
under the spell of Herzl's personality, which came to them,

as it were, trailing clouds of glory from the great world beyond the ghetto; and for them no less than for his western adherents, criticism such as Ahad Ha-Am ventured on was next door to blasphemy. After the *Altneuland* incident the unpopularity of the inexorable critic attained unprecedented dimensions. He became *the* enemy of Zion, and some of the more zealous believers even burned his offending writings in public.

Herzl himself must have thought that a reply was called for, and it was at his request that Max Nordau essayed one in the columns of the official German-language Zionist weekly *Die Welt*. Nordau does not seem to have been at his best on this occasion. Whether misled by a faulty translation, or through genuine lack of understanding, he grossly misrepresented Ahad Ha-Am's views, and treated their author as an unenlightened rabbinical zealot, ignorant of European civilization and its outlook and literary conventions. Particularly maladroit was his handling of the crucial question of the language of the Jews restored to Palestine. Ahad Ha-Am had pointed out that *Altneuland* contained no clear statement on this question, but that internal evidence, for which he gave chapter and verse, seemed to indicate that the language of the masses would be Yiddish, and the upper classes would speak European languages, principally German. Nordau thought, or affected to think, that the benighted critic was ignorant of the convention by which the writer of a story makes his characters speak in the language in which the story is told, without thereby suggesting that that is their actual language. This was really unpardonable, and Ahad Ha-Am had no difficulty in tearing Nordau's defense to tatters in a spirited rejoinder. This affair naturally did not help to narrow the breach between him and the Zionist Organization; but it is characteristic of his indifference to personal attacks that it did not diminish his personal respect for Nordau.

%; 4 ;%

In the following year, 1903, the Zionist Organization faced its almost fatal crisis. Hopes of a charter from the Turkish Government for Jewish mass settlement in Palestine under international guarantees had faded away, and Herzl, haunted by the spectre of Jewish misery and insecurity in eastern Europe, had been driven to seek a home of refuge elsewhere. He had turned to the British Government, with the result that he was able to come to the sixth Congress, in August, 1903, with an offer from Great Britain of a territory in East Africa for Jewish settlement, with a Jewish governor and internal autonomy.

Although this proposal had the tremendous advantage of Herzl's strong personal advocacy, it had a stormy passage in the Congress. During the preceding two years Herzl's position in the movement had been somewhat weakened by an embryo revolt against his somewhat dictatorial methods and his indifference to cultural questions. This opposition, of which Chaim Weizmann was one of the leading spirits, was in fact a reflection of Ahad Ha-Am's ideas, which had more influence in the Zionist Organization than he himself perhaps recognized at that time. The East Africa proposal brought matters to a head. To many of the old Hovevé Zion, the very idea of a Jewish national settlement elsewhere than in Eretz Israel was no less abhorrent than would have been a suggestion that they should change their religion. They refused to be reassured by Nordau's protestations that East Africa was only a temporary resting-place, that Palestine remained, and would always remain, the goal of the movement. They were shocked into a realization of the bitter truth which Ahad Ha-Am had for years been preaching to deaf ears, that "western" Zionism and their own rested on different philosophies and had been held together artificially. A proposal to send out a commission of inquiry to examine the offered territory and report to the next Congress obtained a substantial majority, but 178 delegates, or well over one-third of the total, cast their votes against it; and when the result of the voting was declared, these withdrew and held a separate meeting of their own, at which tears were shed for their lost Palestine. Even Herzl's personal entreaties availed only with difficulty to bring these "Zion Zionists" back to the Congress.

Ahad Ha-Am's reactions to the events of the sixth Congress are on record both in an article which he published shortly after the Congress, under the title *Those Who Wept,* and in a letter[9] written about the same time to an unnamed correspondent, which he subsequently included in the published selection of his correspondence. Both are written in a white heat of moral indignation. He sees in the East Africa proposal confirmation of the forebodings he had expressed five years earlier in connection with the prospectus of the Jewish Colonial Trust, and finds the unforgivable sin of the dissentient Congress delegates in their having allowed themselves to be persuaded to return to the Congress. Political Zionism, he says, is dead: "In Basle, on the first of Ellul, 5657, this Zionism was born, and in Basle, on the first of Ellul, 5663, its 'soul' departed from it, leaving nothing but a name emptied of all meaning and a program with a new, far-fetched interpretation." Basle Zionism has tried, and inevitably failed, to combine two incompatible ideals, that of the restoration of Jewish national life in Palestine, and that of the speedy establishment of a Jewish State. The devotees of the State ideal, no longer professing Zionism, will continue for a time their vain search for a territory in which that ideal can be fulfilled; and new champions of the true Zionist ideal will arise, who will not again allow themselves to be deceived into thinking possible its early realization by diplomatic means.

As we all know now, his gloomy prophecies were happily not realized. The Territorialist movement came into being, as he had foretold, and spent itself, as he also foresaw it would, in a fruitless search for a substitute for Palestine; but the political Zionist Organization did not die, and even survived the cruel blow of the untimely death of Herzl, which happened before the commission of inquiry presented its report on the East Africa territory—an unfavorable one— to the seventh Zionist Congress in August, 1905. The survival of the Organization was secured by the action of a group of Russian leaders, who, though they had thrown in their lot with Herzl, were in a very broad sense Ahad Ha-Amists. At the head of them was Menahem Ussishkin, who was fundamentally a Hovev Zion in Ahad Ha-Am's sense of the term, but was less "spiritual" than Ahad Ha-Am, and more ready to appreciate the benefit that Zionism could derive from the political experience and connections of the western newcomers to the movement. After the sixth Congress Ussishkin and his colleagues threatened to withdraw from the Zionist Organization, taking all the Russian Zionists with them, and to call an opposition Congress, unless Herzl undertook in writing to abandon the East Africa scheme. Herzl did not accept their demand; but his death shortly afterwards, coupled with the secession of Zangwill and his territorialist group, left those political Zionists who remained faithful to the Organization, as many did, in no position to dominate it as he had done. During the next few years, though formally the program remained unchanged, and there was a protracted struggle for control between the "political" and the "practical" wings before the latter finally prevailed, the emphasis shifted from diplomatic manoeuvering to practical and cultural activities; and this development received a powerful impetus as a result of the Turkish revolution of 1908, since the pronounced nationalism and modernism of the Young Turks made it impossible for Zionism to persist in avowing even by implication political designs on Palestine which had not seemed incongruous in the days when Turkey had been "the sick man of Europe."

It was of course due to the Turkish revolution rather than to Ahad Ha-Am's influence that in 1909 the official organ of the Zionist Organization went so far as to declare that the Organization had never contemplated a Jewish State (of which there was no explicit mention in the Basle Program). But whatever the cause, the Zionist Organization became more and more like a Herzlian body with an Ahad Ha-Am soul. The triumph of practical sense over ideological differences was finally achieved in the "synthetic Zionism" of Chaim Weizmann. Ahad Ha-Am himself remained formally outside the Zionist Organization, but the old hostility lost its edge. In 1911 he was present as a visitor at the tenth Congress, after having been absent from all the earlier ones except the first; and a few years later he was among the counselors of the Zionist leaders who were responsible for the first political achievement of Zionism in the Balfour Declaration.

Ahad Ha-Am's published letters show that he watched the transformation which began to come over the Zionist movement after Herzl's death with a certain degree of satisfaction. He wrote in this sense to Klausner as early as October, 1905, and added: "Zionism is in process of freeing itself from the messianic illusion, and it is bound as a matter of course to eject all the foreign elements which joined it only because of its messianic features." The emergence of Zangwill's Territorial Organization showed that he was right to some extent; but the defection of the "foreign elements" was not so extensive as he expected it to be, and the organizational union of East-European and western Jewry, which was one of Herzl's outstanding services to the Jewish people, remained a reality. Ahad Ha-Am did not make

sufficient allowance either for the ability of men less logical
than himself to ignore the demands of strict consistency, or
for the extent of his own influence both on many of the
leaders of Zionism and on a large section of its rank-and-file.

❧ 5 ☙

Herzl and Ahad Ha-Am stand out as the protagonists
of two antithetic conceptions of Jewish nationalism. Far as
they were removed from one another in almost every important respect, whether of background and education or of
character and temperament, they were yet at one in
the radicalism with which each attacked that aspect of the
Jewish problem in which he was particularly interested.
Herzl, aroused to an assertion of his Jewishness by "the
plight of the Jews," saw the futility of the conventional
palliative measures of piecemeal emigration and diplomatic
representations to anti-Jewish governments. He realized that
even the best-intentioned and most influential of philan-
thropists could not solve the problem, and that what was
needed was a national effort for national independence.
Ahad Ha-Am, concerned primarily with "the plight of
Judaism," was the first to appreciate the dimensions of that
problem, to diagnose its underlying causes, and to offer
a comprehensive solution in place of the superficial expedients by which it had been shelved rather than solved.
He saw that Judaism could not be fitted into the framework of the modern world by an attempt to forget or conceal its national character, and could not be made viable
by mechanical reform of religious practice, or by the encouragement of an archaeological interest in the Jewish
past, or by the imposition of a "mission" on the scattered
and harassed remnant of a people which had lost its home
and its independence. He realized that nothing less would
suffice than a revolution in Judaism, with a shift of em-

phasis from the past to the future, and a reinvigoration of the national sentiment and the national hope. But given the necessary reorientation of the Jewish heart and mind, *Jüdische Wissenschaft* and the "mission" theory would be purged of the taint of assimilationism and become positive factors in Jewish life. The study of the national past would cease to be the preserve of dryasdust scholars in ivory towers, and would be pursued, within the general framework of Jewish education, in the spirit of a deep attachment to the past as part of the continuing chain of experience and spiritual achievement of a living people. The metaphysical fantasy of the "mission" theory, which taught that the Jews had to be scattered over the world in order to fulfill, by their mere existence, the divine purpose of bringing light to the nations, would be replaced by the legitimate ambition of the Jewish people, restored to independent spiritual creativity in its own home, to become once more a force making for the progress of humanity. (In conversation he illustrated the difference between his own view and that of the "missionists" by a commercial analogy with the two types of traveling salesman: on the one hand the representative of a well-established manufacturing concern, who shows prospective clients specimens of the products which his firm can supply in quantity, and on the other hand the itinerant peddler, who has nothing to offer except what he carries on his back.) And in an independent Jewish life, emancipated alike from the restrictions of the ghetto and from the "slavery in freedom" which is the concomitant of assimilation, religious reform would come about spontaneously and would proceed along lines determined by the spirit and character of the Jewish people, and not by the psychological urge of a minority to appear as little unlike the dominant type as possible.

ᵉ⸱ 6 ᵉ⸱

Ahad Ha-Am reacted against political Zionism with his heart no less than with his head, and attacked it at times with a bitterness which he rarely injected into his other controversial writings. He exposed the weaknesses of the Zionist Organization without making allowances for the difficulties by which it was beset, and he failed sufficiently to appreciate the capital importance of the contribution made by its founder and leader, despite all the defects of his Zionist philosophy, to the national revival. Not unnaturally, his negative attitude was deeply resented by Herzl's followers, and they were more anxious to silence his inconvenient criticisms than to understand what precisely were the grounds of his quarrel with the new Zionism. An oversimplified version of the difference between "political" and "spiritual" Zionism gained currency, and has persisted till the present day. Herzl, it was supposed, stood for a Jewish State, which meant independence and freedom for the harassed millions of Jewry and an end to the "Jewish problem"; Ahad Ha-Am was opposed to a Jewish State, and wanted only a "spiritual center," which meant, so far as one could understand the idea at all, the settlement in Palestine, with no economic or political basis for their existence, of a handful of Jews, who would devote themselves entirely to cultural pursuits, and would thereby in some mysterious way exert a beneficial influence on Judaism in the diaspora.

This was, as we have seen, a complete travesty of Ahad Ha-Am's views. He was not opposed to a Jewish State, though he refused to believe that a Jewish State could be established in the near future, or could rapidly solve the material problems of the Jewish masses; and the "national spiritual center" that he desired was conceived as a normal society of men and women, and a culturally autonomous and freely developing Jewish community, in which all the other Jewish communities in the world would have a special interest, and which would serve them all as exemplar and stimulus.

Throughout all the years of his polemic against political Zionism, he was wont to complain of being misunderstood, and even intentionally misrepresented, by the orthodox Zionists; and in 1907 he wrote an essay, under the title *Words and Ideas,*[10] with the express object of removing all ground for misunderstanding in the future (though with little hope of success). He propounded a characteristic psychological explanation of his apparent failure, despite the most strenuous efforts, to make his meaning clear.

> When a man hears an opinion which runs counter to his way of thinking, he is apt unconsciously to grasp the novel opinion in an incorrect form: he will change the meaning of this or that word until it becomes not difficult for him to refute the opinion by unsound arguments, in which again one word or another is used incorrectly. And all this counterfeiting is done by the thinking apparatus automatically, without the knowledge of its owner, by virtue of its inherent tendency to work at any given moment in accordance with the dominant requirements of the subliminal self at that moment.

This, he suggests, explains why his critics refuse to understand the self-evident fact that when he speaks of Palestine as a "spiritual center" he is using the adjective "spiritual" only of the type of relationship that will exist between the center and the circumference, and does not mean that the center itself will have no material needs or interests. But the essay did little if anything to convince orthodox Zionists that the "spiritual center" was intended to be, as he had written years earlier, "a true miniature of the people of Israel," wherein would be found "the genuine type of a Jew, whether it be a rabbi or a scholar or a writer, a farmer

or a craftsman or a businessman." Two years later an unnamed friend—apparently the Ben-Avigdor already mentioned—suggested the publication of a kind of précis of the
three volumes of *At the Crossroads,* and Ahad Ha-Am was
much attracted by the idea, thinking that a small volume
consisting of extracts from his various essays, systematically
arranged under appropriate headings, might be read by
many who would not trouble to read three volumes; but
the plan was stillborn.

The misunderstanding of his attitude to the question of
a Jewish State was no less endemic. Soon after the first
Zionist Congress he wrote (in *Jewish State and Jewish
Problem*) that Hibbath Zion (by which, of course, he meant
his own version of Zionism) "wants a Jewish State and be-
lieves in the possibility of the establishment of a Jewish
State in the future"; and a year later, even more explicitly
(in an essay called *Three Stages*): "There is only one national right which can satisfy our national requirements,
and without which we can never completely realize our
aims: namely, that we become the majority in the one
country to which we have an indisputable historic right."
Yet it was (and indeed still is[11]) widely believed that his
goal of a "national spiritual center" was set up as an alternative to that of a Jewish State, and that he wanted nothing
more than—in the terms of his own caricature of the popular notion of spiritual Zionism—to settle in Palestine "a
dozen *batlanim* to occupy themselves with spiritual nationality".

It is doubtful, however, whether the inattention to statements like those just quoted, though it gave him legitimate
ground for complaint, was in any large measure responsible
for his unpopularity in the Zionist world. Ordinary men
and women were likely to be less impressed by occasional
pronouncements of that kind than by the fact that they
were only occasional, and seemed to run counter to the
general tenor of his ideas. It was exceptional for him to re-

mind his readers in so many words that a Jewish State had
any place in his scheme of things, or that even in a spiritual
center life would necessarily have its material aspects. In
spite of his years of participation in the practical work of
Hibbath Zion, it was felt that his characteristic and abiding
attitude was that expressed when he said (in *The Spiritual
Revival*): "The establishment of a single great school of
learning or art in Palestine, or of a single academy of language and literature, would in my opinion be a national
achievement of first-rate importance, and would contribute
more to the attainment of our aims than a hundred agricultural settlements." And when in *Words and Ideas* he triumphantly quoted his list of the types of Jew that would
be found in the spiritual center of the future, to prove that
he had made provision for bread-and-butter occupations, it
was noticeable that the rabbi, the scholar, and the writer
preceded the farmer, the craftsman, and the man of business. He might well be thought to be paying no more than
lip-service to the things that for ordinary folk were all-
important.

At bottom the objection to his criticisms of political Zionism reflected the plain man's instinctive sense of a radical
difference of outlook and interest. The plain man felt that
Ahad Ha-Am, in spite of his realism and practical sense,
and in spite of his unquestioned devotion to the re-
establishment of Jewish national life in Palestine, did not
belong wholly to the world of every day, and, when he
spoke his real mind seemed not to be fundamentally concerned with its problems so much as with "the latter end
of days." There was in his complex personality a touch of
the apocalyptic visionary, which erupted every now and then
into the activities and controversies of the workaday Zionist
world.

11

LAST
YEARS
IN RUSSIA

On giving up the editorship of *Hashiloah* Ahad Ha-Am returned to the world of commerce, but this time as a salaried employee. Before the expiration of the notice of resignation which he gave to Ahiasaf in October, 1902, he was offered by the Wissotzky firm a position as inspector of the outlying branches of the company's far-flung organization in Russia. The matter had been arranged without his knowledge by one of his close friends, A. E. Lubarski, who had himself been in the service of the firm for a number of years. The offer was made, as he wrote to Dr. Bernfeld, "in the most tactful manner," and the position was a responsible one, with a salary which would enable him to live in comfort, though not in luxury, and would also leave him some time for study and writing. He accepted the post, though he can scarcely have found much satisfaction in the prospect of a return to commerce without even the compensation of being his own master. For the time being his predominant feeling was one of profound thankfulness for his escape from the "humiliations and heartaches" of the last six years, and he did not express any misgivings about the future.

The new post, which he held for five years before his transfer to London as manager of the Wissotzky office there, involved frequent journeys throughout the length and breadth of Russia, not without an element of danger when conditions were disturbed. Some of the published letters of this period are dated from exotic places like Tiflis and Baku; but his home remained always in Odessa. His elder daughter, Leah, was married at some time during this period to S. Pevsner, one of the moving spirits in the modern development of Haifa, and went to live in Palestine with her husband; the younger girl and the boy had not yet completed their education.

In practice his new post turned out to be something of a disappointment. The constant traveling which it involved not only taxed his physical strength, but severely reduced the opportunities for study and writing on which he had counted when he accepted the post. A letter to Dubnow written in January, 1904, after a year's experience of his new mode of life, shows him as dissatisfied as ever:

> It is about a month since I returned home, and I have not had even a week free for myself and my own work. On my return I found the manager left all alone, as his two deputies had both gone away . . . , and of course I was at once given the honor of filling both their places. I have to sit in the office from morning till evening and sign hundreds of letters and documents, till I am heartily sick of my own name. I have only three hours each evening for my correspondence and reading papers and books. So you can reckon out how much is left for literary and public work. All the same, I did try to write something, but when I finished it I realized the truth of the talmudic adage that one who would impart knowledge must first pray [for a clear mind], because when I read over what I had written, I found it much below my usual standard, and discarded it. I don't know how long this state of things will last, but anyhow I have lost the whole of this winter, in which I hoped to do a great deal.

Dubnow had left Odessa in 1903 for Vilna, where he was lecturing on Jewish History in an institute for higher education, and in 1907 took up a similar position in St. Petersburg. He was unable to understand how Ahad Ha-Am could reconcile himself to a life which left him so little time for the things that mattered. He himself had an insatiable love of learning and an inexhaustible capacity for work; he was in the habit of spending twelve hours or more a day at his desk. He made various attempts to lure his like-minded friend away from the uncongenial world of business, suggesting at one time that Ahad Ha-Am should come and lecture in the institute in which he himself taught, at another that he should join the editorial staff of the Russian-language Jewish encyclopedia, on which work began in 1906. These suggestions were tempting to Ahad Ha-Am, who was condemned to look with longing from outside into the "fairer world" of learning and research; but he felt that he could not do anything serious in the field of scholarship without giving up his present livelihood entirely, and he could not bring himself to do that. Apart from his temperamental caution, his experience with *Hashiloah* had confirmed his distaste for depending on the Jewish public for his living. At bottom his independence of anything that could be even remotely regarded as charity mattered more to him than any other purely personal consideration, and to it he sacrificed the possibility of realizing his literary ambitions.

Just before entering the Wissotzky firm he had written to a friend that now, having returned to private life, he intended to carry out an idea of seven years earlier. He would give up writing on current topics and "concentrate on some subject of importance, work at it for a few years, and leave something worth while for posterity." But he added with characteristic caution: "Whether I shall succeed I do not know. Possibly I am unfit for any large-scale and protracted work; possibly, too, I have been so corrupted by the hurly-burly that I cannot hold my peace when I see things done that seem to me wrong. All this is possible, and experience

will tell me what I am and what I can do." The event justified his forebodings, and he was never able to concentrate
on writing a book. And, with three notable exceptions, the
essays he wrote during the post-*Hashiloah* period in Odessa
were concerned with current topics.

It was not only the demands of the tea business that kept
him away from his study. A great deal of what spare time he
could find was given up to public work, which he could
not abandon, though it brought him neither pleasure nor
profit. The habit of attending committee meetings had become too ingrained to be altogether shaken off, try as he
might to escape. He became less regular in his attendance
at meetings of the Central Committee of the Hovevé Zion,
which had become too bureaucratic for his liking; but he
was an active member of at least two other committees of
importance, on which Zionists and assimilationists sat together in uneasy association. One of these, called the "National Committee," was apparently a Zionist body which
was concerned with local Jewish affairs, and on it he found
himself sometimes in conflict with the political Zionists.
When, for example, at the end of 1903, they supported the
candidature of a Zionist who was entirely innocent of Jewish knowledge for the post of "official" Rabbi of the Odessa
community, Ahad Ha-Am regarded their attitude as an insult to Judaism. He seems to have been somewhat less unhappy on his other principal committee, which was that of
the "Society for the Spread of Enlightenment," a nation-
wide body devoted to the cause of Haskalah. Here he was
engaged in a running fight against the assimilationist advocates of the "Russification" of the Jewish schools, and
he raised his voice in and out of season in favor of a more
full-blooded Jewish education, with emphasis on the Hebrew language and Jewish history and culture. The fortunes
of battle fluctuated; at the beginning of 1904 we find him
thinking of resigning from this committee in despair, but
a year later he sees hope of making headway against the

assimilationist communal leaders. This struggle left its mark on his collected writings in the shape of his own Hebrew translation of a speech on *National Education,* which he delivered at an important conference called by the Society in 1902, and which even today retains its interest and value as a powerful statement of the nationalist position on the essentials of Jewish education.

In 1903 he had occasion to protest against the pusillanimity of the leaders of Russian Jewry, not excluding the Zionists among them. That was the year of the Kishinev pogrom, which, condoned if not actually instigated by the tsar's government, focused the attention of the civilized world for the time being on Russian anti-Semitism. The reaction of the Jewish communal leaders did not seem to Ahad Ha-Am to be worthy of the Jewish people, and, as usual, he made no attempt to conceal his dissatisfaction. In his opinion, the occasion demanded a firm declaration of the rights of the Jews as human beings, not a servile plea for mercy. His protest was unavailing, but he had the satisfaction of taking part in the promotion of a self-defense organization to protect the Jews in the event of further attacks, which did in fact follow that of Kishinev. He himself drafted the circular letter which was sent to the Jewish communities in Russia in this connection, and as a result of which some of the subsequent pogroms found the Jews readier to fight back than they had been at Kishinev. Here again there was the inevitable difference of opinion between him and his associates: he was for having the circular signed with the names of those responsible for the appeal, including of course his own, but was overruled by his more prudent colleagues, who decided in favor of anonymity.

His sense of what Jewish dignity demanded was again asserted when, at the end of 1903, after a serious pogrom in Homel, the Russian Government brought the attacked Jews to trial as the guilty party. There was an idea of inviting him and his friend Dubnow to help in the defense, and Ahad Ha-Am's attitude was expressed in a characteristic letter which he wrote to Dubnow when he heard of this possibility:

> Do the Homel people think that you or I will be allowed to say *all* that has to be said? If I receive an invitation, I will answer that I want to appear as the defendant, and to reply in the name of the whole Jewish people to the lying charges which they will heap upon us; and that if they can promise me unequivocally that I shall be able to speak my whole mind without let or hindrance, and to say frankly what we feel about the villains who persecute us and have the impudence to look for further excuses in the name of justice—well and good; but otherwise let them seek other defenders, who can bow their heads and talk the language of beggars.

In 1905, the year of the first Russian revolution, which brought about the grant by the tsar of some semblance of constitutional government, he was drawn for once into the arena of internal Russo-Jewish politics. The promulgation of a constitution for Russia in August of that year, and the subsequent preparations for the elections to the first parliament (Duma), which met in April of the following year, aroused great hopes and stimulated feverish activity in the Jewish community. Opinions were divided as to whether the Jewish cause would be best served by treating the question of Jewish rights as a separate issue, or by throwing the whole weight of Jewish support behind the progressive Russian parties in their struggle against the reactionaries. Most of the leaders of Russo-Jewish thought, including some of the Zionists, favored the latter alternative. The Jews, they thought, would automatically obtain the advantages of the triumph of liberalism, and ought therefore to submerge their particular interests in the battle for the wider ideal. Ahad Ha-Am took the other view. Though not a member of the League for the Attainment of Equal

Rights for the Jewish People in Russia, of which Simon Dubnow and Vladimir Jabotinsky, 1880-1940—later to become the founder and leader of the Zionist Revisionist Organization—were among the leading spirits, and which included national as well as individual rights in its program, he was in sympathy with its aims, and spoke at one of its conventions. He also expressed his views in the columns of the *Voschod,* the principal Russian-language Jewish weekly, overcoming for once his objection to writing in a language other than Hebrew, because it was particularly the assimilationist wing that he was anxious to address on this issue. His view was that the Jewish question in Russia was *sui generis,* that the Jews must fight for their own rights, and that by figuring prominently among the supporters of the progressive parties they would play into the hands of the reactionaries, who would be only too glad to be able to represent the revolution to the anti-Semitic masses as a movement for which the Jews were responsible.

He and Dubnow were pilloried in the Russo-Jewish press as narrow nationalists incapable of looking beyond their sectional interests; but they were justified by the event, at least negatively. What would have happened if the Jews had taken the independent line which they advocated is a matter for conjecture; but at any rate their support of the Russian progressive parties brought the Jews little gratitude and no tangible advantage. Pogroms continued after the grant of the constitution, and one of the worst of them happened in Odessa in November, 1905, when after two days of fighting the military intervened to help the rioting mob against the Jewish self-defense forces. On that occasion Ahad Ha-Am did not suffer personally; but eighteen months later, after a bomb outrage which rumor falsely attributed to a Jew, he was attacked and beaten up by a policeman in the street. Fortunately he was not seriously injured, and he was able to write sarcastically to Dubnow, the non-Zionist champion of national minority rights for

Jews in the diaspora, about this personal experience of the
blessings of Jewish autonomy.

❧ 2 ❧

In the summer of 1906 he reached the age of fifty, and
among many letters of congratulation which he received
from various parts of the world was one written on behalf
of a number of Jewish scholars in the United States of
America by Dr. Solomon Schechter, who had then been
for some years the President of the Jewish Theological
Seminary in New York. The two men were not personally
acquainted (they did not meet till 1910), and Schechter,
who was by some years the elder, had left his native Rumania many years before Ahad Ha-Am's first appearance
in print; but the name and fame of Ahad Ha-Am had by
now spread to the Jewish communities of the West, and
Schechter was among his admirers. They were both of
hasidic stock and upbringing, and there was between them
a fundamental identity of outlook, though they differed
markedly both in temperament and in their attitude to
religion.

Earlier in the same year, Schechter had extended to Ahad
Ha-Am, through his old friend Lubarski, who was by that
time in charge of the New York branch of the Wissotzky
firm, an invitation to become head[1] of the Dropsie College
for Hebrew and Cognate Learning, which was then about
to be opened in Philadelphia. Ahad Ha-Am's reply shows
how deeply he was stirred by the prospect thus held out to
him. He reproached Lubarski half-seriously for having re-
called to life the ghosts of old longings which he had forgotten. He would love nothing better than to give the rest
of his days to learning and literature; but he is concerned,
as ever, for his spiritual independence. The new institution
will inevitably have to take account of public opinion, and
he doubts whether at his age he can begin to bend the

knee before that "despotic queen," to whom he has never owed allegiance. Moreover, as he has been a stranger to regular studies for many years, and has never seen the inside of a university, he doubts whether he could successfully pass without training or preparation from a tea-merchant's business to the headship of an institution of higher learning. Still, he does not give Lubarski a negative reply, but seems to wait, perhaps half in hope and half in fear, for Lubarski or Schechter to resolve his doubts. In the event nothing came of this interesting proposal, whether because of Ahad Ha-Am's indecision, or because of objections raised by some of Schechter's anti-nationalist colleagues. It was no doubt just as well from Ahad Ha-Am's point of view. In spite of the enormous care he always took to avoid treading on religious corns, it seems highly doubtful whether a man who cared so little about the minutiae of religious observance, not to speak of his shortcomings in the matter of religious feeling and belief, could possibly have held a position of responsibility and leadership in an institution which, he thought, had a theological orientation. Some years later, after he had settled in London, Schechter again invited him to come to Dropsie College, this time for the purpose of delivering a course of ten lectures on Jewish ethics. Ahad Ha-Am accepted the invitation, though not without misgivings as to his ability to fulfill the assignment; but in the end circumstances compelled him to cancel the arrangement, and he never visited America.

Both Schechter's invitation and the birthday greetings indicate that by 1906 Ahad Ha-Am already had a considerable following in the United States, although few American Jews can have read him in the original Hebrew, and very few of his essays had as yet been translated into English. It may be assumed that, in addition to Lubarski, Israel Friedlaender[2] had helped to make his views and ideas known to the thinking section of the American Jewish public. In a letter written at the end of 1903 he rebukes Lubarski for having used his name in an advertisement of the Wissotzky firm which sought to gain it credit for employing men of learning and culture in its service; and obviously Lubarski would not have been guilty of this indiscretion if he had not expected the name of Ahad Ha-Am to mean something to the public which he was addressing. Ahad Ha-Am himself was very much alive to the growing importance of the great center of Judaism and Jewish life in the United States; and a letter to Israel Friedlaender written on the same day as the one just mentioned says that he has long been anxious to visit America and study the condition of Judaism there. He seems even to have had some hope that there might be an occasion for him to spend some time in the United States on behalf of his firm, but this hope, like so many others, was doomed to frustration.

More than two years later, in a letter to Lubarski—written apparently a few hours before Lubarski's letter containing Schechter's invitation reached him—he outlined a plan, which had evidently been discussed between them already, for a weekly or fortnightly paper designed to bridge the vast gulf which separated the two great Jewries of Russia and the United States, and to enable them to understand one another's conditions and problems. The paper was to be trilingual and to be issued in two editions, one in English and Yiddish for America, and one in Hebrew and Yiddish for Russia. The Yiddish section, designed primarily for emigrants and prospective emigrants from Russia to America, would be common to both editions and would contain news and useful information; the other section would contain articles by experts on all aspects of Jewish life in Russia and in America, and these articles would be translated from English into Hebrew and vice versa as required. Nothing more seems to have been heard of this original idea, the implementation of which might have done something towards restoring contact between the East-European

Jews who had found a home in the New World and those who had remained behind, and possibly might have acted as a brake on the assimilation of the former.

⁂ 3 ⁂

Though disappointed in his hope of being able to devote a substantial amount of time to literary work, Ahad Ha-Am did not allow his other occupations—business, public work, and correspondence—to cut him off completely from "the shrine of literature." During the five *Wanderjahre* he wrote no more than about ten articles and essays, many of them quite short. Most of these were on matters of current interest or debate, and some of the earlier ones—including the reply to Nordau about *Altneuland* and the stinging rebuke to the Russian delegates at the sixth Zionist Congress—were connected with his campaign against political Zionism. One other, also mentioned above, was an attempt to explain what he meant by a "spiritual center." But the period is really notable for three outstanding essays, *Moses, Flesh and Spirit,* and *The Supremacy of Reason.* The first two of these appeared in 1904, the third in 1905.

Moses,[3] by common consent his finest essay, is a kind of lay sermon on the prophet as the supreme Jewish type, most perfectly exemplified in the ideal figure of Moses, which he regards as "a creation of the Jewish spirit" creating in its own image. The prophet is the uncompromising champion of absolute truth and justice, who cannot lay down his burden, but must devote himself entirely to the service of an ideal which is unattainable in our imperfect world. The kernel of the essay is a brilliant (and judiciously selective) retelling of the biblical story of Moses in the light of this conception; and throughout there is an undercurrent of reference to the Jewish people as the people of the prophets, which has accepted their ideal as the basis and justification of its national existence, and whose present striving for a national rebirth betokens a new stirring of the prophetic spirit within it.

Flesh and Spirit[4] is a philosophico-historical disquisition in the manner of the group of *Fragments* written ten years earlier, on the attitude of Jewish thought to asceticism, which Ahad Ha-Am regards as foreign to the spirit of Judaism. As usual, he soon lifts the discussion from the individual to the national plane, and illustrates his thesis by examples drawn not from the conduct or teaching of individuals, but from the conflicts between sects or parties in Jewish history and in contemporary Jewish life. Just as in Roman times the true spokesmen of the Jewish people were neither the Essenes, who in their exaggerated spirituality turned their backs on political life, nor the Sadducees, who cared only for the material aspects of statehood, but the Pharisees, the true heirs of the prophets, who took the middle line, so in our own day, he asserts, the Jewish people will neither renounce nationhood with the theorists of the "mission of Israel," nor follow the proponents of a purely political nationalism, but will take the middle course of spiritual Zionism, and look forward to a third Jewish State of which the guiding principle will be, as was that of the prophets in the first and the Pharisees in the second, the ennobling of the material life by the spirit, alike in the individual and in the nation.

The year in which both *Moses* and *Flesh and Spirit* appeared in *Hashiloah* was the seventh centenary of the death of Maimonides, which occurred in December, 1204. The anniversary was the occasion of tributes to the great philosopher by Jewish scholars all over the world; and Ahad Ha-Am was moved to pay his own tribute to the medieval thinker who had been to him a beacon of light in his early struggles towards freedom of thought and judgment, and to whom, more than to anybody else, he felt that he owed his intellectual emancipation. He was himself not so thoroughgoing a devotee of pure reason as he represents Maimonides to have been; but in character and temperament there was more than a superficial resemblance between the two men. A burning passion for truth, a lofty morality, a love of order and clarity in thought and its exposition, and a dislike of mysticism were common to both. They were alike in their all-absorbing devotion to the Jewish people. A scholar who afterwards joined issue with Ahad Ha-Am's estimate of Maimonides says of the medieval philosopher that he held a stern theory of life, but objected to asceticism; that he cultivated a philosophic insensibility to the chances and changes of life, but revealed himself on occasion as a man of warm and tender feeling; that he learned to meet malicious charges without excitement or resentment; that he was opposed to all forms of amusement as unworthy of rational men; that he had no appreciation of nature, and considered village life as obviously inferior to life in town; that he had no liking for poetry or light literature; and that "his was a great and somewhat lonely spirit that dared to dwell apart from the world."[5] Ahad Ha-Am might almost have sat for this portrait.

His tribute to Maimonides was paid first in an address, delivered in Russian, to the local Jewish Club in Odessa, and was subsequently elaborated into a Hebrew article, long by his standards, which appeared in *Hashiloah* under the title of *The Supremacy of Reason*.[6] The title indicates his view that Maimonides, despite his religious orthodoxy and his gigantic labors in the field of Jewish law, was a complete rationalist. The bulk of the essay is a highly condensed yet admirably lucid exposition for the general reader of the main features of the philosophy of Maimonides. He stresses the supreme importance attached by Maimonides, from the religious and the moral point of view, to the purely intellectual apprehension of the truth about the universe, and maintains that, unlike the generality of religious philosophers, who make reason conform to revelation, Maimonides aimed at justifying revelation by showing that its truths were in conformity with those established by metaphysics. Other Jewish thinkers place Judaism above reason; Maimonides identifies it with reason. This view of Ahad Ha-Am's is no more orthodox than most of his views were, but he had a thorough knowledge of his subject, and could hold his own against learned criticism, as witness a long letter[7] to Dr. Israel Friedlaender in reply to observations made by him after the reappearance of the essay in the fourth and last volume of *At the Crossroads* in 1913.

The Supremacy of Reason is Ahad Ha-Am's solitary excursion into the field of pure scholarship. It had no ulterior motive, no design of influencing opinion on any live issue. It was written with the sole purpose of doing honor to the memory of a philosopher of the Middle Ages, and making a contribution to the understanding of his system. But the publicist in Ahad Ha-Am could never be entirely suppressed. Even in this scholarly piece of writing, which is in parts heavy going for the lay reader, he begins with some introductory paragraphs in which there is an oblique animadversion on political Zionism, and ends by raising, and answering in the affirmative, the question whether Maimonides was unconsciously what we should now call a Jewish nationalist.

❧ 4 ❧

Ahad Ha-Am never enjoyed robust health, and an indoor life, a worrying disposition, habitual overwork and excessive cigarette-smoking and tea-drinking were not calculated to improve his physical condition. While he lived in Odessa he used to spend his summer vacations at the country home of his friend Mordechai Hacohen near Homel, where Dubnow was also a frequent guest; but there is evidence that most of his time there was spent in writing and discussion of serious topics, and he had little relaxation. He habitually drove himself too hard, and was impatient of idleness. We have seen that he was ordered to rest because of nervous trouble in 1898, and that his strength was heavily taxed by the mission to Palestine in 1899-1900. The nervous trouble recurred in an aggravated form six or seven years later, when the strain of two or three years of traveling all over Russia, sometimes in disturbed conditions, had been added to the other factors inimical to his health. He spent much of the winter of 1906-7 in Moscow for business reasons, and was under medical treatment there for a liver complaint; but in the following spring an Odessa specialist found that there was nothing wrong with his liver, but that he had some nervous trouble, for which he needed rest, hydropathic treatment and a sea voyage. He accordingly left Odessa for Palestine in May, and spent three weeks with his married daughter in Haifa. For once he had a complete rest, and did not visit a single settlement. In the notes on his visits to Palestine which are incorporated in the *Reminiscences,* this particular visit is commemorated only by what he describes in a footnote as "a little lyrical outburst."[8] This is worth reproducing (in the necessarily inadequate medium of a translation) if only because it would be difficult to believe that it was his if we had not his own word for it. The heading is *On the Top of Carmel:*

> Once more I have been in Palestine—have been there and yet have not been there. This time my object was not work but rest, and so, instead of visiting the scenes of activity, I have sought out a secluded haven of rest on the top of Carmel, and have not seen the *yishuv* and its centers.
>
> Yet I feel in every fiber of my being that this time too I have been in Palestine: nay more, it almost seems to me that *only* this time have I been in Palestine. If any diaspora Jew about to visit Palestine were to ask me now what he

should do to get the pure flavor of the land, with all its sweetness and all its bitterness, I should reply: Ignore Jaffa and its offshoots, with their noise and bustle, and go up to the top of Carmel. Stay there for a few days, alone with your thoughts, holding whispered converse day and night with the winds that come up to you from the depths of the primeval ocean, with no human being to interrupt the whispering and drive away the spirit-winds with the raucous sounds of every day.

I sit on the top of Carmel at nightfall and turn my eyes westward, to where the sun is sinking into the ocean. How strange is all that I see about me! Nothing remains of all my ancestral inheritance here, not even a tiny ruin. The house in which I live, the trees in whose shade I shelter, the lovely vineyards all around—everything is newly made by strangers, who have come from afar to favor the sacred dust. But I—what or whom have I here? With anger in my heart I turn my eyes away and gaze beseechingly on the sun, which alone still shines and still sets in this place as it used to shine and to set thousands of years ago, and alone saw my ancestors here in the days of their prosperity. Let the sun, then, be my witness that I am no stranger here.

The sun reddens and hastens to hide in the depths as though ashamed to remember those days, when the children of Israel used to bow down before it in worship, and build altars to it, and prophets used to prophesy in its name on top of Carmel.

Not less surprising than the poetic vein in which these lines are cast is the invocation by the spiritual Zionist of his remote sun-worshiping ancestors, rather than of the Law and the prophets, as proof of his being no stranger in Palestine. There is no other known point of contact between him and the present-day section of Israel's youth, known as "Canaanites," who claim a national link with the pre-Exodus inhabitants of their country.

This holiday ended with a strange episode, perhaps the only one in his life that could be dignified with the name of an adventure. He had reached Constantinople on his way home, and had actually boarded a ship bound for Odessa, when a telegram was handed to him. It turned out to be a warning from his friends that it would be dangerous to return to Odessa; so he landed again, and traveled to Vienna, and thence to Carlsbad, with the result that he did not arrive home until September. It appears that the police had searched his house, possibly for some reason connected with his part in encouraging Jewish self-defense two years earlier, and his friends judged that it would be prudent for him to stay away for a time. Nothing more was heard of the affair. This false alarm had the result of lengthening his holiday, but notwithstanding this he returned home in little better condition than when he had left it. He seems to have had some fear of being a semi-invalid for the rest of his life, but he recovered, and it was not until some years later that he had a serious breakdown.

In October, 1907, he was again in Moscow on the business of his firm, and thence after a few weeks he traveled, alone, to London, which was shortly to become his home. The time had come for him to leave Odessa, where the unknown student of twenty-one years earlier had become famous throughout the Jewish world as the inspirer and philosopher of his people's cultural renaissance.

His public career during those years in Odessa was rendered remarkable not only by the exceptional qualities of mind and character which it revealed, but by the exclusiveness of his self-dedication to the cause of the national rebirth. That cause was the pole whose magnetic attraction determined the direction of all his activities, in literature and public work alike, and to it he devoted the whole of his intellectual gifts and the vast store of knowledge which he had acquired. He might have written with distinction on many subjects of general interest, not to speak of Jewish history and thought, in Russian or German, or even eventually in English; but he chose to write only for his own people, in its own little-known language, and on the central problem of its existence. Tending, as always, to go to extremes, he shut himself within the four walls of Jewish life with a thoroughness that might seem scarcely consistent with the humanism which was an integral element in his philosophy; but the reproach of narrowness would have had no terrors for him. He had met it—not, of course, with explicit reference to himself, but in its more general bearing— more than once in his essays, and particularly in *Priest and Prophet* (1894), one of the *Fragments,* where he first put forward an idea to which he was to recur ten years later in *Moses.* The Prophet is there represented as a spiritual giant, a moral superman, who is essentially one-sided, and cares for nothing in life except the ideal to which his whole being is devoted; and "Prophecy is, as it were, the hallmark of the Jewish national spirit." The prophetic character of the Hebrew mind, he suggests, is revealed in its bent towards concentration on a single aim, in contrast to the Greek preference for a type of life of which complexity and many-sidedness are the characteristics. Naturally, his own allegiance was given to the Hebraic ideal, and by that his conduct was guided. Again, in the abovementioned essay, *The Spiritual Revival* (1902), he rounds on the "broad-minded" anti-nationalists who condemn Jewish nationalism as "petty tribalism," and argues that a creative artist who works among a people to which he is not attached by his deepest roots is less likely to produce the best of which he is capable than one who works in the cultural environment of his own people. There is thus, he suggests, some loss to humanity, as well as to the Jewish people itself, through the assimilation which leads Jews, including many of the most gifted, to forsake their own cultural heritage; and the Jewish people can best serve humanity as well as itself by cultivating its own vineyard.

His intense Jewishness, at the core of which glowed his *grande passion,* the love of Zion, not only determined the scope of his literary and public work: it governed his private and social life as well. His circle of friends consisted entirely of those who were interested, like himself, though not necessarily with his extreme concentration, in the Jewish national revival. He lived, according to one who was close to him in his Odessa days, in a sort of Zionist ghetto. In course of time he became the central figure of the distinguished group of Hebrew writers and Zionist workers known as the Odessa group, and its members constituted his world. For them he kept open house on Friday evenings; with them he discussed projects and problems of common interest, and argued about political Zionism, on which few if any of them shared his extreme views; and from among them were drawn his more intimate friends, with whom he spent his limited hours of relaxation. What time he could spare from work and the society of his friends was given mostly to reading, for he remained an inveterate student long after reaching manhood. His private and domestic concerns seem to have had a low place in his scheme of priorities. He was, in his own way, attached to his children, and especially to the younger of his two daughters; and he was interested in their Jewish education. But his absorption in the national movement and the things of the mind left him little opportunity for family life.

12

LONDON

EXILE

The visit to London in October, 1907, was an exploratory one, occasioned by a suggestion of the heads of the Wissotzky tea firm that he should exchange his inspectorship in Russia for the position of manager of their recently-opened London office. He had not been in the British capital since 1893, and he had then left it with his Anglophile leanings somewhat subdued as a result of his brief contact with English life. Nonetheless, the prospect of living in England had very great attractions. It was, in marked contrast to Russia, a free country, and the home of a people whose common sense and tolerance were proverbial. His own thought had been profoundly influenced by the British moral philosophers, and their straightforward empiricism appealed to his love of clarity and distrust of mysticism far more than the obscure profundities of the German metaphysicians. Above all, there was the lure of the British Museum Library for such a book-lover as he was. On the other side there was the parting from his old friends, and the abandonment of the familiar surroundings of Odessa, where he had lived for over twenty years, and had become the center of a circle of friends and co-workers in the Jewish national cause, for a virtually unknown city in a strange country. For a man with his conservative habits, to whom friendship meant so much, this heavy disadvantage might well have seemed to outweigh all the attractions of London, not excluding even the British Museum. However, he did not refuse the offered position out of hand, but decided that it would be wise to go to London for a trial period of three or four months before committing himself definitely.

In London he found, or there was found for him, a pair of rooms in an unpretentious lodging-house in the west-central district, very near the British Museum, and not too far from the Wissotzky office in Mincing Lane, the center of the tea trade in the City. There were numbers of people in London, mostly recent arrivals from eastern Europe, to whom his name was well known and his arrival was a matter of interest. Some of these were Hebrew teachers or Yiddish journalists, who had read his works and been influenced by his ideas; and there must have been many Zionists of the rank and file who had heard of him because of his controversy with political Zionism, and whose feelings towards him were oddly compounded of dislike for the enemy of the Zionist Organization and admiration for the foremost Hebrew writer and thinker of his day. Among the British-born and English-educated section of the Jewish community, which at that time numbered few Zionists and fewer readers of modern Hebrew, his name was as yet scarcely familiar, though not entirely unknown. Anglo-Jewry lagged behind in all matters connected with Hebrew and Jewish scholarship; and there was as yet nothing in English on the scale of Israel Friedlaender's German translation of a number of Ahad Ha-Am's essays, a volume of which had been published in 1904 by the *Juedischer Verlag* in Berlin, under the title *Am Scheidewege.* However, an English version of three of his *Fragments,* by Lilian Ruth Bentwich, daughter of Herbert Bentwich, the well-known English Hovev Zion and Zionist, and shortly to become Israel Friedlaender's wife, had appeared in the London *Jewish Chronicle,* with a brief introductory note, in 1905, and had subsequently been reprinted in pamphlet form; and shortly before his arrival in London the 1907 *Annual* of the

Union of Jewish Literary Societies had contained a translation by the present biographer of an article of his, *The Time
Has Come,* which had appeared in that year in a Hebrew
miscellany published in Jerusalem. He had also, it seems,
letters of introduction to some prominent members of the
Anglo-Jewish community in London; and a letter to Ravnitzki written after a few weeks there tells how he has
begun his round of visits to the "bigwigs," at the rate of one
a week, which is as much as he can manage, with "due observance of English etiquette," which is "very important."

It is clear from his letters to friends that during the exploratory visit to London he was treated as a distinguished
stranger and welcomed on all hands; but it is equally clear
that he was lonely and unhappy, and felt completely out of
his element. In letters to his friends he gave his impressions
of English Judaism with his usual forthrightness. "Judaism
in our sense of the word," he wrote to Dubnow, "is in
galuth here much more than in Russia. There are Jewish
meetings, including Zionist meetings, there are literary societies, and even Hebrew-speaking societies. But in all these
things there is no breath of life. You feel at once that it is
only a foreign plant brought here from afar, which has obtained a superficial hold on the soil by artificial means, but
has no real roots." There was of course Zionism, but it was
mostly of the political variety, and had no attraction for
him. He attended a Zionist Conference in Manchester, and
was well received, but came away disheartened by the
paucity of interest in Jewish culture and the prevailing
atmosphere of pettiness and personal animosities. The only
ray of light that he could find in "western" Anglo-Jewry
was in a handful of young men of English birth and education, Zionist or near-Zionist in their outlook, in whom, as he
wrote, Judaism by some miracle had not died, and who
would have liked to bring about a revival, but were not allowed to do so by the "despotic" Jewish community.

Notwithstanding the highly discouraging impressions of his five-months' trial, he decided to accept the Wissotzky managership in London—remarks in some of his letters suggest that he had little real choice in the matter—and after returning to Russia for a month he was back in London in May, 1908, accompanied this time by his younger daughter, who, after a disagreeable period of hotel life, found and furnished a comfortable house in the northwestern suburb of Belsize Park. There after a while they were joined by his wife and son, and the family was complete, the elder daughter being already settled in Haifa.

He was only too soon confirmed in his impression that London would never be a real home for him. To be at home meant to be in a congenial Jewish milieu, and this he could not find in the British metropolis. There was no lack of readiness on the part of the Anglo-Jewish community to take him to its heart, but it was not in him to respond. Not only was he shy, and unable or unwilling, at fifty-two, to adapt himself to the social conventions of a new environment. A deeper reason lay in the gulf which separated Judaism as he understood it from the synagogue-Judaism of an assimilated western community. From his point of view English Judaism was a museum-piece, an affair of tombstones and epitaphs. He had no interest in rabbis or ministers of religion as such, and Jewish scholarship was but poorly represented in England. And of course he could not mix socially with people with whom he had no serious interest in common. He had, as we have seen, made some contacts with Anglo-Jewish families during the trial months, but when he settled in London he did not attempt to develop a single one of them, except that with the Bentwich family. So during the whole of his fourteen years in London he remained almost a complete stranger to the assimilated section of the Anglo-Jewish community, apart from the few men of the younger generation, mentioned above, who were in a broad sense his disciples, or were at least interested

in the problems which engrossed him and able to understand his views.

He was scarcely less a stranger to the other, the "foreign,"
section of London Jewry. No doubt it was less assimilated
than the "English" section, by which, as he was quick to
observe, it was treated with patronizing contempt; but its
yiddishkeit had scarcely more appeal for him than Anglo-
Judaism. Early in 1909, after he had lived in London for
some months, he had occasion to disillusion Klausner, who
apparently thought that he was living in a paradise of comfortable material conditions and personal security, with
large numbers of Russian Jews around him, and had no
ground for complaint.

> Of *my* Russian Jews [he wrote], there are only two or
> three, who visit me once in several weeks. I have no con-
> tact with the rest of the Russian Jews, not only because
> in practice I do not live in the same city (London is not
> one city, but a whole country, and it is an hour's journey
> by train from my home to the Russian Ghetto), but—and
> this is the main reason—because all that large commu-
> nity has no resemblance to those Russian Jews who are
> like us and to whom we feel we belong. Here you will
> find only the two extremes: either ignoramuses with a
> smattering of jargonized [*i.e.,* yiddishist] socialism, or
> "observant" Jews of the driest Lithuanian type. As to the
> Zionists among them, I had better say nothing.

The only kind of milieu in which he could feel fully at
home was that of Europeanized and Zionized maskilim of
the Odessa type; and such were scarcely to be found in the
London ghetto. There were, however, a few of them scattered over the vast area of the metropolis, and these formed
his circle. He had scarcely any other society, apart from the
handful of new acquaintances already mentioned, except
when one or another of his old friends from Russia or
Palestine came to London on a visit. Weizmann was in Man-

chester, and visited London only on rare occasions before 1914.

His isolation was not only social; he took no part in communal or public activity of any kind. Apart from lack of time, he did not feel qualified, as a stranger ignorant of the local conditions, to intervene in the affairs of the Anglo-Jewish community, or even of English Zionism. The small band of devotees of the Hebrew linguistic and literary revival not unnaturally hoped that the presence in London of the greatest of living Hebrew writers would give their work a much-needed fillip; but they were disappointed. He regarded Hebrew speaking in the diaspora as artificial, and only out of politeness would he converse in Hebrew with anybody who addressed him in that language. He could not see a living Hebrew movement, or even the beginnings of one, in the activities of a handful of enthusiasts, without means or influence in the community, to whom nobody outside their own circle paid any heed. Not long after his arrival in London he was persuaded to address a Hebrew meeting, to which his great reputation attracted many who did not ordinarily participate in such functions, and his address was heard with great appreciation by a large audience; but that was an isolated exception to his self-imposed rule of aloofness. Some years later he was among those who put their names to a circular heralding the establishment of a Hebrew Club in London, and he was an active member of the club during its brief span of life. He did not respond to occasional invitations to collaborate with the local Hebraists in projected literary undertakings, or help the Hebrew movement in any other way.

Thus the fourteen years of his life in London passed by without leaving any impression on Anglo-Jewish life on the one hand, or on the development of his own thought or interests on the other. He was in England without being of it. His personal contacts were almost exclusively with old

friends and colleagues of the Odessa days, and with a few
English Jews who had come under the influence of his ideas
before they made his personal acquaintance. Outside that
small circle there was nobody to whom it was a fact of
significance that the philosopher of Zionism was now living
in London. He did not appear at public functions, or give
interviews to journalists, or write for local periodicals. His
influence on Anglo-Jewry, such as it was, continued to be
exercised, as before, through his Hebrew writings, in the
original or in translation, and through Russian Jews who
had been his disciples before they left eastern Europe. And
he on his side found no new inspiration or stimulus in English Judaism. With the possible exception of his extended
review of Claude Montefiore's book on the Gospels, which
contains some introductory sentences about the remoteness
of contemporary English Judaism from the Jewish spirit, he
wrote nothing in London that might not equally have been
written in Odessa.

He could no doubt have entered into the general cultural
life of the British capital, and made non-Jewish friends, had
he been so disposed; but if he had lived in a sort of Zionist
ghetto in Odessa, a city in which he was really at home, he
was obviously not tempted to venture outside the limits of
Jewish life in a strange city like London. The non-Jewish
staff of his city office liked and respected him, but there is
no indication that he had contact with any of them outside
business hours.

The story of his life in England is strikingly different
from that of another distinguished Jew from the continent
of Europe whose arrival in London preceded his by a quarter of a century, and who held views akin to his on the character and destiny of the Jewish people, though he was a
religious Jew and remained within the four walls of traditional orthodoxy. Solomon Schechter, a native of Rumania,
was born, like Ahad Ha-Am, of a hasidic family, but un-

like him moved westward at an early age, and obtained the
university education which the other was denied. Temperamentally he was as warm, ebullient, and irrepressible as
Ahad Ha-Am was cold, reserved and retiring. When Schechter was brought to London by Claude Montefiore in 1882,
still in his thirties, he was not, as Ahad Ha-Am was in 1908,
the bearer of a name famous throughout Jewry: he was
practically unknown outside a small circle of Jewish scholars. His knowledge of the English language and English
conditions was small. Yet within a few years he was publishing articles in English, and in 1896 he produced the first
volume of his *Studies in Judaism,* a book which ranks
among the classics of Jewish literature in the English language. Soon after his arrival in London he made contact
with a group of Jewish intellectuals, and became their unquestioned leader. Though he was as downright as Ahad
Ha-Am in his condemnation of the sterility and philistinism
of Anglo-Jewry, and no less emphatic in his advocacy of the
unpopular cause of Jewish knowledge, he entered fully into
the life of the community, and became one of its leading
figures. He spent twelve years as Lecturer (and subsequently
Reader) in rabbinics at Cambridge, where he was a figure
of note in the university as well as a powerful influence on
successive generations of its Jewish undergraduates. His
work on the Cairo Geniza manuscripts made him interna-
tionally famous. He had left his mark on Anglo-Jewish life,
and to some extent on English cultural life in general, when
he left England in 1902 to become the head of the Jewish
Theological Seminary in New York; and before long he
was the most dynamic force in the Jewish life of the United
States. The reasons for this piquant contrast lay partly in the
temperamental differences between the two men; but probably Ahad Ha-Am's avowed secularism would in any case
have made it impossible for him to become a spiritual leader
of the Anglo-Jewish community.

❧ 2 ❧

After settling in his London home, Ahad Ha-Am had to wait many weeks for the arrival of his books from Russia. When at last the books were arranged on the bookshelves which lined the whole of his study, he allowed himself to hope, as he had recently written to Dubnow, that he would be able to resume his old way of life. The lack of friends, he thought, would be a positive blessing, because there would be nobody to worry him when he wanted to write or study; and he was looking forward to making good use of his reader's ticket for the British Museum reading-room.

Unfortunately these hopes, like so many that he entertained at different times, were not fulfilled, and the move to London turned out to be something of a tragedy. Psychologically, to be torn up by the roots, sundered from all his old friends, and transplanted into a very different environment was a more serious wrench than probably he realized himself. Physically, the English climate never agreed with him, and although he had no serious illness before 1919, his health underwent a gradual impairment, especially during the years of World War I. The underground journeys to and from the City, occupying an hour and a half a day, and the noise and gloom of the City itself, in which he had to spend the whole day five days a week, and which he was wont to describe as "hell," imposed a severe nervous strain upon him; and his annual summer holiday of a month or two at an English or continental watering-place did not always suffice for reinvigoration. What was still worse for a man to whom his mind was of so much more importance than his body, he found serious study almost impossible. The great reading room, on which he had pinned his hopes, closed at too early an hour for him to be able to make much use of it after business hours; and his high sense of responsibility would not permit him to play truant from the office while it was open, though it is not impossible that he could have allowed himself a certain license without detriment to the interests of his employers. So he spent seven hours or more daily in "hell" on five days of the week (he never went to the City on the Sabbath except in case of emergency); and he returned home in the evening with shattered nerves, unable to settle down to intellectual work, and for the most part fit only for reading the papers and fulfilling in exemplary fashion the obligations of a conscientious correspondent to his numerous friends abroad—in Russia, the United States, and Palestine.

In such circumstances the paucity of friends on the spot, with whom he could hold personal converse, was scarcely the blessing that he had impulsively told Dubnow it would be. He did not welcome solitude at times when he was not engrossed in study or in literary work. His wife, too, had not many friends, and never overcame the drawback of an inadequate command of English; nor, in any case, did he look to her for intellectual companionship. His loneliness was intensified not long after the settlement of the family in London, when the son and daughter left home to pursue their studies at distant universities, and thereafter were only occasional sojourners under the parental roof. Thus conditions in London were no more conducive to his personal happiness than to his literary productivity. But he made small demands on life, and did not wear his heart on his sleeve. To outward appearance his earlier years in London, before World War I, were tolerably happy.

Those still alive who knew him in his London period will remember best the gatherings in his house on Friday evenings, when he was "at home" to his friends, in accordance with his old Odessa practice. The guests were a variegated and multilingual company, with a sprinkling of ladies among the men, and often included one or more of his old friends who happened to be in London. Chaim Weizmann,

on a brief visit from Manchester, was occasionally among
them, and now and again there would be other Zionists or
Hebrew writers of importance, along with the smaller fry.
The conversation of the groups into which the guests divided themselves was conducted in a variety of languages—
Hebrew, Yiddish, English, Russian—and flitted "from grave
to gay, from lively to severe," and the host would move from
group to group, listening to their talk and now and then
interposing a comment or an anecdote in his quiet way.
Whatever he said, whether in more serious or in lighter vein,
was worth attention, but he was not overfond of the sound
of his own voice, and liked to listen at least as well as to talk.
He had not the conversational brilliance of a Shmarya Levin
or a Bialik, and left behind him no scintillating trail of epi-
grams and *bons mots*. His spare physique and gentle voice
and manner were not those of a dominating figure. Yet those
Friday evening gatherings in his home bore the impress of
his personality, and their atmosphere reflected the deep-
rooted Jewishness of his outlook and interests.

❧ 3 ❧

The various committees which had taken up so much of
his time in Odessa naturally ceased to have any claim on
him when he moved to London; and his attitude to the
Anglo-Jewish community and to English Zionism was such
as to preclude his seeking local substitutes for them. His
services were, however, enlisted in the cause of one Palestinian project, which occupied a good deal of his time from
his first arrival in London until the eve of the outbreak of
World War I.

When Kalman Wissotzky died, in 1904, he left instructions in his will that an institution to commemorate his
name should be established once every five years, and set
aside for this purpose a capital sum which would provide
100,000 roubles (say, £10,000) at the end of each quinquen-

nial period. The first institution was due to be established in 1909, and a year or so earlier Ahad Ha-Am, whom Wissotzky had appointed one of the trustees of his charitable bequest, suggested to the testator's son, David Wissotzky, that the first 100,000 roubles should be used for the creation of an institution in Palestine. David Wissotzky scented Zionism in this idea, and turned it down; he wanted the bequest to be used for some philanthropic object in Russia. It may be surmised that Ahad Ha-Am would not condescend to attempt to overcome his objection; but others tried and succeeded. Dr. Paul Nathan, Secretary of the German philanthropic organization, the Hilfsverein der deutschen Juden, which maintained a number of schools in Palestine, had just visited the Holy Land, where he was inspired by what he saw of the *yishuv,* and conceived the idea that a technical school would be of great value for its development. Nathan, who was under no suspicion of Zionist learnings, joined Shmarya Levin[1] in approaching David Wissotzky with a suggestion that his father's bequest should be devoted to the establishment of a technical school in Palestine, and their mission was successful. Wissotzky abandoned his idea of spending the bequest money in Russia, and an agreement was entered into under which the Wissotzky trust and the Hilfsverein were to be jointly responsible for the implementation of the technical school project, the German organization undertaking to provide whatever funds might be found necessary to supplement the bequest money. It was decided to set up a Kuratorium, or board of governors, representative of both parties, to put the scheme into effect. Ahad Ha-Am and Levin were original members of this body, together with Nathan and other representatives of his organization. Later it was strengthened by the addition of Yehiel Tchlenow, and of some prominent American Jews, including Solomon Schechter and Jacob Schiff, the latter of whom made a liberal contribution to the funds of the enterprise. Ahad Ha-Am was chosen as one of the members of the small inner executive committee, and the scheme involved him, as the principal representative of the Zionists on the board, in many journeys to Berlin, and a vast amount of correspondence and negotiation, during the next five or six years.

From the outset the board agreed that it would be necessary to establish a secondary school as a feeder for the technical school, and plans were accordingly drawn up for buildings for both schools to be erected on a site which was provided by the Jewish National Fund at Haifa. During the next three or four years considerable progress was made with the buildings, and some appointments were even made to the teaching staff of the secondary school, which was to be opened first. But as the time for opening drew near, the fundamental differences of outlook which divided the Zionist and the non-Zionist members of the Kuratorium inevitably revealed themselves, and the scheme broke down. Ahad Ha-Am's part in the proceedings—a novel one for a man of his strong views and rigid adherence to principles—was that of a mediator between the official Zionists and the assimilationists (who included the Wissotzky heirs as well as the German members); and he was the better able to exert a moderating influence because he was not formally a member of the Zionist Organization. But even his wisdom and tact could not achieve the impossible. In those pre-Balfour days Zionism was still anathema to most of the influential Jews in the western communities; and it would have been little short of miraculous if Zionists and non-Zionists had succeeded in carrying out a joint enterprise of importance in Palestine, even had there not been the complicating factor of political ambitions which were no concern of Zionism or the Jewish people.

Ahad Ha-Am had realized from the outset how wide was the gulf between his own standpoint and that of the Hilfsverein. He had, as he wrote to Ussishkin in March, 1908, a great struggle with himself before he finally decided that it would on the whole be better to have a technical school run in the philanthropic spirit of the Hilfsverein than to have none at all. He was very strongly impressed by the potential value of such a school, not only for the Jewish development of Palestine itself, but also from the point of view of the Jewish position in the Middle East; and it was obvious that for financial reasons the project could not be carried out by the Zionists alone.

His first contacts with Paul Nathan were somewhat re-assuring, and for a time he allowed himself to believe that serious differences of opinion on the Kuratorium might be avoided; but whatever hopes he had were soon shattered. In 1910 he wrote to Klausner of the difficulty that he and his colleagues had in co-operating with the Germans, and to Lubarski that "it is difficult to keep the peace between fire and water." More than once he was on the point of resigning because of the refusal of the Germans to make any conces-sion to the Zionist point of view. Though he was prepared to stretch points for the sake of peace, there were questions of principle on which he could not budge; and it was not only the Hilfsverein representatives with whom he found himself in disagreement. He had occasion to protest strongly against an attempt by Schiff to prevent Tchlenow's co-option to the Kuratorium on the sole ground that Tchlenow was a Zionist, and also against the same philanthropist's intention to attach to his financial contribution a condition which would have hampered freedom of opinion in the projected school. He objected equally to the attempts made now and then by the Hilfsverein representatives to by-pass the Kura-torium and give the outside world the impression that their organization was in sole control, and to a suggestion of Schiff's that the undertaking should be put under the super-vision of all the Jewish organizations in the western world.

But the two great stumbling-blocks were the questions of the language of instruction and of the place of religion

in the two schools. It was the former of these questions that
in the end led to the resignation of the Zionist members of
the Kuratorium; but the battle over the religious question is
of greater interest for the light it throws on Ahad Ha-Am's
personality and outlook. It was easier for him to compromise on the religious issue than on the question of the
Hebrew language.

It will have been gathered that his position on the question of religion was that of a highly sympathetic and understanding agnostic. Disclaiming any positive religious belief,
he yet retained the reverence of the most conservative of
traditionalists for "the holy things of the nation," which in
his view a good nationalist was bound to respect independently of his personal faith or unfaith; and in practice he was
likely to be aligned with the moderate religionists rather
than with the out-and-out secularists on any concrete question of religious observance. His was a middle-of-the-road
attitude, which may be regarded as a kind of working compromise arrived at between his native skepticism and some
of the less negative elements of his spiritual make-up—his
passion for individual freedom, his strong sense of the crucial importance of historic continuity in Judaism, and his
awareness of the futility of needlessly antagonizing the religious majority.

Thus, for example, he was naturally in general sympathy
with the Tel Aviv High School (Gymnasia Herzlia), which
was opened by Jewish nationalists in 1907, and made history
as the first Hebrew-language secondary school in the world;
and he intervened on the school's behalf with its great
patron, Jacob Moser,[2] when the latter, disturbed by reported
secularist tendencies in the school, was disposed to attach
unacceptable conditions to his much-needed financial contribution. At the same time, he deprecated the introduction
of the disputable theories of the so-called "higher criticism"
into the teaching of the Bible to school-children, and he

gently ridiculed the objection of the more anti-religious teachers to allowing their pupils to keep their heads covered during Bible lessons. Over against this and other examples of his opposition to extreme secularism must be set his equally strong resistance to any suggestion that a Jewish nationalist must necessarily profess religious faith. In 1910, when consulted by Dr. J. L. Magnes,[3] then Rabbi of Temple Emanu-El in New York, about his project of founding a society "to propagate national religion and religious nationalism," he took exception to this formulation of the society's aim. He fully agreed, he wrote, that Judaism was a national religion, but he could not accept "religious nationalism" unless it was simply another way of saying "national religion." "In my view," he said, "our religion is national—that is to say, it is a product of our national spirit—but the converse is not true. If it is impossible to be a Jew in the religious sense without acknowledging our nationality, it is possible to be a Jew in the national sense without accepting many things in which religion requires belief."

The clearest statement of his conception of the relation between religion and nationality in the Jewish tradition is contained in a letter which he wrote in 1913 to Dr. Israel Abrahams,[4] who was, incidentally, almost the only Anglo-Jewish scholar with whom, so far as his published correspondence shows, he was in touch during his London years:

> The answer to the question what Judaism is depends, of course, on the meaning one attaches to the vague terms "Judaism," "religion" and "culture." In the sense in which I understand those terms, I should say that religion itself is only one particular form of "culture," and that "Judaism" is neither the one nor the other, but is the national creative power, which in the past expressed itself in a form of culture which was primarily religious. In what form it will express itself in the future—that we cannot tell.

Holding such views as these, he clearly could not subscribe
to a definition in religious terms of the Jewish aims of the
projected technical school; and at an early stage in the proceedings of the Kuratorium he objected, in common with
his Zionist colleagues, to a draft clause put forward by the
Hilfsverein for inclusion in a document setting forth the
basic principles by which the institution was to be governed.
Among a number of provisions which were expressly stated
to be unalterable was one which, as drafted, laid it down
that it should be the object of the secondary school and the
technical school to educate their pupils as Jews who should
have "an adequate knowledge of Hebrew and Jewish history" and should "be attached by ties of affection and respect
to their religion and to their home in Palestine." In spite of
the recognition of the claims of Hebrew and Jewish history,
and the emphasis on attachment to Palestine, the Zionists
scented assimilationist implications in this formula; and
Ahad Ha-Am suggested the substitution of "their Judaism"
for "their religion"—a change which, as we have seen, was
for him far from being purely verbal. The Hilfsverein representatives on the Kuratorium were unable to accept this
counter-proposal, and suggested the compromise formula
"their religion and their Judaism," to which the Zionists
agreed. Ahad Ha-Am used this formula to set at rest the
doubts of Schechter, who, having been invited to join the
Kuratorium, had felt it necessary, in view of the reputation
of the Tel Aviv Gymnasia, to seek assurances about the position of religion in the projected technical school. It appears,
however, that later the formula was replaced, without any
protest from Ahad Ha-Am, by one which spoke of "conscious Jews, who respect their origin (*Abstammung*) and
religion"—a wording which, with its oblique reference to a
purely racial nationalism, seems no more acceptable from
his point of view than that originally suggested.

One of Ahad Ha-Am's numerous letters to Shmarya
Levin about the technical school project reveals that if the

Hilfsverein had insisted on the wording which they originally proposed, he would have been prepared to accept it
rather than risk jeopardizing the whole undertaking by a
refusal to compromise on this particular point. He defended
this attitude on the ground that "religion" is a vague term,
and all nationalist Jews, except the yiddishist-nationalists of
the socialist organization known as the Bund, are bound to
their religion by ties of affection and reverence, though for
some "religion" means ceremonial observances, while for
others it means Isaiah and Jeremiah. This is a strange defense coming from him, who was the sworn enemy of am-
biguity, and in his polemic against political Zionism had
charged its leaders with stifling discussion of fundamentals
so as not to bring into the open the deep cleavage of opinion
between the "eastern" and the "western" Zionists. The fact
is that he did not attach any importance to the formulation
of the ideas of the Kuratorium about the place of religion
in the schools. He realized that in the last resort the teachers would be the determining factor, and was very willing
to postpone controversy over this delicate issue until the
time came for filling the key positions in the teaching staff.
The vital thing was to avoid a breakdown of the scheme.

He was, understandably, unable to show an equal degree
of flexibility on the other fundamental issue, that of the
language of instruction, on which the scheme finally came
to grief. Though he made many attempts to get this question settled, the Hilfsverein representatives succeeded in
keeping it off the agenda for some years. But at length the
time arrived when it could no longer be shirked, and it then
became evident that they were not prepared for any accom-
modation with the Zionists. They insisted that German must
be the language of teaching not only in the technical school
itself, when it came into being, but also in the secondary
school so far as secular subjects were concerned. They were
prepared to admit Hebrew only for Jewish subjects.

This uncompromising attitude came as a surprise in view

of the previous record of the Hilfsverein, which in its educational work in Palestine had shown a greater readiness than the French Alliance, or even than the Anglo-Jewish Association, to recognize the claims of the revived Hebrew language. Probably there was good ground for the suspicion that their obstinate insistence on German as the language of instruction for the projected new schools was not unconnected with German political ambitions in the Middle East. Be that as it may, the Kuratorium found it impossible to arrive at a generally acceptable solution of the language problem. The Zionist members other than Ahad Ha-Am claimed that from the outset Hebrew should be the sole language of instruction in both the schools. Ahad Ha-Am, as ever tempering idealism with practical sense, was with them only as regards the secondary school. Experience had shown that the Hebrew language was sufficiently developed for the purposes of non-technical secondary education; but there was at that time no parallel experience in the field of scientific and technical subjects, other than mathematics and physics, and he felt that insistence on using Hebrew from the outset for the teaching of all such subjects might prove disastrous. While, therefore, he held out for Hebrew as the only language of instruction in the secondary school, he did not feel it right to insist on Hebrew for the technical school —which was to be opened later—except for mathematics and physics, and for any other subjects for which the teachers might decide from time to time that Hebrew could be used without any practical disadvantage.

The American members of the board supported the claim for Hebrew. But the Hilfsverein representatives were immovable, and they had the whip hand, because their organization could if necessary carry the whole of the financial burden, but without its participation the scheme could not be implemented. Levin and Tchlenow resigned from the Kuratorium on this issue, and Ahad Ha-Am joined them, though with some reluctance, for he was not certain that he could not serve the interests of the project better by continuing on the board, and trying to influence its policy from within, than by resigning. The American members did not resign at once; but their efforts to patch up a compromise were fruitless, and before long they too resigned, and left the field clear for the Hilfsverein. However, World War I broke out the following year, and of course the German organization was never able to attempt to carry out the project.

A by-product of the secession of the Zionist members from the Kuratorium, when their reason for it became public property, was the declaration of a strike by the Hebrew teachers of the Hilfsverein schools in Palestine. Their union forbade them to work any longer for an organization which flouted one of the first principles of the Jewish national revival, and demanded that the Zionist Organization should take over responsibility for the Hebrew school system in Palestine, and thus safeguard it from assimilationist interference. Ahad Ha-Am, who hated *herem,* or excommunication, as one of the most distasteful manifestations of religious bigotry, and did not think that it became any less reprehensible when it was practised by secularists under the more modern name of boycott, protested against the strike; and on practical grounds he deprecated the addition of the cost of running the schools to the already excessive financial burdens of the Zionist Organization. But his protest was unheeded, and his forebodings were not justified by the event. The strike went on, and the Zionist Organization not only established a network of new schools to replace those of the Hilfsverein, but managed somehow to find the money needed for their upkeep. Thus the intransigence of the Hilfsverein on the language question had the unintended effect of speeding up the development of Hebrew education on Jewish national lines in Palestine. And the Haifa Technion, established after the end of the war

under Zionist auspices, is today one of the major agencies
for the training of the scientific and technical personnel on
which the State of Israel depends so largely for the material
well-being of its inhabitants.

$$\approx 4 \approx$$

The abortive technical school project bulks largely in the
published selections from Ahad Ha-Am's voluminous correspondence; but it was not a subject on which he felt called
upon or authorized to write for publication while the delicate negotiations connected with it were in progress. There
is consequently no hint of it in the fourth and last volume
of *At the Crossroads,* which appeared in 1913, and includes
the whole literary output of his London years, about a dozen
essays in all, together with *The Supremacy of Reason* and
three or four other pieces written during his last years in
Odessa. In London, lacking the stimulus of active participation in the national movement, and balked of his hope of
finding time and strength for sustained intellectual labor,
he wrote even more sparingly than in the early years of his
literary career; but the essays of this period include noteworthy expositions of his views both on Zionism and on
Judaism.

Not long before he left Odessa friends of his in Jerusalem
had begun to publish the monthly *Ha'omer,* the first modern Hebrew literary organ to appear in Palestine, and he
had written for publication in it an article (in the form of
a letter to the editor) entitled *The Time Has Come,*[5] which
contained a powerful restatement of the point of view of
spiritual Zionism in the light of the then prevailing circumstances. In the following year, 1908, the Young Turk revolution overthrew the autocratic rule of Abdul Hamid and
established a democratic régime, strongly nationalistic in
spirit; and the Zionist Organization found it expedient to
cease proclaiming its ideal of a Jewish State, and to empha-

size its practical colonization work in Palestine, for which it entertained hopes (soon to be dispelled) of a more sympathetic attitude on the part of the new Turkish Government. This and other developments were the occasion of a second letter to the editor of *Ha'omer,* in which Ahad Ha-Am reinforced his favorite thesis of the importance of the psychological factor in political life by the example of the Young Turks themselves, who had not attempted to overthrow the old order until they had secured adequate popular support for their movement. He proceeded to stress—for once—the value of Jewish cultural work in Palestine from a purely utilitarian point of view.

In another essay written at about the same time for *Hashiloah,* he crossed swords, not for the first time, with his old friend Dubnow. Ten years earlier Dubnow had published, in Russian, a brilliant series of *Letters on Judaism Ancient and Modern,* in which he had expounded the idea of what came to be known as "diaspora nationalism" (or alternatively "autonomism" or "spiritual nationalism"). The Jewish people, he maintained, had long outlived the stage of territorial nationalism, and had become a spiritual nation. They should not seek to concentrate themselves in a country of their own; they might settle in Palestine so far as circumstances permitted, but Palestine could not solve the problem of Jewish survival. The main effort must be to acquire national autonomy for the Jewish communities in the diaspora (or rather in eastern Europe, for the theory was entirely based on the conditions obtaining in that part of the world), and this would be a natural sequel to the acquisition of individual rights by the Jews in western countries. Diaspora nationalism was thus diametrically opposed to political Zionism, which demanded the liquidation of the diaspora, and during the next few years there was much argument in the Hebrew press between the two schools of thought, the one "affirming" the diaspora, and the other, the Zionist, "denying" it.

Ahad Ha-Am, whose position had points of contact with both schools, fired an occasional shot in this controversy from the sidelines, both by incidental references in his published articles, and in private correspondence with Dubnow; and when, in 1907, Dubnow's series of *Letters on Judaism* appeared in book form, with replies to some of his own criticisms, he decided to set forth his views on the question at issue more fully and systematically. For one reason or another he was unable to carry out this intention for some time, and it was not until the spring of 1909 that his article on *The Negation of the Diaspora*[6] appeared in *Hashiloah*.

He was naturally much closer to diaspora nationalism, with its cultural and spiritual emphasis, than to political Zionism; and he once went so far as to tell a correspondent that he would have agreed with Dubnow if only he could have been satisfied that it would be possible for the Jews to attain *complete* spiritual development in the diaspora. That was no doubt an exaggeration, for it is scarcely conceivable that his deep emotional attachment to Zion could have been overcome by rational demonstration. But in any case there was no practical danger of his having to choose, for Jewish national autonomy, even in European countries in which large numbers of Jews had lived for centuries, was clearly a castle in the air. It is true that after World War I the Jews in some of the countries of eastern Europe, including Poland and Lithuania, were granted the cultural rights of a national minority, and for a time there was in those countries an efflorescence of both Hebrew and Yiddish schools; but this triumph of diaspora nationalism was of short duration. The minority rights were whittled away, and before the outbreak of World War II had ceased to exist except on paper.

In his article of 1909, Ahad Ha-Am draws a distinction between what he calls objective and subjective acceptance of the diaspora. The *galuth* is a fact, however distasteful, which cannot be denied; but to acquiesce in it as an immutable fact is a different matter, and the Jewish people as a whole will never accept a theory which involves the sacrifice of its hope for a national restoration. He proceeds to argue that national minority rights in the diaspora could not provide the conditions necessary for a complete Jewish life in the cultural sense, and that in any case they are unattainable, the Jews being nowhere indigenous, as other national minorities are.

Two years later he returned to the charge with a second article, *Rival Tongues*,[7] on the linguistic aspect of the question, the controversy between the partisans of Hebrew and of Yiddish as the national language of the Jewish people. Diaspora nationalism was associated with attachment to Yiddish, which had been the mother-tongue of the masses of Jews in eastern Europe for some centuries; and there were even some extremists (Dubnow was not among them) who were bitterly hostile to Palestine and Hebrew, and solemnly proclaimed (at a conference in 1906) that Hebrew was dead and Yiddish was the national language. Yiddish was Ahad Ha-Am's mother-tongue, and to the end of his days he spoke it fluently and well. He used to write in Yiddish to his mother and his wife (but in Hebrew to his father), and once in his life he was persuaded by Ravnitzki to write a Yiddish article for publication. He did not agree with those extreme Hebraeophile Zionists who wished to ban the use of Yiddish in Zionist propaganda or as a medium of popular literature. It had its utilitarian justification so long as there were Jews who spoke no other language. But both his reverence for historic Judaism and his aristocratic instincts were revolted by the impudent claim that Yiddish was *the* national language, and he would have regarded the victory of Yiddish nationalism as the greatest conceivable calamity. Nor had he anything but scorn for the more modest pretensions of those of the advocates of Yiddish who were content to place it on a par with Hebrew as a second national language. He maintained—not without exaggeration—that

Yiddish had no greater hold on the Jewish people than any of the other languages which circumstances had compelled them to use during the centuries of exile; and he believed, perhaps optimistically, that it would not survive the present century. He always wrote of it as "the jargon," and excused himself on the grounds that not all his readers would understand *yehudith* to mean a Judaeo-German dialect, and that *yehudith* in the Book of Kings had a different significance; but there was probably a psychological reason for his use of the term of contempt.

After the appearance of *Rival Tongues,* in which the attitude here outlined received vigorous expression, Dubnow in a letter took Ahad Ha-Am to task for his *laissez-faire* attitude towards Yiddish, which he would neither encourage nor attempt to kill. Dubnow's view was that Yiddish should be supported because the practical alternative to it was not Hebrew, but the spoken language of the non-Jewish environment, and its disappearance would therefore involve a weakening of the Jewish consciousness. Ahad Ha-Am's reply is not on record; but he may well have been convinced that an attempt to keep Yiddish alive artificially had no chance of success and was not worth making. The events of the last half century have strengthened the objective grounds for that conviction; but Yiddish still has its devotees even among those who have no need for it as a language of speech, and there is no telling what future it may have.

Between the writing of the two essays on diaspora nationalism Ahad Ha-Am made his weightiest single contribution to the philosophy of Judaism in his famous essay on Claude Montefiore's *Synoptic Gospels.* As far back as 1897 he had commented in *Hashiloah,* in one of the notes included in his *Miscellany,* on one of the more extreme manifestations of radical tendencies in English Judaism. The occasion of the note had been the appearance in the *Jewish Quarterly Review,* then still published in England, of various answers

to its invitation to readers to express their views on a proposal by Oswald John Simon, a member of one of the
prominent Anglo-Jewish families, for the establishment of a
new Jewish church, which should cut itself loose from all
that was national in the Jewish tradition, and confine its
doctrine to the universally acceptable religious and moral
principles inculcated by Judaism. Ahad Ha-Am's note,
which he had called *Names That Have Lost Their Meaning,* had dealt mainly with the contribution to this sym-
posium of Miss Sylvie d'Avigdor,[8] who had made it clear
that what she and others were looking for was not so much
the fulfillment of the "mission of Judaism," in the name of
which Simon had spoken, as the satisfaction of their own
psychological need for the removal of the barrier that still
separated them from their non-Jewish environment. He
pointed out that the problem of the younger generation of
English Jews was similar to that of the "young men" in
Russia who demanded "expansion of the bounds" of Judaism,
but that there was an important difference between the two
approaches. The demand of the nationalistic Russian Jews
for "humanity" could be met without danger to Judaism;
but the "religious" English Jews were in effect asking for
the merging of Judaism in "humanity," which must entail
the obliteration of Judaism, even though its name were retained as a label for monotheism and other generally accepted beliefs. He avoided any explicit reference to Christianity, though of course he realized what must in practice
be the result of stripping Judaism, in a Christian environment, of all its national elements.

A dozen years later Dr. Claude G. Montefiore, the distinguished head of the liberal Jewish movement in England,
published a commentary on the *Synoptic Gospels,* avowedly
from a Jewish point of view, with the object of showing that
the teaching of the New Testament could and should be
accepted as part of Judaism. Ahad Ha-Am, now himself in

England, wrote an extended review of Montefiore's book, which appeared in *Hashiloah*[9] (and in English translation in the *Jewish Review*) in 1910. He did not, like other critics, suggest that Montefiore had attacked Judaism, or ignore his numerous admissions that in this or that particular the teaching of rabbinic Judaism was equal, or even superior, to that of the Gospels. Accepting without question the sincerity of Montefiore's professions, he showed that he was unconsciously biased in favor of Christianity, and that his so-called "Jewish point of view" was colored by the influences of a Christian environment.

The bulk of the review is devoted to an exposition of the broad difference, as Ahad Ha-Am sees it, between the Jewish and the Christian religious and moral outlook. The basic commandment of Judaism, he says, is "Thou shalt make no graven image": that is to say, Judaism is absolutely opposed to personification, and rejects equally a deity in human form, and a prophet who says "thus say I" instead of "thus saith the Lord." It leans always to the abstract and the impersonal; and it is concerned less with the salvation of the individual soul than with the holiness of the nation. And as in religion, so in ethics. Judaism does not wish to replace the unlimited egoism of the natural man by unlimited altruism, which is simply inverted egoism, substituting the desires of "the other" for those of "the self" as the criterion of right action: it demands the complete elimination of the personal factor, and the application of the standard of abstract and impersonal justice to all cases alike, including those in which one's own claims are involved. It condemns selfishness, but does not regard self-denial as intrinsically virtuous. In support of his thesis he quotes the Jewish law of divorce as reflecting a social and not a sacramental view of the nature of the marriage tie, and the Jewish preference for the negative form of the so-called "golden rule" as indicating that Judaism, while demanding regard for the rights of others, does not enjoin self-sacrifice except where it is required by the good of society as a whole.

This penetrating analysis of the root difference between Judaism and Christianity as systems of religion and morality is made in no polemical or apologetic spirit. He is not concerned to argue that the Jewish aim, which is the perfection and well-being of a group, and ultimately of the whole human race, is morally superior to the Christian aim, which is the salvation of the individual. The question of relative merit, he says,

> has been endlessly debated; but the truth is that in this matter we cannot establish any scale of values. A man may attain to the highest level in his religious and moral life whether he is inspired by the one aim or by the other. But individual salvation certainly makes a stronger appeal to most men, and is more likely to kindle their imagination and to inspire them to strive after moral and religious perfection.

What Judaism cannot do, he asserts, is to change its character and try to compete with Christianity on its own ground: and to Claude Montefiore, who is inclined to think that "if Judaism does not, as it were, come to terms with the Gospels, it must always be . . . a creed in a corner, of little influence and with no expansive power," he replies:

> A Jew may be a liberal of liberals without forgetting that Judaism was born in a corner and has always lived in a corner, aloof from the great world, which has never understood it and therefore hates it. So it was with Judaism before the rise of Christianity, and so it has remained since. History has not yet satisfactorily explained how it came about that a tiny nation in a corner of Asia produced a unique religious and ethical outlook, which, though it has had so profound an influence on the rest of the world, has yet remained so foreign to the rest of the world, unable to this day either to master or to be

mastered by it. This is a historical phenomenon to which, despite many attempted answers, we must still attach a note of interrogation. But every true Jew, be he orthodox or liberal, feels in the depths of his being that there is something in the spirit of our people—though we do not know what it is—which has prevented us from following the rest of the world along the beaten path, has led to our producing this Judaism of ours, and has kept us and our Judaism in a corner to this day, because we cannot abandon the distinctive outlook on which Judaism is based.

Thus Judaism, as a system of religion and morals, is eternally precluded from accepting the Gospels, because their teachings are at variance with its fundamental postulates.

Another of his capital essays—in effect the last he ever wrote—appeared in *Hashiloah* about two years later, in the spring of 1912. The tenth Zionist Congress had been held in Basle during the preceding summer, and Ahad Ha-Am had attended it as a visitor, breaking at last his long habit of abstention. He had decided to visit Palestine once more in that year, and took in the Congress on his way for the pleasure of a reunion with a number of his old friends. *Sach Hakol,*[10] as the resulting essay was called, summarized his impressions both of the Congress and of the Land. Its generalizations about the *yishuv* were based on much detailed inquiry and observation, as is shown by the notes of this visit which are incorporated in his *Reminiscences.*

The tone and substance of this essay are very different from those of his denunciatory articles of the Herzl days. Of course he is still critical; but for once he is more alive to the brighter than to the darker aspects of the *yishuv.* The new mood reflects his conviction that Zionism, in its own despite, is at last on the right lines. True, the official program is unchanged, the old messianic slogans about "redemption" are still repeated, and Ahad Ha-Amist ideas are still vehemently repudiated. But in fact what is going on in Palestine is the slow creation of that "spiritual center" of which he had for years been preaching the necessity. He is no longer distressed, as he used to be, by the discrepancy between the avowed aim of Zionist work in Palestine and what it is actually achieving.

> Now that I have seen the results of the work so far, I have no such fears as to its ultimate fate. . . . *L'homme propose.* . . . History does not trouble about our program; it creates what it creates at the bidding of our "instinct of self-preservation."

The center which is being created in Palestine will not be, can never be, "a 'secure home of refuge' for our people; but it will surely be *a home of healing for its spirit.*" His dream of twenty years ago is in process of realization, and he is confident of the future. He sees "with his mind's eye this center growing in size, improving in quality, and exerting an ever-increasing spiritual influence on our people, until at last it shall reach the goal set before it by the instinct of self-preservation: to restore our national unity the world over through the restoration of our national culture in its historic home." And to those who wish to know what will happen after that stage of accomplishment has been reached his advice is:

> Ask no questions! In our present state of spiritual disorganization we have no idea of the measure of our national strength, nor of what it will be able to achieve when all its elements are united round a single center, and quickened by a single strong and healthy spirit. The generations that are to come afterwards will know the measure of their strength, and will adjust their actions to it. For us, we are not concerned with the hidden things of the distant future. Enough for us to know the things revealed, the things that are to be done by us and our children in a future that is near.

The development of Zionist policy and sentiment during the years which had passed since Herzl's death had broadly indicated the justice of his criticism of the philosophy of political Zionism in its first phase; and the reception of *Sach Hakol* (which was translated both into English and into German soon after its appearance in Hebrew) by the public interested in such matters showed that his point of view was widely shared. The article was, however, attacked in the official Zionist organs, not without misrepresentation of its author's views. Despite the clear indication in the passage quoted above that he saw the full development of the "national spiritual center," which was still in the future, only as a stage on the way to the complete realization of the national aims, the official critics took the line that for Ahad Ha-Am the establishment of a few agricultural settlements and cultural institutions was the final goal of Zionism. He protested against this treatment in strongly-worded but friendly letters to Ussishkin and to Alter Druyanov,[11] then editor of *Ha'olam,* the official Hebrew organ of the Zionist Organization—both of them intimate friends—and also defended himself in a short note in *Hatsefirah.*

A more pertinent criticism, to which no reply of his is on record, was that of the organ of the socialist workmen in Palestine, who were engaged in the herculean task of trying to "capture labor"—that is, to replace by Jews the Arab laborers by whom most of the hard work in the Jewish agricultural settlements was still performed. For these young men the creation of a Jewish agricultural proletariat in Palestine was an ideal, the realization of which was essential if the country was ever to become Jewish. Ahad Ha-Am had no sympathy with the idea of a Jewish agricultural proletariat, which did not fit in with his conception of the Jewish character. For him, the rôle appropriate to the Jew in the agricultural sphere was not that of the manual laborer, but that of the gentleman-farmer of the type of Boaz in the book of Ruth. The experiment in collective settlement (*k'vutzah*), which was then in its infancy, he dismissed in a footnote to his essay with a brief reference, which shows no appreciation of its importance or its potentialities. He was too thoroughgoing an individualist to believe in socialism, despite its claim to stand for social justice; and he did not conceal his dislike and distrust of the socialist Zionists who were engaged in "capturing labor." (It is true that their spiritual guide, Aaron David Gordon,[12] was his disciple; but it is no uncommon experience for men of different temperaments to draw opposite practical conclusions from the same fundamental principles.) The issue was further complicated by a moral question at which he hinted in his footnote: whether Jews, who complain of anti-Jewish discrimination in the economic life of other countries, could decently claim a monopoly of agricultural labor in Palestine. Denying as he did the possibility of "capturing labor," he might think it superfluous to discuss the morality of the policy; but he cannot be said to have faced fairly and squarely the question how, under the conditions then obtaining, it could ever become possible to obtain a Jewish majority in Palestine, which he had admitted to be a necessary condition of the "spiritual center" ideal, if the basic physical work was to be left indefinitely in non-Jewish hands. There seems to have been here a conflict between the demands of his strong moral sense and those of his equally strong conviction of the Jewish people's paramount need for a self-subsistent center in its historic land.

The visit to Palestine in 1910 produced, in addition to *Sach Hakol,* an article on the Gymnasia Herzlia in Tel Aviv (which for some unknown reason he insisted on calling Jaffa), based on personal observation of its work and discussions with its teachers. The article is characteristic in being much more sparing of praise than of criticism, for which he found grounds in what he considered the inadequate amount of attention given to the Judaism of the post-biblical period, and in the "higher critical" approach to the Bible itself.

The fourth and final volume of the collected essays also contains the attack on Brenner mentioned in an earlier chapter, and one or two pieces of no special note; and it ends with a collection of documents relating to the B'né Mosheh, published under the title of *Nissayon shelo hitzliah,* which means an unsuccessful experiment. Thus the last volume of his collected essays ended, as the first had begun, with a negative title.

Special interest attaches to one literary product of the London period which he decided, after much consideration, not to include in his last volume. This was a bunch of ten short aphorisms, about which he wrote to Druyanov in August, 1910: "I may tell you *in confidence* that I have recently been jotting down now and then stray thoughts in the form of aphorisms. The few I have already committed to writing seem to me good, and if, as I hope, I am able to add to them during my holiday, when I shall be alone and undisturbed, I will send you some of them for *Ha'olam,* not over my name, but over the initials. A. H." In the ten aphorisms which appeared in *Ha'olam* a few weeks later over these initials, and with the title *Remazim,* or "Hints," there is no reference to any specifically Jewish question, and nothing even to indicate Jewish authorship except the language and a single parenthetical reference to "us Jews." They are the fruit of much reflection on human life, but not on Jewish life in particular, by a mind of great acumen and psychological insight. One of them may serve as a specimen:

A healthy man naturally loves life, but he may hate his love of life, which nature has implanted in him willy-nilly. So when a man professes to hate life, and yet does not commit suicide, you are not to suspect him of hypocrisy. It may be that he is only mistaking his hatred of the love of life for hatred of life itself. Observation will convince you that this mistake is made in connection with many kinds of hatred: a man imagines that he hates the object, when what he really hates is only his love of the object.

Ahad Ha-Am's published letters show that he was in two minds about these aphorisms. He did not know whether he chose anonymity because he was sure that everybody would recognize his hand, or because he wanted the authorship to be a secret. He had intended to write more aphorisms, but was discouraged when he found that the first ten attracted scarcely any notice. To Mosheh Smilanski,[13] one of the few who did notice them, he wrote that because of the lack of interest on the part of the reading public he had abandoned his original idea of publishing further installments, but if he wrote any more, he would keep them in manuscript for inclusion in the fourth volume of his essays. When that volume was about to appear, he decided, as we have seen, against including in it the ten aphorisms already published; but a dozen years later they were printed, along with some other small pieces, in an appendix to the sixth and final volume of the letters which he selected for publication.

This ambivalent attitude towards his solitary excursion into the domain of Pascal cannot be without significance. Taken in conjunction with the account of his spiritual evolution in the *Discarded Old Manuscript,* and with one or two other pointers, it suggests that his dedication of all his literary gifts to the ideal of Hibbath Zion and to the Hebrew language was not so inevitable as might have been thought, and was achieved only after a struggle, which left its mark in a sense of frustration and disappointed ambitions. There remained perhaps in his mind an undercurrent of impatience with the limitations, in regard both to subject-matter and to language, which he had imposed on his pen.

13

WORLD WAR
AND
NATIONAL HOME

In 1912 the normal tranquility of his domestic life was shattered by a blow as cruel as any that could have befallen him: his second daughter, Rachel, married a Russian writer, Michael Ossorgin, whom she had met during her years of study abroad. He saw in intermarriage the most deadly of all threats to Jewish survival, and his favorite daughter's act of treason—for it was nothing less in his view—confronted him with a painful choice. In the end his sense of national duty prevailed over paternal affection, and he broke off relations with his daughter (but did not compel his wife to do the same). *Der Staat hat keine Töchter,* "the State has no daughters," he quoted to Smilanski, whom he had informed of the catastrophe, and who had urged in the daughter's behalf the right of the individual to pursue his own happiness. But the struggle and the estrangement cost him untold agony, which ate into his heart the more because his habitual reticence forbade him to betray his suffering.

The blow stirred into activity his latent longing to leave the diaspora for Palestine; but he had to abandon hope of that consolation for the time being. The breach with his daughter was healed ten years later; and Mme. Ossorgin afterwards returned to her people. She spent the last years of her life, which ended in 1957, in legal practice in Jerusalem.

Two years after this calamity in the house he suffered a
blow of a less private character, but one not less overwhelming in its impact on the foundations upon which his spiritual life rested, in the outbreak of World War I. The idea
of global warfare has by now become so much a common-
place of our everyday thought and speech, that it is difficult
to realize how impossible it was for Ahad Ha-Am, less than
half a century ago, to fit the fact of a war between the
civilized powers of the modern world into his scheme of
things. With all his realism and distrust of utopianism, he
had the nineteenth century's implicit belief in human progress as part of the order of nature; and war in Europe
meant a relapse into barbarism, which conflicted with that
faith. What was even worse, the horror of the slaughter
which was involved was not mitigated for him by a belief
that this war was a simple conflict between right and wrong.
The association of despotic Russia with liberal Great Britain
and France in what purported to be a struggle for liberty
and justice seemed to him a hollow mockery of the truth.
Always an enemy of advertisement even in the best of
causes, he was revolted by the war propaganda, which not
only incited nation against nation, but debased the lofty
ideals of a supra-national morality by pressing them into the
service of selfish national ends. The Jewish people, he
thought, the people of the prophets, the standard-bearer of
the prophetic ideal of absolute truth and justice, should have
cried out against this iniquity; but in fact Jews in all countries were as loud as their neighbors in repeating the accepted slogans. Morality had ceased to exist, and violence
and hypocrisy had usurped its throne. Sentiments such as
these found expression in savage letters to his friends, to
one of whom he wrote with envy of Shackleton, the ex-
plorer, who had got away in time to the South Pole—"the
only place which is certainly out of reach of the stench of
humanity."

A sharper edge was lent to his anguish, as the war pro-

ceeded, by the appalling sufferings—appalling by the modest
standards of those days—which it brought on the Jews in
Europe, and especially by the devastation of Ukrainian
Jewry, to which he belonged by birth and the associations
of his early years, and to which he always remained deeply
attached. His mother had died in 1908, and it is not known
that any of his relatives or close friends suffered in the
tragedy of the Ukraine; but nonetheless it fell upon him
with the weight of a personal bereavement. On one occasion,
when there was a particularly harassing report of massacres
in the Ukraine, he was so far beside himself, and found the
need for action of some sort so compelling, that he suggested to Sokolow, who was in London at the time, that they
should go together to the Chief Rabbi and ask him to proclaim a day of fasting for his community. The violence of
his reaction to the war, and of the language he used about
it in private correspondence, reveals for once the intensity
of the emotional volcano which smoldered behind a normally calm and dispassionate exterior.

He did not publicly express such sentiments, or any sentiments, about the war. As a writer he was reduced to complete silence. In spite of censorship and other difficulties,
Jewish self-expression was not rendered absolutely impossible: there was here and there an organ of opinion in
Yiddish or Hebrew in which journalists and writers could
publish their views about the position and the after-war
hopes and prospects of the Jewish people. Many readers
would have liked to know what Ahad Ha-Am thought on
these matters; but they were disappointed. The catastrophe
was too overwhelming, and the future too dark, for calm
reflection and objective assessment; and for a man who believed in telling the whole truth without regard to consequences, it was impossible to write for publication so long
as war conditions rendered full and free expression of opinion impossible. So he resisted all invitations to address the
Jewish public on the burning questions of the hour; and

there was little point in writing about anything else, even if he could have found the necessary detachment and peace of mind. Throughout the whole of the war he produced nothing except a Hebrew translation of Pinsker's *Auto-Emanzipation* and a short contribution (which appeared first in Russian and only later in Hebrew) to a special issue of the Russian Zionist paper *Yevreiska Jizn* commemorating the twenty-fifth anniversary of Pinsker's death, which fell in 1917.

Thus for practical purposes the war put an end to his literary career. It also greatly intensified, as was inevitable, the difficulties and harassments of his daily life in the city as manager of a branch of a foreign business. His physical health, always peculiarly sensitive to disturbances of his emotional equilibrium, suffered a setback from which he never fully recovered. And yet—so inextricably are the black and white threads interwoven in the pattern of human affairs—the calamity which caused him so much suffering was also indirectly the source of the one ray of hope that somewhat relieved the gloom: for when Turkey, then the overlord of Palestine, entered the conflict as Germany's ally, it became possible to hope that the martyrdom of East-European Jewry might be rewarded by some recognition of Jewish national rights when the war was over.

❧ 2 ❧

There was, as has been mentioned, a close friendship between Ahad Ha-Am and Chaim Weizmann, who on the outbreak of war in August, 1914, when he was a Lecturer in Chemistry at the University of Manchester, at once realized the necessity of taking steps to secure that the Zionist case should have a sympathetic hearing after the Allied victory of which he was confident. On his own initiative Weizmann embarked on a series of interviews with British leaders of public opinion and statesmen for the purpose of

winning sympathy and support for the Zionist idea; and
Ahad Ha-Am was in his confidence from the outset.
Throughout the three years which elapsed before the issue
of the government pronouncement of November 2, 1917,
known as the Balfour Declaration, which pledges British
support for the establishment in Palestine of a National
Home for the Jewish people, he was consulted by Weizmann on every issue of consequence (with the not unimportant exception of the Jewish legion, about which something
will be said below). He also had frequent discussions with
Sokolow, who ran in double harness with Weizmann from
the beginning of 1915, when he and Tchlenow found their
way from Berlin to London at the instance of the Zionist
Executive, of which both were members. He was, however,
much closer to Weizmann than to Sokolow.

Thus it came about that the one-time implacable enemy
of political Zionism played a part of some importance, if an
unobtrusive and mainly unrecorded one, in the molding of
Zionist policy during the period which culminated in the
first great triumph of the movement in the political field.
That triumph might not have been won if the Zionist leaders had put forward political demands which, though they
had a basis in history, were outside the range of practical
politics. The moral support and wise counsel of the veteran
champion of realism and moderation strengthened the hands
of Weizmann and Sokolow in their resistance to Herzlian
stalwarts who were for demanding the immediate establishment of a Jewish State and unrestricted Jewish immigration
into Palestine.

By the beginning of 1917 the efforts of Weizmann and
Sokolow to win the sympathy of British statesmen for Zionist aims had made sufficient headway for the government
to appoint an emissary (Sir Mark Sykes) to enter into
formal negotiations with the Zionist leaders on its behalf;
and in July of that year, when the issue of a pro-Zionist declaration by the government was being seriously considered,

Weizmann and Sokolow thought it desirable to bring into being a consultative committee, consisting of leading Zionists then in England, and representative of the various shades of Zionist opinion, to provide them with some sort of constitutional backing. The Zionist Organization, being an international body, was of course unable to function normally during the war, and the two spokesmen had strictly no authority to negotiate on its behalf. True, Sokolow had a certain *locus standi* as a duly elected member of the Zionist Executive, by whom he had been sent to London for the purpose of furthering the cause; but Weizmann, who was in effect the senior partner in the combination, had held no official position in the movement when he began to approach British statesmen, and his subsequent election to the Presidency of the English Zionist Federation could not confer on him the status which he lacked in the absence of a mandate from the Zionist Congress. In the abnormal circumstances of the time, the election of a truly representative body to speak for the Zionist Organization was out of the question, and a nominated Political Committee seemed to be the best available substitute. Such a body could not, however, be saddled with the responsibility for deciding on crucial issues of Zionist policy, and it was made clear from the outset that the functions of the Committee were to be purely advisory.

Ahad Ha-Am, though not in the organizational sense a Zionist, was invited to become a member of the Political Committee, and was in principle willing to accept the invitation. He raised no objection to the limitation of the Committee's functions, but he demanded a formal assurance in writing from Weizmann and Sokolow that it would be able to express its views on all questions that might arise, and only when that demand was complied with—not, it seems, without some reluctance on Weizmann's part—did he agree to come on the Committee. His influence on the conduct of Zionist affairs at that critical time, which was due primarily to the qualities which had won him his unique eminence in Jewish life, and secondarily to his personal relations with Weizmann, was neither enhanced nor diminished thereby; but his membership of the Committee did involve him in a serious conflict with Weizmann during its brief life, which automatically ceased with the issue of the Balfour Declaration, after it had devoted most of its attention to the preparation and discussion of various alternative drafts of that document. The occasion of the conflict was Jabotinsky's attempt to obtain the sanction of the British Government for the formation of a Jewish legion to fight with the Allied forces against the Turks in Palestine.

With the entry of Turkey into World War I, the attitude of its government to the Jewish development of Palestine, hitherto no more than passively obstructionist, became one of active hostility, and many of the leading members of the *yishuv* were driven into exile. In these circumstances it was natural for some of the younger and more vigorous spirits to wish to participate as Jews in the military operations of the Allies against Turkey; and the Zion Mule Corps fought with distinction in the ill-starred Gallipoli campaign of 1915-16. The Corps was raised by Joseph Trumpeldor (1880-1920), a former officer in the Russian army; and on its disbandment he embarked on the more ambitious project of raising a Jewish legion to fight on the Allied side. Trumpeldor visited London in the latter part of 1916 to further his project (which did not come to fruition), and evidently consulted Ahad Ha-Am about it, for Ahad Ha-Am's views are expressed in a letter to Trumpeldor, dated November 9th, which is included in his published *Letters*. Though he intensely disliked fighting, he was not a pacifist; and he expressed no objection in principle to a Jewish legion. He stipulated, however (and Trumpeldor apparently agreed), that it must be available for service on any front, and not on one only; it must not be demonstratively aimed at Turkey alone. At the same time he made it clear that, unlike Trumpeldor, he attached little importance to the project. The existence of a Jewish legion would in his opinion be of very little value for the solution of the Palestine question; and the Jews had already given sufficient evidence of their fighting qualities in all the armies engaged in the conflict.

In the following year, when Jabotinsky, acting entirely on his own initiative, approached both the Jewish public and the British Government with a similar proposal, it found little support even among Zionists in Great Britain, and Weizmann himself was hostile. Later, however, he changed his mind, and, though he made no public pronouncement on the subject, it was widely believed that in his confidential talks with British Government representatives he was using the promise of a Jewish military contribution to the Allied cause to strengthen the case for an official declaration of sympathy with Zionist aims. A situation in which the President of the English Zionist Federation allowed it to be thought that he was secretly supportng a scheme to which the majority of members of the Federation were opposed, and on which the Federation's Executive had not declared itself, could obviously not be allowed to continue indefinitely. Yet Weizmann did not bring the question of the legion before the Executive; nor did he of his own volition ask the Political Committee for its views. There were, however, rumblings of discontent on the Committee, some of whose members were known to hold opinions contrary to those attributed to Weizmann on this matter, and at length it was placed on the Committee's agenda.

An invitation to a meeting at which the legion question was to be discussed reached Ahad Ha-Am, with an explanatory memorandum, while he was on his summer holiday at Buxton, and he at once wrote Weizmann a letter, dated August 17th, in which he said that he had for some time been preparing himself to write to him fully on "this painful subject," but had decided to wait until they could meet, because he did not yet feel able to discuss it calmly. Now he

wanted to say only that in his opinion the Zionist Federation would have to make a public statement on its attitude
to the legion project, because the public naturally assumed
that the government could not possibly have failed to consult Weizmann and Sokolow on a proposal of this kind put
to them by a free-lance. He added a brief statement of his
own views, which had apparently undergone some modification since his correspondence with Trumpeldor some
months earlier. He thought it highly desirable that there
should be Jewish soldiers on the Palestine front in the British (or if possible the American) forces, but he regarded
the idea of a separate Jewish force as "an empty demonstration," fraught with danger to the Jews in Palestine and in
Turkey generally, and also to the future of Jewish development in Palestine if after all that country should remain in
Turkish hands after the war.

It is not known whether, or how, Weizmann reacted to the
letter; but on September 4th Ahad Ha-Am was among those
present at a meeting of the Political Committee at which the
legion question was discussed, and the attitude adopted by
Weizmann at that meeting brought matters to a head.
What that attitude was may be gathered from a longish
letter which Ahad Ha-Am wrote to Weizmann immediately after the meeting (and which, together with the letter
of August 17th and that of September 5th, still to be mentioned, appears in the published selection of Ahad Ha-Am's
correspondence in his own Hebrew translation of the Russian
original). The letter begins by reminding Weizmann of the
pledge which he and Sokolow had given, that the Committee would be able to express its views on all questions that
might arise, and points out that if Weizmann now tells the
Committee that he will not even listen to its views on this
particular question, he is reducing the whole affair to a
meaningless fiction. If, then, Weizmann has definitely decided not to take part in the next meeting of the Committee,
because he does not wish to hear unpalatable views ex-

pressed on the legion project, he, Ahad Ha-Am, will regard that as a breach of the undertaking given, and will be compelled to resign from the Committee. He goes on to refer to Weizmann's change of opinion on this question, the reasons for which he has never been told, and says that until that day's meeting he had felt sure that Weizmann had not committed himself to support of the project in his talks with the government. At the meeting, however, he had, unless deceived by defective hearing, heard Weizmann use some such expression as "I have built on this foundation" in a context in which it could mean only that Weizmann could not agree to a public dissociation of the Zionist Organization from the legion scheme, because it had played an important part in his conversations with the government. If Weizmann had actually used such an expression, and if his interpretation of it was correct, he thought that the proper course would be for Weizmann to communicate this to the Committee at its next meeting. This would alter the whole situation, and the discussion would take a new turn, since nobody really wanted to destroy Weizmann's work.

The tenor of Weizmann's reply is clear from a further letter written to him by Ahad Ha-Am on the following day, September 5th, which has become historic. In this letter Ahad Ha-Am says that he is writing, for the first time in all the years of their friendship, "not just as a friend (that I should not consider right on this occasion, for the simple reason that the tone of your letter is that of a breaking-off of relations), but as an older colleague, who was in the line of battle while you were still at school, and who has almost certainly had some influence, direct or indirect, on your attitude to Jewish problems." He continues:

> As such a colleague, I tell you that what you contemplate doing is, in the fullest sense of the term, a stab in the back[1] to the whole Zionist cause. I do not express any opinion here on the causes that have led to your decision. One cannot judge of what one does not know; and you must

admit that your vague references to unpleasantnesses
which you have suffered or are suffering, and which in
any case are only of a personal and incidental character,
cannot be regarded as adequate explanation of such a
step. But whatever the causes, it is your duty to think not
of them, but of the consequences of this step. A man of
your wisdom cannot fail to see that the result of your
resignation will be to discredit the Zionist leaders in the
estimation of those on whom the fate of the movement
depends in this difficult hour. Not because you are the
only man who could do the job, and no substitute could
be found. Nobody is absolutely irreplaceable; and if you
gave up the job for some reason beyond your control, like
a severe illness or some other mishap, that would certainly
be very regrettable, and a great blow to the cause; but in
that case the work would be carried on by others, not
completely ruined. On the other hand, if you had from
the outset met the authorities as a duly appointed representative of the Zionist Organization (as Sokolow did
afterwards), your resignation would not have seemed to
the other side so astonishing, because they are familiar
with the principle of election, and are used to changes
of personnel by which one emissary replaces another.
Normally it is not the personality that matters, but the
credentials. But your position is exceptional. You took up
the job not as the duly appointed representative of some
corporate body, but as a private Zionist. Thanks to your
personal qualities and to favorable external circumstances,
you became in a comparatively short time almost the symbol of Zionism for many people of influence. And suddenly one fine day you announce that you are no longer
in the business, that you have resigned! To whom have
you handed in your resignation? Who, having chosen
you, has the right to accept your resignation? It was circumstances that chose you, and circumstances will release
you in due course, when complete success or failure makes
your job no longer necessary. But till then you cannot
leave your post without creating in the minds of those
with whom you have negotiated so far a most unfavorable

impression of Zionists—and perhaps of Zionism—and nobody will be able to carry on what you began.

You of course know that tomorrow the Committee will
meet to discuss this question. I think it my duty to inform
you that at that meeting I propose to suggest the dispatch
of a letter to you more or less on the following lines:

We did not appoint you, and we cannot accept your
resignation. From the outset you assumed as a volunteer
the highly important function which you have so bril-
liantly fulfilled. Now, while the battle is at its height,
you want to resign without leave. We cannot keep you
against your will, but we pronounce your action—if you
proceed with it—an act of treason; and of such an act we
are confident that you are not capable.

I do not think it necessary to explain to you that such an
action on your part would be moral suicide. That is your
private concern, and you fully understand the position.

It is possible that this letter may cause you to break with
me completely and absolutely. For my part I will continue to entertain for you feelings of the sincerest friendship, as I have done hitherto, because it is not my habit
to allow even the sharpest differences of opinion on public
affairs to intrude on private relationships.

This incident is only one, though by far the most dramatic
and important, of a number in which Ahad Ha-Am was
able to use his unique moral authority over his friends for
their good. The biblical precept "thou shalt surely rebuke
thy neighbor" is so little in harmony with the conventions
of polite society as to have become almost a dead letter, un-
regarded except by prigs and busybodies. Ahad Ha-Am,
who was neither, not only observed it whenever necessary,
but had the rare gift of being able to do so without self-
righteousness or censoriousness. His letter to Weizmann
about the legion affair, with its restraint and its felicitous
wording, is a model of how such an unpleasant letter should
be written, if written it must be. He wrote as an older to
a younger friend, without any attempt to conceal the sever-

ity of his disapproval, but equally without any hint of
either pressure or entreaty; and he concluded with the
assurance of his unalterable friendship. The last sentence
of his letter has been criticized, and certainly it seems to
push a laudable principle to excessive lengths. Is it either
right or possible to retain one's personal attachment to a
friend who has been guilty of what one condemns as treason?
Ahad Ha-Am's regard for logical consistency forbade him
to admit any exception to the rule that a man's personal
feelings and his views on public questions must be kept in
separate watertight compartments; but it may be doubted
whether even he, if he had been put to the test, could have
lived up to his principles in this particular case. Fortunately
he was not put to the test. Weizmann not only did not withdraw from the conduct of Zionist affairs, but remained
Ahad Ha-Am's close friend. In this he acted as Ussishkin,
Bialik and many more had done at one time or another
after coming under the same mentor's rod.

In the discussions of the political committee about the
draft of the declaration of sympathy which the government
was to be asked to sign, Ahad Ha-Am's principal concern
was to secure that it should be made clear that whatever
rights might be granted to Jews in Palestine should belong to the Jewish people as a whole, and not merely to the
handful of Jews already settled in the country. He expressed
a personal preference for leaving the government to suggest
its own formula, on the ground that this would indicate
how far Great Britain would be prepared to go; but the suggestion met with little or no support, and he did not press it.

When the Balfour Declaration was finally issued, Weizmann showed his sense of what was appropriate to the historic occasion by taking the document to Ahad Ha-Am on
its receipt. The philosopher of Jewish nationalism found
legitimate cause for rejoicing in the explicit recognition, for
the first time in two thousand years, of "the Jewish people"

as a corporate body towards which international obligations could be undertaken. The precise nature of the obligations, in the political and in the practical sphere, mattered less to him than the acknowledgment by the world that the Jewish people was no longer a vagrant without a fixed address. That acknowledgment could never be erased from the page of history, whereas detailed political and practical arrangements could and must be modified as circumstances changed.

As to the immediate value of the declaration, as distinct from its long-term implications, he was better armed than men of more sanguine temperament against the seductions of wishful thinking. He realized, as so many at that time did not, that the declaration, which spoke of "the establishment in Palestine of a National Home for the Jewish people," and expressly safeguarded the rights of the non-Jewish inhabitants of the country, meant what it said and no more. When the four volumes of *At the Crossroads* were reprinted in 1921, he took the opportunity to set forth his views on the meaning of the declaration in a new preface written for the occasion.[2] He revealed for the first time that the draft submitted by the Zionists to the government had spoken of "the reconstitution of Palestine as the National Home of the Jewish people," and pointed out the substantial difference between this and the formula actually adopted—"the establishment in Palestine of a National Home for the Jewish people"—from the point of view of the extent to which Jewish rights were in fact recognized. "The government," he wrote, with a characteristic touch of irony, "thinks, it would seem, that when a people has only the moral force of its claim to build its national home in a land at present inhabited by others, and has not behind it a powerful army or fleet to prove the justice of its claim, that people can have only what its right allows it in truth and justice, and not what conquering peoples take for themselves by armed force, under the cover of various 'rights'

invented *ad hoc.*" The Arab inhabitants of Palestine were
in possession, and the Jews would have to share the country with them on terms of equality. The declaration did not
contain any promise of a Jewish State, as many had fondly
imagined, and the messianic era had not arrived. Moreover,
the promise was a vague one, and what it was going to
mean in practice would depend on the good will of the
mandatory power. His preface ends with a valedictory
reiteration of the lesson of patience and perseverance which
he had been preaching, first to the Hovevé Zion and later
to the Zionists, for thirty years:

> At this great and difficult moment I appear before my
> readers—perhaps for the last time—on the threshold of
> this book, and repeat once more my old warning, on
> which most of the essays in this book are a commentary:
> Do not attempt to reach the goal before the conditions
> necessary to its attainment have been created; and do not
> disparage the work which is possible at any given time in
> the existing conditions, even if it will not bring the
> Messiah today or tomorrow.

Over a year after the issue of the Balfour Declaration and
the end of the war, when the Zionists had to prepare their
case for the Peace Conference, Ahad Ha-Am was again in
unofficial co-operation with the leaders of the national
movement. A letter of December, 1918,[3] to Weizmann reveals him as watchdog of the historical right of the Jewish
people to Palestine. He had been led to expect that the
draft of the Zionist demands would contain a clause expressly mentioning Jewish national rights. When the draft
reached him, he found in it no such clause, but only an
incidental mention of Jewish "claims," without even the
word "national." He protested energetically against this
omission, urging that a clear and unequivocal endorsement
of their historic national right was the most important thing
that the Jews could seek from the Peace Conference. It
might almost seem as though the mantle of Herzl, who had

been so insistent on international recognition of the aims of Zionism, had fallen for the nonce on the shoulders of his great critic. And a draft which Ahad Ha-Am prepared at that time of the obligations which should be imposed on the mandatory power includes a provision that such conditions shall be created as will promote the continuous expansion and development of the *yishuv* into a Jewish commonwealth.

The attainment of an independent Jewish state not at a single bound, but after a period of preparation under tutelage, was in accordance with the views that he had always advocated; and so far the Balfour Declaration and the mandate justified his political prescience. He had implicit faith in the willingness and ability of Great Britain to carry out the obligations of the mandate, and he no doubt hoped for the gradual development of the national home into a Jewish State which would be Jewish in the qualitative sense, and would be a "national spiritual center" so long as a large diaspora persisted. What he could not foresee was the cataclysm which would on the one hand destroy the great centers of Jewish life in Europe, whose plight had stimulated Herzl to demand a Jewish State, and on the other hand bring about political conditions in which the idea of a Jewish State in Palestine would cease to be chimerical. But if the course of events has dealt unkindly with his gradualist philosophy, it has done nothing to call in question the correctness of his diagnosis of the Jewish problem. "The plight of Jewry" is no longer the nightmare that it was before the terrible holocaust of the 'forties; but "the plight of Judaism" remains, and the unexpectedly speedy transition from National Home to Jewish State does not of itself affect the justice of his conviction that the most urgent need of the still scattered Jewish people is for a "national spiritual center."

❧ 3 ❧

During the early years of the war Ahad Ha-Am put up
a good fight against the steady deterioration of his health—
not, however, by taking special care of himself, but by dis-
regarding medical injunctions to do so. He was no hypo-
chondriac, though some of his friends suspected that his
troubles were more imaginary than real, and his fresh com-
plexion gave an illusory appearance of health. Towards
the end of 1916 he made light of his troubles in a letter to
Barzilai, in which he wrote that after consulting doctors
great and small he had come to the conclusion that it was
best to keep clear of them. "So long as a man is able to
stand on his feet and is not in constant pain, the best thing
he can do is to forget his health and carry on as usual."
Worrying about one's health and one's symptoms, he
thought, could only bring on illness and shorten life. But in
a letter to Hacohen at the beginning of 1918 there is a fore-
shadowing of trouble to come. "In these terrible [war] years,"
he writes, "I have aged (not so much physically as mentally)
at least ten years. I feel completely broken and shattered,
though outwardly I go on living as before, and the only
difference is that I spend my free time in reading papers
of all kinds and in all languages. It is a long time since I
read a book, and of course I don't write a line." And in
the autumn of 1919 he fell seriously ill, was practically confined to the house for three months, suffering supposedly
from arteriosclerosis, and then, under doctor's orders, went
to Switzerland, where he spent three more months in
a Montreux sanatorium. A specialist whom he consulted
in Berne found no sign of serious arteriosclerosis, but diag-
nosed nervous trouble and emphysema of the lung. It is not
clear which of the conflicting medical opinions was right;
but he had unquestionably become an invalid, and he returned from Switzerland scarcely better than when he went

there. It is significant that his published letters include none dated between the end of May, 1920 and the end of March, 1921.

In the autumn of 1919 he had been invited by the Ukrainian Government to be one of a commission of experts which it proposed to set up to enquire on the spot into the recent anti-Jewish pogroms in that area. Ussishkin and two other Jews who had received similar invitations declined them on political grounds. Ahad Ha-Am saw no justification for this, but was compelled for his part to decline on grounds of health. In a private letter to a friend he wrote that he could not have borne, and perhaps could not have survived, the strain of seeing the devastation of the country he knew so well, and hearing accounts of the unexampled atrocities which had been committed.

Despite his enfeebled condition, he was able to write the new preface already mentioned in the summer of 1920; but he was unfit for anything else, and his sole remaining hope now was that he might recover some measure of health in Palestine. To settle in that country had been his ambition since early manhood, but all his attempts, from the first one in 1893 onward, had been baffled by obstacles which he was unable to overcome. The last attempt before the war had been made in 1912, when he had tried to come to an arrangement with the Wissotzky firm which would have permitted him to spend most of his time in Palestine while still retaining his managership in London. That scheme went the way of all the others, and it was only after World War I, when he reached the age of retirement on pension, that removal to Palestine became a concrete possibility. He had actually planned to leave England in the autumn of 1920, but his serious illness earlier in that year necessitated postponement of his departure, and it was not until the end of the following year that he actually sailed for Palestine, accompanied by his wife and son. Even then there were apparently difficulties, and he would have deferred his departure still further if not for pressure from his (non-Jewish) doctor, who not only urged him to go as soon as possible, but, knowing what Palestine meant to him, assured him that once there he would recover his health. So he was able to quote as applicable to himself a rabbinical saying that the Jews would return to Palestine under compulsion.

He landed in Palestine in the early days of 1922, probably hoping against hope that the doctor's forecast would prove correct. He had decided against settling in Jerusalem, partly because its climate would not suit him, and partly because he disliked religious fanaticism, and probably had not forgotten the days when the zealots of the Holy City had slandered the B'né Mosheh. He made his home in Tel Aviv, the first Hebrew city of modern times, where several of his old friends were settled, and the spiritual climate would be congenial. The physical climate and living conditions proved in the event to be less so; but to them he gave no thought beforehand.

14

TEL AVIV

Tel Aviv, established in 1909 as a Jewish suburb of Arab Jaffa, had grown considerably in the intervening dozen years, but still, in 1922, had less than 20,000 inhabitants, and was mainly a residential townlet built round the Gymnasia Herzlia, on behalf of which Ahad Ha-Am had once intervened with a patron uneasy about its attitude to religion. The Gymnasia stood at the junction of Herzl St. and Ahad Ha-Am St. The naming of the latter, in the days of Tel Aviv's infancy, had drawn from its eponymous hero the sarcastic remark that the Palestine Jews, who so far had reviled his name with their lips, would now tread it underfoot. When he came to settle in Tel Aviv, its municipal Council, at the head of which was his old friend Meir Dizengoff,[1] decided to provide him with a house next to the Gymnasia; and after a few uncomfortable months of boardinghouse existence he and his wife were able to move into their own home. Their son and daughter-in-law settled in Jerusalem, where the son had obtained a post in the education department of the mandatory government.

Some of Ahad Ha-Am's oldest and closest friends had preceded him in settling in Tel Aviv, and beyond his immediate circle he was universally known and revered throughout the *yishuv* as the philosopher of Zionism and the father of the modern renaissance of Hebraism. He was treated on all hands with the greatest respect and deference. The High Commissioner, Sir Herbert Samuel (now Viscount Samuel) and his Chief Secretary, Sir Wyndham Deedes, hoped that his moral influence would help them in the difficult task of maintaining good relations between the different elements of the population. He himself had seemingly good reason to hope that he would be able, in such congenial surroundings, to contribute in one way or another to the progress of the "national spiritual center" of his dreams.

In fact he found himself condemned from the outset to something not very far removed from complete inactivity. His health did not improve in Palestine, as a too sanguine doctor had prophesied it would. He suffered from no specific disease, at least in the first year or two, but his nerves had gone to pieces. He complained bitterly of the noise of Tel Aviv and the stifling heat of its summers. The heat he could escape by taking refuge on Mount Carmel during the worst months; but, although the municipal authorities considerately barred the neighborhood of his house to traffic during the hours of his afternoon siesta, he found the noise of the busiest corner of the city insufferable, and became a victim to insomnia and a slave to the sleeping-draught. His trouble seems to have been largely psychological, but it was none the less serious for that. The few letters of this period which were published after his death are full of laments about his unhappiness, his inability to work, his sense of being useless, his desire for release from a life which has become a burden. Little more than a year after his arrival in Palestine he wrote to Dubnow:

I am crushed and broken, and sunk in a dejection which I can never shake off . . . I live here among my dearest and most intimate friends; affection and respect are lavished on me from every side, my children are very near at hand, and for the present I can study in peace and quiet: and all this in Palestine, of which I have dreamt all these years. And in these ideal conditions I sit and long—for London! I don't mean for the friends I left there—there may be three or four such—but just for London, for its busy streets and market-places, for the gloomy City in which I spent so many years without light or air, for the choking fog, and so forth. These longings, painful enough in themselves, trouble me still more because they seem to me a sure sign of some disease of the spirit: otherwise such a thing would not be possible.

As time went on definite troubles, neuralgia and emphysema of the lung, developed, and there were periods when he could not even use a pen, and had to dictate what few letters he wrote. But the root of the trouble was some "disease of the spirit," some psychological maladjustment, which perhaps had its origin in early frustrations and inner conflicts.

In such conditions sustained activity of any kind was obviously impossible. He had perforce to reconcile himself to that unpalatable fact; but complete idleness would have been insupportable, and a middle way had to be found. He allowed himself to be elected to the Municipal Council of Tel Aviv (of which he became the first freeman) initially as a nominee of all the parties, and later as head of the General Zionist list, and for a time attended its meetings and used his great moral influence on occasion to keep within bounds the partisan zeal of its members. He also served on the governing body of the Gymnasia (which he used regularly to visit during the morning break for tea and conversation with the teachers), and on one or two other bodies. He was even selected as one of the representatives of the *yishuv* at a meeting of the Zionist General Council which was to take place at Karlsbad in the summer of 1922; but he was compelled to decline the nomination on health grounds. Later he was keenly interested in the preparations for the opening of the Hebrew University, and in particular of the Institute of Jewish Studies, one of the three research institutes which formed its original nucleus.

The university was naturally of exceptional importance to him. In 1918, when its foundation stones were laid, he had expressed, in an English letter to Weizmann,[2] his "deep satisfaction and heartfelt joy on the occasion of this his-

torical event," and his hope that the university would not be
"a mere imitation of a European university, with Hebrew
as the dominant language," but would endeavor from the
very beginning "to become the true embodiment of the
Hebrew spirit of old, and to shake off the mental and moral
servitude to which our people has been so long subjected in
the diaspora."

The Institute of Jewish Studies, in which Judah L. Magnes, now settled in Jerusalem, was the moving spirit,
was opened in the winter of 1924, but ill-health and in-
clement weather prevented Ahad Ha-Am from attending
the opening ceremony, and he had to be content with sending Magnes a message of good wishes, written in a spirit of
enthusiasm and optimism such as he rarely evinced. In the
following year, when the university was formally opened
by Lord Balfour, he had a place of honor on the platform,
but the state of his health did not permit him to be among
the speakers; nor is there any printed record of what he
thought and felt on the realization of one of his most cherished projects. He was greatly impressed by the opening
ceremony, though earlier he had not been in favor of the
grandiose scale on which it was planned, and in particular
had disapproved, on grounds of security, of the decision to
invite Balfour and other distinguished foreign guests to
take part in it. His forebodings were justified in a measure
by Arab demonstrations against Balfour in Palestine, and
subsequent more violent ones in Damascus; but fortunately
nothing serious happened.

Though the state of his health severely limited the extent
of his participation in public affairs, he was able to keep
well informed about all that was going on around him.
This is evident from such of his letters to friends in Europe
as have been published[3] since his death, and also from the
very few short pieces that he wrote for publication during
his Tel Aviv years. Among these is a letter to the newspaper
Ha'aretz in which he expresses his horror and shame at the

killing of an innocent Arab child by Jewish youths in re-
prisal for Arab attacks on Jews. He also contributed a brief
note to a volume published in Jerusalem in 1923 to commemorate the First Zionist Congress on its twenty-fifth
anniversary. In this note he proclaimed for the last time
his long familiar *credo*. Recalling his battle with political
Zionism, he reaffirmed his old conviction that no charter or
declaration could bring about the fulfillment of Jewish
national aims so long as there was not a strong national
determination to achieve them. The pending ratification of
the British Mandate for Palestine, he wrote, would greatly
enlarge the opportunities open to the Jewish people; but
how if it proved that the will to take advantage of them
was lacking? After the first Congress he had written: "Opponents of the Jewish State doubt whether it will be possible to secure international consent to the establishment of
the State; but a much more difficult question is, as it seems
to me, whether in our present moral condition we should
be fit to accept the consent if it were forthcoming." Now,
aged and ailing and approaching his end, he repeats this
reminder of the importance of the moral factor for the
benefit of those who can hope, as he himself cannot, to see
the better times that are in store.

Though not reduced to absolute inactivity, he had, for the
first time in his life, not enough to do; and he might have
sunk before long under the sheer weight of boredom if not
for a happy inspiration of one of his old friends, Ravnitzki,
who suggested that he should prepare for publication a
selection of the vast number of letters which he had written to all sorts and conditions of people during his active
career. This would enable him to feel that he was usefully
occupied without unduly taxing his limited capacity for
work.

He found Ravnitzki's suggestion attractive. He had rejected the idea of writing his autobiography, because he—
of all men!—was not confident of his ability to preserve ab-

solute objectivity in writing about himself, and feared that
he might unintentionally distort the truth and mislead the
public; but that objection did not apply to the publication
of letters written years ago without any thought of their
ever being read by any but the recipients. Technically the
project was feasible, because ever since 1896, when *Hashiloah* began to appear, he had religiously kept a water-press
copy of every letter he had written; and he was justified in thinking that the labor involved would be worth
while from the point of view of the public which was interested in him and his work and ideals. He felt, too, that
he was probably better qualified than any literary executor
could be after his death to decide which letters were worth
publishing.

He had been in Tel Aviv only a few months when he set
to work on the project. He went carefully through the vast
collection of letters, decided which were to be published,
and which parts of those chosen were to be omitted, and
finally copied in his own hand the selected letters and extracts. The work soon became too much for him, and he
engaged a secretary recommended by Ravnitzki, a young
man named Johanan Pograbinski, to do the copying after
he himself had made the selection. Pograbinski has recorded
in articles published in the Hebrew press his recollections
of Ahad Ha-Am, whom he had read "with religious awe"
while still a boy in Russia. After their first interview, he
tells us, his joy at having found work which would save
him and his family from hunger was eclipsed by the thrill
of being chosen to help Ahad Ha-Am in the preparation of
his letters for the press. In the editorial side of the work
Ahad Ha-Am had the constant assistance of his old friends
Ravnitzki and Grazowsky, and he was largely guided by
them in his final decisions as to inclusion and exclusion.
In the result the *Iggeroth Ahad Ha-Am,* which appeared
in six volumes published at intervals between 1923 and
1925, contained no more than about 1700 letters, not all

of them reproduced in full. The great majority had been written in Hebrew, but some were translated into that language, by Ahad Ha-Am himself, from the Russian, German or English originals for the purpose of the publication.[4]

The first volume has a preface in which the genesis, purpose, and scope of the collection are explained. As to its scope, he evidently regarded it as self-understood that he would not be expected to pander to the vulgar taste for the trivial and the sensational. "Of course," he writes, "I have included only letters which have in my opinion a certain value, from one point of view or another, as material for the history of Hebrew literature and of the national movement, or of the participants in these activities, in my time." He adds that probably two-thirds or even more of the letters of which he has copies will be excluded, and many of those included will be printed only in part. The omission or curtailment of a letter may be due to either of two causes: its failure to satisfy the criterion of historical value, or its containing something which could not be published without showing some person, alive or dead, in an unfavorable light. This second consideration was one of cardinal importance for Ahad Ha-Am, who, though few could be more plain-spoken or hit harder in controversy about ideas and opinions, was sensitive to a degree about casting reflections on anybody's character.

The application of his twofold test of fitness for publication may well have robbed the *Letters of Ahad Ha-Am* of some of the interest that they might have had for those avid for intimate revelations; but for the avowed purpose with which their author selected them with such meticulous care, that of enlightening posterity about the history of the Jewish national movement and of modern Hebrew literature, and about the outstanding personalities in those two spheres of activity, they are of unique and permanent value. The recipients of the letters included most of the leading

Hovevé Zion, Zionists and Hebrew writers of Ahad Ha-Am's time, as well as a number of well-known Jewish scholars and many people less distinguished; and his correspondence touched on a wide variety of subjects, from the philosophy of Maimonides to the projected purchase of a piece of land near Jerusalem for Jewish settlement, from the Kantian categorical imperative to Maurice Maeterlinck, from the ethics of advertising to the "natural method" of teaching Hebrew. The *Letters* are especially rich in information about the inner history of the B'né Mosheh (he was able to include some letters from the Society's archives written before 1896), of *Hashiloah,* of the technical school project, and of the Zionist deliberations which preceded the issue of the Balfour Declaration.

For us to-day, however, the main interest of the *Letters* lies in the light they shed on Ahad Ha-Am's own personality and character. Written with no thought of publication, they reveal much more about him as a human being than his articles and essays, in which he endeavored to remain on the plane of impersonal argument and exposition. In the *Letters,* though his temperamental restraint is not shaken off, he is more spontaneous than he could be when he wrote, "like a High Priest ministering in the Holy of Holies," for the public. If he does not appear in négligé, at least he is not always in evening dress; and his motives for censoring the letters before passing them for publication did not include falsification of the spiritual self-portrait which they present. As printed, they do not hide his weaknesses: they reveal his irascibility, his pessimism, his touch of pedantry, and his proneness to exaggerated reactions and hasty judgments, no less than his immense integrity and moral strength, his magnanimity, his good-nature, and his affection for his friends. We learn something, too, though not much, about the details of his personal life, and in particular about his constant overwork and indifferent

health. Sometimes, writing to a correspondent who has
criticized one or another of his essays, he summarizes in
a sentence or two views on some important question of
Judaism or Zionism which are expressed in fuller detail,
but less crisply, in his published work; and now and then
he throws off an opinion on some extraneous matter of general interest.

Not unnaturally, one of the strongest impressions left by
the *Letters* is that of their author's unusually extensive reading and retentive memory. He is familiar with Steinthal and
Guyau, with De Candolle's *History of Science and Scien-
tists,* with Collins' abridgement of Herbert Spencer, with a
little English book on village life in Palestine, with books
by Gradowsky and by Starke on nationalism, with the work
of Fischel, Ratzel and Weiss in the field of ethnology, with
Horace, and with Lucian and the Church Fathers (his
reading during air-raids in World War I). He shows much
more than a layman's acquaintance with philological theory.
And of course evidence abounds of his familiarity with all
branches of Jewish knowledge, from Bible and Talmud to
the recent fruits of *Jüdische Wissenschaft.* When nearing his
sixtieth year, he remembers having seen in Fuenn's Bible
dictionary, published thirty years earlier, an anticipation of
the explanation of a difficult passage in Isaiah propounded in
a letter written to him by a Jewish scholar in London. These
are only a few random illustrations of the encyclopaedic
learning which he acquired and retained.

The concentration of interest on Ahad Ha-Am's philosophy and doctrines is no doubt responsible for the comparative neglect of his *Letters,* which are much less widely
known than they deserve to be. Quite apart from their historical value, there is scarcely one that does not bear the
stamp of the writer's individuality in some turn of thought
or expression. They can be read for the most part only in
the Hebrew in which they were originally published; but
for those to whom that is not an insuperable obstacle they

provide an opportunity of contact, through the medium of the printed page, with an exceptionally live and many-sided personality.[5]

The collection of *Letters* ends with Ahad Ha-Am's departure from London at the end of 1921, which seemed to him to be a natural stopping-point. He was, however, able to include a number of letters, mostly concerned with the B'né Mosheh, anterior to the date at which he began to keep copies. After his death some seventy letters written during his last years in Palestine were published by the Beth Ahad Ha-Am—the institute for students established in his Tel Aviv house, with a library of which his books form the nucleus—together with his *Reminiscences,* and a few much earlier letters—and they are our principal source of information about his life during his Tel Aviv years. Many of them, letters of a sick man chafing under enforced inactivity, make melancholy reading.

With the publication of the sixth volume of the *Letters* in 1925, his occupation was gone. His friends again came to his rescue by suggesting that he should dictate to his secretary reminiscences of his early life to supplement those which he had written many years before; and they eased his task by formulating specific questions for him to answer. This dictation continued intermittently until almost his last day. He was also persuaded, in 1926, to collaborate with Ravnitzki in the selection of passages from his essays for separate publication as a sort of compendium of his teaching; and when that task was accomplished, he had neither the will nor the strength to embark on another. His mind, however, remained clear to the very end.

❧ 2 ❧

After his retirement from the managership of the Wissotzky branch in London he remained a member of the firm's directorate; and this connection was one of the reasons for his only visit to Europe after he had settled in Palestine. The other reason was Mrs. Ginzberg's desire to take a cure at Bad Nauheim. They left Palestine in the middle of 1923, and spent two or three months in Germany and a few weeks in London. He had hoped to attend the Zionist Congress, but was unable to do so; nor, to his intense disappointment, was he even able to see his old friend Dubnow, then living in Berlin, because there was a general strike in the city at the time of his proposed visit, and he was dissuaded by his daughter Rachel, to whom he had now become reconciled, from risking what might prove to be a nerve-shattering experience.

The only other noteworthy event of his years in Tel Aviv was his seventieth birthday, which fell at the end of July, 1926. He would have liked the day to pass unnoticed, but his friends in Palestine insisted on a modest celebration, in which he participated. The birthday was also marked by his disciples and admirers throughout the Jewish world. He received thousands of letters and telegrams of congratulation, and public meetings and special supplements to Hebrew papers in many countries paid tribute to his unique contribution to Hebrew literature and to the Jewish renaissance. He derived a certain satisfaction—as who would not?—from these manifestations of affection and esteem; but he was glad when "the noisy days" were over and he could return to the quiet routine of his daily life. There was a sudden and surprising improvement in his health, and he busied himself with the arrangement of his papers and plans for literary work; but it was not to be for long. In October he wrote to a friend that, although he had not recovered his health, he was still not without hope of being able to contribute something to the national revival; but very soon afterwards, in a letter which was apparently his last, he told another friend that his hopes of recovery were dwindling.

The end came, almost suddenly, on January 2, 1927 (28th Tebeth, 5687). On the day before, a Sabbath, he had been visited by a number of friends, with whom, though not feeling well, he was able to converse without difficulty, passing from Hebrew to Yiddish or German as necessary. That night he obeyed his doctor's order to go to bed, instead of sleeping in an armchair, as he had been accustomed to do for the last year; but on retiring he told his secretary that he knew he would not get up again. The next morning he was no more, having passed away at a very early hour. He was laid to rest on the same day in what is now the Old Cemetery of Tel Aviv, amidst the mourning of the Hebrew city, which was shared by the whole of the *yishuv* and by thousands in the diaspora.[6]

His grave is next to that of Max Nordau, his opponent of earlier days, as though to symbolize the reconciling power of their common ideal.

15

PHILOSOPHY OF
JUDAISM AND
THE SPIRITUAL
CENTER

Ahad Ha-Am was nothing if not a critic, and his criticism of contemporary Jewish movements and philosophies was penetrating and relentless. He exposed the weaknesses of the Hibbath Zion movement, with its pathetic attempt to reclaim Palestine for the Jewish people by small-scale agricultural settlement, without adequate means or political security; of the Haskalah ideology, with its indiscriminate aping of European models; of Political Zionism, with its blindness to the profounder elements in Jewish nationalism; and of assimilationism, with its corollary of "slavery in freedom." The negative aspects of his criticism were sufficiently emphasized, especially in the case of Political Zionism, to give those whom it hurt some excuse for decrying him as a purely negative and destructive force; but in fact his negations were grounded in a positive philosophy of Judaism and Jewish history, in the light of which alone they can be seen in their true perspective. His philosophy was a highly individual one, the originality of which lay in its being an amalgam of fundamental Jewish beliefs and ideals with the theory of evolution, which he accepted unquestioningly as the key to the interpretation of the phenomena of social and national life no less than of those of the physical universe. Insofar as that theory is inconsistent with the traditional Jewish dogma of revelation, it may be said that his philosophy was not only eclectic, but was a mixture of mutually contradictory ideas. Moreover, his interpretation of Judaism and Jewish history was no doubt affected by his personal equation, his intellectualist and anti-mystical bent. But the Judaism which enveloped him from his earliest years had deeper and stronger roots in him than any doctrine encountered in later life could acquire, and it was the dominant element in his unusual synthesis. His was an inherited Jewish voice with an acquired Darwinian inflection.

As a writer he was seldom, if ever, concerned with the past for its own sake, and it was no part of his purpose to teach, still less to propagate, Judaism as a system of belief and observance. His preoccupation was with the practical problems of the Jewish people, and he approached those problems not as one having, so to speak, a professional interest in Judaism, as rabbi or teacher or preacher, but as a plain Jew, concerned as such for the well-being of the people to which he belonged. He was not a scholar who left his ivory tower now and then for an excursion into contemporary problems, but a publicist with an exceptionally generous endowment of learning and philosophic depth. A disproportionate amount of his time was spent in controversies on Hibbath Zion and Zionism, and it was exceptional for him to choose a subject from the field of Jewish beliefs or the Jewish past rather than from contemporary Jewish life. His philosophy of Judaism and Jewish history, nowhere comprehensively and systematically expounded by himself, has to be pieced together from these exceptional essays—notable among which are the eight *Fragments, Flesh and Spirit, Moses, The Supremacy of Reason,* and *Judaism and the Gospels*—and from longer or shorter excursuses and scattered observations in his more controversial writings and in his published *Letters.*

Jewish opinion in his day was much exercised by the question whether the Jews are essentially a nation or a church—a question which we should now regard as primarily one of semantics. He stood squarely on the side of the nationalists, and indeed made nationalism the basis of his whole philosophy. Historically he could find no justification for the idea that Judaism ever had been, or ever could be, a purely religious differentiation. The Jews had certainly been a nation in ancient times, with a land, a language and a politico-economic organization of their own; and they had never renounced their nationhood. They would continue to be a nation—than which in his view no higher form of human association existed—so long as there were Jews alive who were not content to forget their national past and abandon the hope of a national future. In his view, however, the essential activity of a nation was the expression in thought and action of its distinctive character or spirit, of what might be called its individuality. Its political and economic activities were subsidiary to its cultural self-realization, which meant "the expression of universal human values in the terms of its own distinctive spirit." This conception of the nation as a basically cultural group, and of the relation between the individual nation and the human family as one in which each nation's life is an attempt to embody in its own particular fashion ideals which are common to humanity as a whole, is pivotal to his outlook, and is what redeems his intense Jewish nationalism from the charge of tribal narrowness.

He was, however, less concerned to enlarge on the universalistic aspect of his nationalism than to insist on the unique character of the nation to which he belonged. For this uniqueness he sought an explanation not in a purposive supernatural intervention in human affairs (though he did not in so many words deny that possibility), but in the working of normal historical forces. At an early stage of its national career, he held, the Jewish people, its independence continually threatened by neighbors more powerful than itself, had realized the futility of depending on physical force for its survival, and had come to put its trust in the spirit. Taking for its watchword "not by might, nor by power," it was set apart from the nations of the earth, which believe in force and live by the sword; and it is in the realm of the spirit, of religion and morality, that its most characteristic contributions to human civilization have been made. The doctrine of the superiority of the spirit is associated in Jewish tradition with the prophets, and particularly with Moses, the "lord of the prophets" and the national lawgiver. Ahad Ha-Am is not troubled by the question of the historicity of the prophets, or of the validity of their claim to direct converse with the Supreme Being. He represents them as the embodiment of the highest aspirations of the Jewish people, as, indeed, projections of itself, created in its own image. Prophetic Judaism, with which is associated the religious progress of the nation from belief in a tribal deity to pure monotheism, is thus for him the purest and truest expression of the Jewish national spirit.

Here and there in his essays he indicates what he regards as the fundamental characteristics of prophetic Judaism. Prominent among these is the conception of the relation between the spiritual and the material aspects of human life as one of mutual interdependence. Ancient Hebrew thought, as reflected in the Pentateuch, knew nothing of a soul which survives the body; and though that idea found its way into Judaism at a later stage, when the national fortunes were at a low ebb, and the individual craving for immortality could no longer find its satisfaction, as it had done of old, in the belief in an endless future for the nation, the doctrine of bodily resurrection, and not that of a nonphysical immortality, still expresses the characteristically Jewish attitude to the problem of life after death. For Judaism body and spirit are united in a partnership in which each is essential to the other; but the spirit plays the leading part in the combination, the ideal aim of which is to sublimate the physical to the level of the spiritual. Jewish teaching, intensely spiritual though it is, has always refused to regard the body as intrinsically evil, or to countenance mortification of the flesh. Since the loss of national independence, ascetic ideas have no doubt gained a footing in Judaism; but asceticism as an ideal is no less repugnant to Jewish ethics than the opposite extreme of unbridled sensuality.

The principle of the interdependence of spirit and matter applies, however, only to human life and institutions. In regard to what lies beyond, the hallmark of Judaism, as Ahad Ha-Am understood it, is its resolute rejection of any intrusion of the material into the realm of the spiritual. The God of Judaism belongs wholly to that realm. He is the ideal of absolute perfection, to which no human being can in the nature of things aspire; and consequently no human being can participate in His divinity, or claim to speak for Him except as a human being chosen by Him to be His messenger to mankind.

The Jewish conception of the relation between God and man has its counterpart in the sphere of ethics, where the bent of Judaism towards the abstract demands the exclusion of all personal considerations from the moral judgment, and aims at replacing the egoism of the natural man not by altruism, which is merely egoism stood on its head, but by strict objectivity in all cases of conflicting claims, including those in which one of the parties is oneself. The social ideal of justice, which is "truth in action," is for Ahad Ha-Am the supreme expression of the Jewish spirit, and absolute devotion to that ideal, rather than any specifically religious illumination, is the outstanding characteristic of the Hebrew prophets. The prophet is distinguished from other men by the one-sidedness of his self-dedication to the service of justice, and his inability to acquiesce in anything short of its unreserved acceptance as the rule of human conduct.

He is an extremist: he will make no concession to human weakness. And since he is precluded by his very nature from abandoning the struggle for his ideal, he is doomed to be forever, in Jeremiah's words, "a man of strife and a man of contention to the whole earth." His teaching is inevitably rejected, because he will have all or nothing. In so far as his ideas have any practical influence on society, it is thanks to another, less extreme type of idealist, called by Ahad Ha-Am the priest, who shares the prophet's ideal, but is prepared to compromise with life, and to forgo one-half of the ideal in order to secure acceptance of the other.

The ideal of absolute justice is universal, knowing no distinction between Jew and Gentile; but the prophets who proclaimed it and served it were at the same time devoted sons of their own people. They threatened their people with dire punishment for its backslidings, but had faith in the ultimate triumph of its better instincts, and promised it reward and salvation in the latter end of days. In the spirit of the biblical picture of the relation between the prophets and the people, but with characteristic disregard of its supernatural elements, Ahad Ha-Am adumbrates the idea that the Jewish people, having accepted the prophets as its spokesmen, has thereby pledged itself to the service of their moral ideal. It has taken upon itself the mission of establishing the rule of righteousness first in its own national life, and then, by example, in the life of humanity as a whole. It cannot lay down its mission, or find abiding peace or fulfillment except in its accomplishment, though the craving for temporal satisfactions may now and then tempt it to rebel against the yoke. And since its ideal is unattainable in the conditions of human life, it must carry on the struggle until victory comes "in the latter end of days." Thus in effect the time-honored belief in the election and the eternity of Israel is re-affirmed, and its theological basis is not explicitly denied.

The religious and ethical principles of Judaism, enunciated by Moses and the later prophets, were elaborated into a system of law and life, known comprehensively as Torah, while the people still lived in its own land; and when the loss of political independence at length became inevitable, the national will to live, or instinct of self-preservation, was able to find in this Torah a temporary substitute for the territorial basis of the national life. The people followed the Pharisees, who were the true heirs of the prophetic teaching, in preferring exile to the abandonment of its own way of life and ideals, which would have meant spiritual death. Its Torah gave it the possibility of preserving its separateness in alien lands until the day of the promised redemption should dawn. But the day of redemption tarried, and as the years lengthened into centuries, and the hostility of the outside world subjected the power of endurance of the scattered and defenceless people to the cruelest of tests, the unique system of belief and conduct which was its sole bulwark became ever more intricate and more jealously guarded. The nation lived on its past, and every iota of its hallowed tradition had to be carefully preserved, lest the slightest departure from the old ways should impair its distinctiveness and jeopardize its chance of survival. The creative spirit of the nation was all but crushed under the weight of the law, and the current of its spiritual life was stagnant. But the old faith still lived, and the hope of restoration to the ancestral land in God's good time still gave the nation strength to endure its martyrdom.

In the eighteenth century, however, the ancient faith, and the hope which it nurtured, began to show signs of weakening. This was a result of the spread of liberal ideas in some of the countries of the western world, and the consequent modification of their age-long attitude of hatred and suspicion towards the Jews. The ensuing civil emancipation of the Jews in those countries made the first serious breach in the solidarity of the Jewish people, which had been unified, in spite of geographical dispersion, by the transmission from generation to generation of its spiritual heritage and its own pattern of life. The minority of emancipated Jews, exposed to the full force of assimilatory influences, lost their sense of belonging to their own people, and ceased to desire to preserve its traditional ways of life and thought unaltered; and their example stimulated a movement among the majority still penned in European ghettoes for the pursuit of cultural assimilation, in the hope that it would in course of time be rewarded by the grant of the rights and opportunities already enjoyed by their envied brethren in the west. The disappointment of that hope, and the persistence of anti-Semitism in the West after the emancipation, could not repair the breach which had been made in the unity of the Jewish people, or restore its old certainty as to its own character and destiny. To the material sufferings to which it had long been accustomed there was now added a new problem, "the problem of Judaism," the question whether, and in what form, Judaism could or should be preserved in the modern world. The Jewish people stood at the crossroads, confused by the conflicting views of its counsellors, and unable to decide which of them to follow. Some were for clinging to the old ways and the old isolation from the world. Others, going to the opposite extreme, advocated assimilation. Others again saw the only hope of salvation in the re-assertion of Jewish nationhood and an attempt to re-establish Jewish national life.

Ahad Ha-Am's views on Judaism and Jewish history naturally aligned him with the third group. The old ghetto life, apart from its intolerable material drawbacks, did not afford scope for the free activity of the national spirit, without which true life was not possible. The assimilated Jews, whose possibility of free self-expression was not hampered by artificial restrictions, were estranged from their own tradition. Hence the only possible road to healthy survival was that of nationalism, and it was in the Hibbath Zion movement that he saw the national will to live manifesting itself. With that movement, accordingly, he became actively associated. But he was quick to realize that the Hované Zion were going about their task in the wrong way. Their movement was languishing because they were neglecting to lay the moral and psychological foundations on which alone it could have any hope of success. The agricultural colonization of Palestine by Jews could have no real significance as a contribution to the solution of the problem of the Jewish people—as distinct from the material problems of individual Jews—unless it was the expression of a re-awakening sense of a common national history and a common national destiny. Hence the first concern of the leadership must be for the "spiritual revival" of diaspora Jewry, to which the establishment of a healthy nucleus of freely developing Jewish life in Palestine could make a vital contribution because of the enduring magic of the Holy Land and its associations. Palestine could and must become the "national spiritual center," to which the whole people would look with affection and pride as the home of the authentic type of Jewish life, and which would powerfully stimulate that process of renewal and regeneration which was necessary before it could repair the devastation wrought by centuries of persecution and assimilation, and could become capable of the united effort required to achieve its full national restoration.

This doctrine of the "national spiritual center," in which the secular and religious aspects of Jewish nationalism are subtly blended, gave to Hibbath Zion, the Love of Zion, a scope and significance immeasurably wider and more august than it had for the mass of those who under its banner were trying to settle Jews on the land in Palestine and to promote Hebrew culture. He sublimated the movement, in the words of an already quoted passage in one of his early essays, from "a part of Judaism," or "something added to Judaism," into "the whole of Judaism, but with a different focal point." By establishing a direct link between the modern Jewish national movement and the Judaism taught by the Hebrew Prophets, "spiritual Zionism" places the practical program of the movement in a new perspective. The Jewish colonization of Palestine, the Hebrew revival, the building up of a national spiritual center, and later of a Jewish State, are seen as serving no less exalted a purpose than to preserve the Jewish people and enable it to be worthy of the ultimate consummation foreshadowed in the prophetic promises. Behind the critical realist in Ahad Ha-Am, the relentless enemy of facile enthusiasm and hopefulness, who afterwards condemned political Zionism for its promise of an early advent of the Messiah, there lurked a visionary, rarely revealed to the world in his essays, whose gaze was fixed on that remote future in which the earthly Jerusalem no longer obscures the bright vision of the heavenly Jerusalem. Fundamentally his Hibbath Zion was no less messianic than Herzl's Zionism; but his was the infinitely patient Messianism of the traditional Jew.

His "spiritual" approach to Zionism had been anticipated in some respects by other nineteenth-century Jews, and most notably by Moses Hess (one of the founders of the Communist movement) in his now classical *Rome and Jerusalem,* written in German and published in 1862, and by Peretz Smolenskin in articles in his monthly *Hashahar* and in his well-known book *'Am Olam,* "The Eternal People" (1873) and other works. Both Hess and Smolenskin wrote before the emergence of any kind of organized Zionist activity. Hess, like Ahad Ha-Am after him, attacked the assimilationist ideals and practices of western Jewry as both servile and futile, ridiculed the notion of a "mission" which could be accomplished by the Jewish people only so long as it remained in dispersion, stressed the essentially national and historical character of Judaism, and condemned the Reform movement for its mechanical trimming of the ceremonial code to suit the tastes and standards of a non-Jewish environment. He too regarded Palestine as the only conceivable home of the restored Jewish State which he advocated, and thought of it not as a home of refuge, but as a national center, the value of which would not depend on the number of Jews it held. Smolenskin expressed broadly similar views; and the term "spiritual center" is used by both writers, though without any special emphasis. There were enough superficial resemblances between Ahad Ha-Am's ideas and Smolenskin's for the former to have been regarded by some of his contemporaries as a disciple of the latter.

It is not possible to determine the extent of Ahad Ha-Am's debt, if any, to either Hess or Smolenskin. Always sparing of personal references in his published writings, he nowhere mentions Hess or his book; and the name of Smolenskin occurs only in one of the footnotes to his *Reminiscences,* in which he repudiates the suggestion of discipleship, and declares that he never saw Smolenskin's *Hashahar* or his books until after he had settled in Odessa, when he was over thirty, and his views, derived from quite other sources, were fully formed. He must, however, have read both Hess and Smolenskin during his Odessa years, and it seems unlikely that the ideas they had advanced were wholly without influence on his thinking. But the fact, if it is a fact, that he was in some measure indebted to them, or to other thinkers of the generation immediately preceding his own, in no way affects his right to be regarded as the true father of the "spiritual Zionism" with which his name is associated. He may have used material derived from others, but the finished product was of his own design and fashioning, and bears the impress of his individual genius.

⁂ 2 ⁂

Students of Judaism and Jewish history, Jew and Gentile alike, generally assume that neither can be properly understood except on the theory that both began with a divine revelation. Ahad Ha-Am did not explicitly reject that standpoint; but his philosophy is not easily reconcilable with it, and is in effect a challenge to accepted beliefs. He relegated religion to the status of "one of the forms of culture," and held that Judaism was something wider than either, being "the national creative power, which in the past expressed itself in a primarily religious culture," but might conceivably express itself in quite a different form in the future. He recognized historic Judaism as a national religion, but would not accept the description of Jewish nationalism as a religious nationalism. Moreover, his nonreligious temperament and outlook led to a certain onesidedness in his treatment of the historical manifestations of the Jewish spirit. Anti-mystical and distrustful of emotion, he was insensitive to the appeal of devotional literature and of the poetry in which the yearning of the individual soul for communion with the infinite finds expression; and his nationalism was so thoroughgoing that he seems to have expected all the spiritual needs of the individual Jew to find their satisfaction in the love of Zion and the service of the Jewish people. He was inspired by those books of the Bible which emphasize the ideal of social justice, and assign to the Hebrew nation a key position in the world-drama of moral progress; but he can scarcely be imagined as going for spiritual sustenance or comfort to, say, the twenty-third Psalm. Yet that too is presumably an authentic product of the Jewish spirit.

This notwithstanding, there was much in common, as regards fundamentals, between his standpoint and that of so orthodox a thinker as Solomon Schechter. The man of religion and the agnostic were at one in recognizing the supreme authority of what is called in Hebrew *k'lal Israel*, the collective historical experience of Jewish life, as transcending theological dogma. They appealed to this authority under different names; for Schechter it was "Catholic Judaism," whereas Ahad Ha-Am spoke in the name of "the Jewish people," *'am Israel*, a designation which connotes a less limited range of relevance. The emphasis is different, but in both cases "the center of authority," as Professor Bentwich writes with regard to Schechter, "is removed from the Bible and placed in some living body."[1] Schechter was able to combine belief in divine revelation with a critical attitude—possibly more critical than Ahad Ha-Am's—to the Bible text; Ahad Ha-Am was more uncompromising in his evolutionary historicism, and his reaction against the quasi-mystical Hasidism in which both were nurtured was more extreme than Schechter's. It would be idle to attempt to minimize the differences between the two, especially in their attitude towards religion, which Schechter, as a believer, regarded as the source of morality, and Ahad Ha-Am did not; but in the perspective of *k'lal Israel* the differences count for less than the points of agreement. And each of them had a strong regard and esteem for the other. Professor Bentwich tells how Schechter, passing through London in 1910, refused even to deposit his baggage before he had paid his respects to Ahad Ha-Am, with whom he was not yet personally acquainted; and he also records Ahad Ha-Am's admiration for Schechter as an exponent of rabbinic Judaism who presented the ideas of the Sages in a plain and straightforward manner, without the glosses and interpretations by which other scholars were wont to distort them.[2]

Not all upholders of the religious point of view have the breadth and tolerance of a Schechter. Despite Ahad Ha-Am's scrupulous avoidance of any appearance of hostility to religion, and his not infrequent championing of the orthodox point of view against its outspoken opponents, he was not exempt from theological attack in his lifetime; and in our own day there are some who seek to saddle him with the responsibility for tendencies among the Israeli youth which he would have condemned no less sincerely than those who are, as he never was, officially in charge of the religious and moral training of the rising generation.

❧ 3 ❧

During Ahad Ha-Am's lifetime, as we have seen, there was a great deal of misunderstanding about the implications of his "spiritual center" formula in relation to Palestine itself. That misunderstanding still persists, and is possibly ineradicable, but it is now of no significance except in a purely historical sense. On the other hand, the complementary question as to the implications of the formula for diaspora Jewry, which was little discussed in his time, has become one of practical moment now that the State of Israel is a fact, and the relations between it and diaspora Jewry give rise to great searchings of heart throughout the Jewish world. What exactly did the thinker who gave currency to the expression *merkaz le'umi ruh'ni* mean by the "spiritual" influence which he expected the center to exercise on the circumference?

In Ahad Ha-Am's terminology the adjective *ruh'ni* has a much wider connotation than that which ordinarily attaches to the English word "spiritual" by which it is translated. He uses *ruah* to embrace everything in human life that is non-physical, so that instincts, feelings and desires, which we should normally think of as belonging to the realm of the psychological rather than of the spiritual, are for him no less "spiritual" than are thoughts and ideals, intellectual activities and moral aspirations. When, therefore, he said that the relation of Palestine to the diaspora would be, or should be, that of a "spiritual center"—that is, a focal point which would radiate influence on the "spirit" of the scattered Jewish people—he was not thinking solely in terms of what we are apt to call the "things of the spirit," of religion, morality, literature, art, music and so forth. He was thinking also, and indeed *primarily,* of influence of what we should rather call a psychological character: of the evocation by the national center of a strong sentiment of affection on the part of the diaspora Jews, and the stimulation among them of an active determination to be associated with it in one way or another and to strive for its progress and well-being. Only on the basis of such a psychological appeal would it be possible for the center to exercise an influence that can be called spiritual in the narrower sense—an influence, that is, on the inner spiritual and cultural life of the diaspora Jews, on their reading and their thinking, their literary and aesthetic activities and predilections, their religious and moral ideas, aspirations and conduct.

In the references—not numerous—to be found in Ahad Ha-Am's published writings to the question how precisely diaspora Jewish life is going to be affected by the influence of the "spiritual center," the kinds of influence here distinguished as "psychological" and "spiritual" are mentioned side by side, and apparently put upon the same level. Thus, in a letter to Dr. Ehrenpreis[3] written in 1904, he says that the influence of the center on the Jews of the diaspora "will be spiritual only, in the sense that it will strengthen their morale, increase their sense of unity, and provide a suitable content for their life as Jews." Again, in the essay of 1907, already referred to, which he wrote with the express purpose of removing misunderstandings about what he meant by a "spiritual center," we read:

> The influence of the center will strengthen the Jewish national consciousness in the diaspora; it will restore our independence of mind and self-respect; it will give to our Judaism a national content which will be genuine and natural, unlike the substitutes with which we now try to fill the void.

In neither of these passages is any special emphasis laid on the "spiritual" influence, that which will give the diaspora

Jews "a suitable content for their life as Jews," or in other words will endow their Judaism with "a national content which will be genuine and natural," as distinct from the "psychological" influence by which their self-respect and their sense of unity will be strengthened. His philosophy was such that he probably would not have admitted even the theoretical possibility of an intensification of the Jewish consciousness unaccompanied by a revival of Judaism, or of either of these developments without a strong emotional stimulus.

Further, the word "spiritual" as a translation of Ahad Ha-Am's *ruh'ni* is obviously not to be read as carrying the religious or quasi-religious implications that cling to the word in ordinary English usage. He had no desire to interfere with the purely religious side of Judaism, and even had, as we have seen, an active dislike of Reform; but he regarded as un-Jewish the development by which, among assimilated Jews, prayer and ceremonial have come to be treated as though they constituted the whole of Judaism, to the neglect of other elements which, in terms of the modern antithesis between "religious" and "national"—an antithesis which is of course inapplicable to traditional Judaism—have to be placed in the latter and not in the former category. He wrote in 1910 to Dr. J. L. Magnes, in a letter to which reference has already been made:[4]

Experience everywhere, and especially in America, has shown that the synagogue by itself, as a house of prayer exclusively, cannot save Judaism, which, unlike other religions, does not depend on prayer. Nor can the separate house of study, which is intended for young people in search of knowledge, serve as an instrument of *popular* education. What we have to do is to revert to the system which our ancestors adopted in days gone by, and to which we owe our survival: we have to make the synagogue itself a house of study, with Jewish learning as its first concern and prayer as a secondary matter. Cut the prayers as short as you like, but make your synagogue a haven of Jewish knowledge, alike for children and for adults, for the educated and the ordinary folk.

No doubt he expected that the attachment of the diaspora Jews to their national spiritual center, and their contact with the new type of Jewish life developed in it, would furnish a powerful stimulus in the direction of the emancipation of the synagogue from its exclusively religious function, so that it would fit naturally into the new pattern of Jewish life which he desiderated. This pattern would be basically "national," of course, in the cultural and non-political sense of that word, and would merit that description both because of the deep emotional attachment of the diaspora Jews to their center and to the Jewish people, and also because, under the influence of the center, the distinctive achievements and values of the Hebrew spirit would come to play a far more significant part than hitherto in the shaping of their lives in the intellectual, religious and moral spheres.

Ahad Ha-Am's Zionism was thus much more exacting, in its demands on the Jewish people as a whole and on the individual Jew, than the purely political Zionism of Herzl and his followers. He could not accept *as an ideal* the establishment of a Jewish State, in which the victims of anti-Semitism in its cruder and more violent forms would find refuge and scope for a free life, while the emancipated Jews remained for the most part in the countries of their birth or adoption, to be peacefully absorbed into their surroundings within a comparatively short time. He realized that Palestine could not take in more than a fraction of the number of Jews living in his day, and he was not prepared to regard the early disappearance of the rest of the Jewish people as inevitable. He demanded nothing less than a far-reaching revival—almost a re-creation—of Judaism in the sense of a national culture: a development which would

affect the Jews in the diaspora as well as those in the national center, and would involve on the part of the former
a very considerable measure of reorientation of cultural
interests and moral standards, as well as some emotional re-
adjustment. Instead of being allowed to lay down the
burden of Judaism, the diaspora Jews were to be stimulated
by the influence of their national spiritual center to an ac-
centuation of their Jewishness, involving both a great extension of the area of their personal lives within which the
differences between them and their non-Jewish neighbors
had significance, and a heightened sense of belonging to
the Jewish people. As he wrote in one of his essays on
Diaspora Nationalism, the "pull" of the national center was
to "transform the scattered atoms" of Jewry "into a single
entity with a definite and self-subsistent character of its
own."

❧ 4 ❧

The course of history has belied in important respects
the expectations on the basis of which Ahad Ha-Am put
forward his doctrine some sixty or seventy years ago. Essentially a believer in slow evolution and gradualness, he expected the "national spiritual center" to attain its influence
on the diaspora as one result of a lengthy process of nation-
building in Palestine, which would be accompanied by, and
would promote, a correspondingly slow but sure reorientation of the diaspora Jewish heart and mind towards Palestine and the Jewish people. In his picture of things to come
the attainment by the center itself of political independence
and state sovereignty, though expected to come about in
the fullness of time, was relegated to a shadowy future.

For a time, indeed, it seemed that his forecast was being
justified by events. After his visit to Palestine in 1911, he
formed the conclusion, as we have seen, that the Zionist
movement, though still professing to aim at an early and

complete solution of the whole "Jewish problem," was in fact creating the national spiritual center of his own ideal; and the process continued, at a somewhat accelerated pace, during the period of the British mandate. But then came the disturbances in Palestine in the 'thirties, the destruction of European Jewry during World War II, the abandonment of the mandate by Great Britain, and the establishment of the Jewish State only fifty years after the first Zionist Congress, before the spiritual reorientation of the diaspora had progressed to anything like the extent which he would have regarded as necessary in the pre-State period. These events have affected the situation, from the point of view of the "spiritual center" theory, in two opposite ways. On the one hand, many of the most vital elements in the diaspora of Ahad Ha-Am's day have been either wiped out, or cut off from contact with the national center and with the Jewish people as a whole; and the relative size and importance of that segment of the diaspora Jewry which lives in conditions of emancipation, with all that they mean for the future of Judaism, are far greater than ever before in history. On the other hand, the birth of the State of Israel and its early struggles have done more than the Zionist work of the preceding sixty or seventy years to focus the attention and affection of diaspora Jewry on Palestine (Israel), which *in the psychological sense* now fulfills the function of a spiritual center to a far greater extent than it did in the days of the British mandate. Whether the emotional response evoked by the emergence of the State of Israel will prove to be more than evanescent, and to what extent it can provide the foundation for a more far-reaching cultural revival than has been achieved so far, are questions on which dogmatism would be unwise; but most of us would agree that the way in which they are answered will determine the future of diaspora Jewry, in so far as its survival or disappearance depends on the Jews themselves. Thus the question of the need for a "national spiritual center" of Jewish life is no less a live issue today than it was when it was first so challengingly formulated by Ahad Ha-Am two generations ago.

16

HIS PERSONALITY AND INFLUENCE

Ahad Ha-Am's shyness, and his detestation of all forms of publicity, which he carried so far as to refuse on one occasion to permit the publication of his photograph in a philanthropic cause, kept him withdrawn from the public eye, and made him something of a legendary figure even during his lifetime. His regular use of a completely impersonal pen-name in his literary and public work, and his constant preoccupation with ideas and avoidance of personalities, all helped to foster the impression of remoteness and to discourage interest in him as a creature of flesh and blood. Today we see him in a different perspective, and it seems natural to seek to know what manner of man he was as well as to understand and appraise his teaching. For this purpose the six volumes of his *Letters* and his fragmentary *Reminiscences,* all published during the last years of his life, provide valuable information which was not available to his contemporaries; and the *Letters* in particular enable us to realize how little truth there was in the legend which represented him as a kind of thinking machine, with none of the passions or the weaknesses of ordinary mortals. The *Letters* reveal a highly emotional character, and one of great complexity and not a few contradictory characteristics.

His physical appearance (which he himself refused to

regard as a matter of legitimate interest to his readers) was
unmistakably that of an intellectual and a thinker. Short-
legged and somewhat below average stature, he had a large
head, surmounted by a broad dome of a brow, and tapering
away to a narrow chin with a close-cut, slightly sandy beard.
The nose was small, the cheekbones high, the deep-set eyes
behind the pince-nez alert and smiling. He was of spare
physique and by no means robust, though a high com-
plexion gave the appearance of good health. His delicate
fingers, quietness of manner, deliberate speech and sparing
use of gesture bespoke the reserve and sensitiveness of an
aristocrat of the spirit. He looked, as he was, the sworn foe
of anything slipshod, sham, vulgar or insincere.

A high seriousness and sense of responsibility were
among his outstanding characteristics. He was the typical
talmid hakham, for whom time not spent in study or in
some other purposeful pursuit is time wasted. He was entirely innocent of self-importance or pomposity, but had
none the less a strong sense of personal dignity, and he expected from others the same respectful treatment which he
invariably accorded to them. His sensitiveness on this point
showed itself particularly in his dread of ridicule. "I can
stand anything with equanimity," he once wrote to a
friend, "insults, abuse, slander or what you will—only not
being deservedly laughed at." To be made a laughing-
stock would have been an intolerable blow to his self-
respect.

Asceticism was contrary to his principles; but if he was
no advocate of self-denial, self-indulgence appealed to him
even less, except in the matter of cigarette-smoking and tea-
drinking, to both of which he was excessively addicted.
Otherwise he seems to have been a model of abstemious-
ness; and in his mature years he was, possibly as the result
of self-discipline, practically free of all craving for the pleasures or amusements by which men are distracted from their

serious concerns. Having no interest in nature, or in any of the arts, he was no lover of the countryside or frequenter of the theater or the concert hall. He had none of the social graces, and did not go to receptions and parties. As a boy he had been fond of swimming and card-playing, and had shed tears over the romances of Kalman Shulman; but all these diversions, and the reading of poetry, were abandoned when he reached years of discretion, if not before. His last surviving pastime was chess, which he gave up in his fiftieth year, having decided that they were right who pronounced it not serious enough to be worth study, but too serious for a pastime. He had an insatiable appetite for intellectual occupation, and he habitually overdrove himself until his health compelled him to take a rest and a cure. He used to grumble about overwork, but there is no reason to suspect insincerity in his admonition in a letter to Klausner of 1913: "Work, work! What else is worth doing?"

His one relaxation was in the society of his friends, to whom he was deeply attached. He was inhibited by his temperamental reserve from giving rein to his emotions—a disability of which he was regretfully conscious—but they were none the less strong, and his affection for his friends was among the most powerful. It was proof against all differences of opinion, and against their occasionally none too courteous expression of dissent from his views. It often found practical expression when a friend, or a struggling young author, needed help; and his generosity did not distinguish between those who shared his views and those who did not.

As a conversationalist he was not brilliant or forceful, but his measured words carried weight by virtue of the wisdom, integrity and rare objectivity with which they were informed. He talked for the most part on serious topics, but in the company of his friends he could relax and indulge in

light conversation, garnished with amusing anecdotes, to
which he was very partial. Hearty laughter was not in
keeping with his character, and he had not the sense of fun
which revels in the sheer absurdity of a comic situation.
His was a satirical turn of humor, most readily aroused by
the irrationality and the oddities of human behavior, but
there was no touch of malice in his satire. He had a great
gift for producing an apposite humorous saying or anecdote to drive home a serious point. When, as happened not
seldom, a course of action adopted against his advice did
not bring about the dire consequences which he had foretold, he would quote in Yiddish an aphorism to the effect
that "an act of folly which turns out well is still an act of
folly." An example of his use of anecdote is the story of
Abraham the Fool at the end of the *Discarded Old Manuscript*. Another, not published, is his ruling on the question
once submitted to him by some anti-religious teachers of
the Tel Aviv Gymnasia, whether they should comply with
the demand of the orthodox patrons of the school that the
pupils must cover their heads during the Bible lesson. They
feared that compliance with this demand might involve a
sacrifice of principle. In reply he told them the following
story. A Jew brought up in the strictest orthodoxy emigrated
from his native Galician village to New York, where in
course of time he became a Reform rabbi. A close friend of
his boyhood days, who had remained in the village and still
conformed to the traditional Jewish way of life, happened
once to be in New York on business, and took the opportunity of visiting his old playmate. Calling on the rabbi on
a Sabbath afternoon, he was shocked to find him smoking
a cigar; and when he too was invited to smoke, his indignation knew no bounds. Whereupon the rabbi said: "What?
You won't smoke? Never mind: one can be a good Jew
even if one doesn't smoke on the Sabbath!" The moral was
that the teachers might, without prejudice to their secularist

principles, emulate the Reform rabbi's tolerance of traditional Jewish practice.

He was of a kindly disposition, and his general mood was cheerful, though he was subject to periods of depression, more especially in his later years of ill-health. Essentially he was a lonely man, living much in his own inner world, intensely introspective, and with enormous power of concentration. He seems to have lacked any natural urge for self-expression and generally wrote, when he did write, rather in obedience to his sense of duty than for the joy of creation. Writing for publication was a difficult and painful process and involved a heavy responsibility.

An able American writer, in a noteworthy recent study of Zionism,[1] dubs Ahad Ha-Am "the agnostic rabbi"; and the description might have been literally, and not only figuratively, correct. Although he did not actually take the rabbinical diploma, it was his father's wish that he should become a rabbi; he received the appropriate education; he had the necessary intellectual acumen and knowledge of the Talmud and Responsa; and in spite of his agnosticism, he possessed most of the other requisites. Far from being aggressively irreligious, he always treated "the holy things of the nation" with reverence, and scrupulously avoided wounding the susceptibilities of the believers. In many ways his personal practice was less remote than his views from the traditional pattern. He did not transgress the dietary laws, or go to work on the Sabbath except in emergency; he observed the Passover *seder* in the traditional fashion; and he went regularly to synagogue to say *kaddish* after his father's death. His published *Letters* show that expressions like "please God," and "thank God," and others from the same mint, came readily to his pen, and in many other ways they reveal a strongly traditional bent. As a rabbi of the old school (not, of course, of the hybrid type with which we are familiar in western countries) he would have had no need of the arts of the preacher or the social mixer, still less of the clergyman's unctuousness; and it needs no great effort of imagination to see Rabbi Asher Zvi Ginzberg winning renown and reverence as one of the greatest authorities of his day on Jewish law, perhaps as the world-famous author of learned commentaries and of inspiring treatises on the moral aspects of Jewish teaching and on the Love of Zion, and setting an example of devotion to learning and truth, of upright conduct, of love of peace and complete freedom from self-seeking and uncharitableness. And as for appearance, an early photograph suggests that he would have looked the part to perfection before the process of westernization left its mark on his dress and his physiognomy as well as on his mind.

The chief obstacle to his becoming a rabbi lay not so much in his lack of religious emotion or conviction, for which he might conceivably have been able to compensate by tightening up his standard of ceremonial observance, as in his rigorous intellectual honesty. Even if he had entered the rabbinate early, his "critical and analytical spirit" would no doubt have led him to skepticism; and since he was incapable of willfully deceiving himself or trying to deceive others, his position would have been intolerable. He could not have attempted to conceal his unbelief from himself by interpreting away the apparent contradictions between the Bible and the findings of science, as the Jewish philosophers of Spain had done in the middle ages: the straightforwardness and clarity of his thought left no room for double meanings. Nor, in the absence of a strong personal craving for religious faith, could he have been tempted to seek refuge in a kind of schizophrenic dualism, like the Italian astronomer-priest mentioned in one of his *Fragments,* whose mind was divided into two water-tight compartments. What was true for one-half of his mind must be true for the other half also; and what he believed true he must profess, regardless of consequences. That was the first law of his moral code, and he had the courage to obey it at whatever cost.

The obligation of truth-telling meant for him, moreover, not only that one must avoid falsehood, but also that one must refuse to suppress the truth even when silence might be more convenient. Diplomacy ranked high among his aversions. Always inclined to go to extremes where morality was concerned, he roundly asserted that "the truth never does any harm"; and at times his attempt to live up to the implications of that hard saying involved a degree of candor which is considered unnecessary, and even undesirable, in polite society. Asked, for example, to attend a meeting called for a purpose with which he was out of sympathy, and for a time at which he had to be elsewhere, he would not be content with the excuse of a prior engagement, but must add a politely-worded statement of the reasons which would in any case have precluded his acceptance of the invitation. This unusual and sometimes embarrassing frankness spared his best friends least of all; but it cost him no friendships, because he was beyond suspicion of ulterior motives or a desire to wound, and his almost superhuman integrity gave him the moral authority of an Aristides. It was, however, in the nature of things impossible for a man of his genuine kindliness to insist on speaking the whole truth and nothing but the truth in all conceivable circumstances. He was once described by a contemporary as having "a stiff neck and a tender heart"; and when the two were in conflict, as often they inevitably were, it was not always the obstinacy of the uncompromising moralist that triumphed. But though he might on occasion hide the truth, or even tell a white lie, to spare the feelings of others, he never deceived himself, or sought to spare himself by deceiving another.

On the other hand, regard for truth and precision in the reporting of facts did not curtail his freedom of expression in the realm of opinion. His judgments, especially his adverse judgments, were often impulsive and expressed in sweeping generalizations which were obviously exaggerated, and could not be defended as literal statements of fact, though they might be broadly true in substance. His disparaging remarks on the Hebrew literature of his day, quoted in an earlier chapter, are a case in point. He found it difficult to resist the temptation to be carried away by his gift for epigrammatic pungency; and for that reason it was his practice never to allow anything that he wrote to be printed before it had been read by one or two friends, whose judgment he trusted, and ruthlessly to cut out any expression which they thought best omitted. Unless we assume that the passage just referred to escaped such scrutiny, it would seem that what was rejected must have been extremely outspoken.

Justice being, according to his own definition, nothing but "truth in action," he was as conscientious in the performance of obligations, great and small, as in faithfulness to facts. A debt unpaid, or a promise unfulfilled, allowed him no rest. When his business failed, he put the duty of paying off his creditors before that of providing for his own future. Carelessness about the fulfillment of promises, and indeed carelessness of any kind, was a feature of the *batlanuth* which he hated. In his revolt against the prevalent imprecision and slipshodness, he tended to go to the opposite extreme of exaggerated attention to minutiae. His meticulous regard for punctuality is illustrated by a story, not necessarily apocryphal, that on one occasion, when he arrived at a conference two minutes after the appointed time, he could not forgive himself until he was assured that his watch was two minutes fast.

Morality, if it is not merely utilitarian, needs for most people a foundation either in religious belief or in philosophical theory. Traditional Judaism of course finds the origin of the moral law in revelation, and Jewish philosophers generally have accepted that belief. Ahad Ha-Am, as he told Schechter in a letter quoted above, gave morality precedence over religion. The progress of religious beliefs, he held, is due to the refusal of a developed moral sense to tolerate old ideas which are felt to be out of harmony with the spirit of a more civilized age, like the *lex talionis*. He was not concerned to inquire how the moral sense came to exist and to develop; he accepted it as a fact. Even, he once argued, if one believed that actions were not intrinsically either moral or immoral, the categorical imperative of morality was a historical phenomenon which required explanation. For once he appears to join hands with Kant. But his implicit belief in the absolute validity of the moral law owed nothing to the German philosopher. It came to him as a part of his Jewish heritage, and was inseparable from his consciousness of belonging to the Jewish people. It was the counterpart in him of the patriotism which loyal sons of a normal nation feel towards the land of their birth and upbringing. Lacking all the material props and appurtenances of the patriotic sentiment, the physical land and the flags and drums, his patriotism was an etherialized attachment to an idealized people, to the country which was no longer its home except in memory and aspiration, and to the law of absolute truth and justice which its prophets of old had enunciated.

The intensity of his Jewish patriotism may be attributable to his hasidic ancestry, but its persistence throughout a life spent outside the Jewish pale probably owes not a little to his special circumstances. Unlike most other East-European Jews, he went through the process of emancipation from the intellectual narrowness and exclusiveness of the ghetto long before he escaped from its physical confines. He never succeeded in entering a university, and the secular studies of his youth and early manhood, pursued in the solitude of a remote Ukrainian village, did not impose on him the necessity of exchanging his mother-tongue for a European language, or accommodating the routine of his daily life

to the requirements of a non-Jewish environment. Until he
reached the age of thirty he lived almost exclusively in the
company of people who spoke Yiddish and followed the
traditional Jewish ways of life and thought; and his literary
language, so far as he wrote at all in those early days, was
Hebrew. When at last he emerged into the Jewish life of
Odessa, with a mind already mature and fully developed
views on the questions in which he was interested, his wide
reading had made him an assimilated Jew in the cultural
sense, but he had not become, and was immunized against
becoming, an assimilated Jew in the psychological sense, or
what is called a "hyphenated" Jew. He never lost the imme-
diacy and spontaneity of the Jewishness of his early years,
or ceased to look out on the world with the eyes of a member of the Jewish people, for whom Judaism is as much a
part of his natural heritage as the color of his eyes: and this
in spite of his temperamental and cultural remoteness from
the Jewish masses, with their simple religious faith, and
their Yiddish pathos and humor. It was no doubt this fusion
of Jewishness and Judaism which moved Bialik to say of
him, in one of his many tributes to the master, "he belongs
wholly to us."

His Jewish patriotism was not only the inspiration of his
universalistic nationalism; it governed the whole course of
his life. He once wrote that the medieval Jew "did not feel
that he was himself, did not feel really alive, unless he was
enveloped in the atmosphere of the Torah"; and the same
was true of himself, with the substitution of "Jewish life"
for "Torah." For a man who spent twenty-one years of his
adult life in Odessa, and fourteen in London, and was engaged in commerce most of the time, he had remarkably
few contacts with the non-Jewish world. It appears from
one of his published letters that he did not even know the
civil date of his own birth until it was accidentally revealed
to him in a letter of congratulation on his sixtieth birthday.

All the time that he could spare from the business of earning his living was spent in the society of Jews and in the service of the Jewish people; and because of his sense of his people's urgent need he overcame his natural inclination for the quiet life of the student and thinker, and spent precious years in the distasteful rôle of a combatant on the battleground of current affairs.

Wholly engrossed as he was in the problems of Jewish survival and revival, he had no occasion to take sides on any issue of political or economic controversy; and his lack of sympathy with socialist Zionsim did not imply any theoretical adherence to the capitalistic system. There was no reason from his point of view why Zionists should not be socialists. But the young men who emigrated from eastern Europe to Palestine with the idea of "conquering labor" seemed to him to be socialists first and foremost, and not to care about the re-establishment of Jewish national life as an end in itself. Moreover, the Hapoel Hatzair group, of whom he fell foul because of Brenner's notorious antireligious article, were socialists. That apart, he was of a too strongly individualistic temperament to be able to tread the socialist path towards his ideal of social justice. His all-party nomination to the Tel Aviv municipal council on his arrival in Palestine was a tribute to his eminence as a national figure; his later nomination by the so-called "General Zionists" alone (there being then no Progressive Party) recognized his real political alignment, so far as he can be said to have had one. He was not unlike a Victorian liberal with a conservative disposition and a rooted dislike of privilege. But he could never have taken an active part in politics, except possibly as an Independent. He was much too nonconformist to accept party discipline or vote with the herd.

His love of independence was, indeed, as potent a factor in the choices by which his career was determined as were his Jewish patriotism and his moral idealism in the shaping of his philosophy. He valued above all things complete freedom to say what he pleased when he pleased; and more than once he declined an offer of a congenial position for fear that by accepting it he might jeopardize that freedom. Equally, his pride revolted against the idea of accepting help that might be tainted, however remotely, with charity. One of the factors in his decision to throw up the editorship of *Hashiloah* was his fear that Hebrew readers who did not want the paper might feel obliged to subscribe to it in order to provide him with a livelihood. A no less costly sacrifice was offered on the altar of independence seven or eight years later, after he had settled in London. In a letter to Eisenstadt of 1910 there is a clear hint that he could at that time have retired from the Wissotzky business and settled in Palestine if he had been prepared to accept financial help. He admits that his refusal to seize the opportunity offered involves the sacrifice of his intellectual powers, which are wasting away in London, as well as of his cherished ambition of settling in Palestine; but he quotes as his guiding principle in life the talmudic adage "Flay a carcass in the street rather than be beholden to others," and concludes: "let everything go to ruin—I will not be a burden on the community or on individual benefactors." It might have been, and possibly was, suggested to him that he had a national duty to cultivate and make the most of his great gifts as a thinker and writer for the benefit of his people; but he apparently put his personal independence first, even when it involved not only forgoing the chance of escape from the "hell" of the City, but virtual renunciation of the hope of crowning his literary career by writing a book of enduring value on Jewish nationalism or ethics.

His conservatism was much more a matter of temperament than of reasoned conviction. He was radical in his criticism of accepted beliefs and policies, and believed implicitly in both the inevitability and the desirability of progress; but he was tenacious of his formed habits and accustomed ways of thinking. His attitude towards the adaptation of the Hebrew language to modern requirements is typical in this respect. He had no sympathy with the purist devotees of unadulterated biblical Hebrew, and even advocated a modernized grammar. But his tolerance of neologisms was unduly limited, and in his own writing he sometimes preferred to go on using a word borrowed from German or Russian even after Ben-Yehuda or some other innovator had introduced a satisfactory new formation from a Hebrew root to take its place. His published *Letters* indicate that with the passage of time he insensibly became more amenable to the influence of what he once sarcastically called "Jerusalem Hebrew"; but in the matter of the transliteration of borrowed words he remained obstinately old-fashioned to the end, retaining what was in effect a Yiddish system long after it had been generally discarded in favor of one which made the borrowings look rather more like Hebrew and less like Yiddish. In the light of his contempt for Yiddish as a literary language, there is a certain piquancy about this particular manifestation of his conservative temperament.

His blend of radicalism and conservatism is nowhere more apparent than in the gradualism and anti-interventionism of his evolutionist philosophy of life. On the one hand, he rejected entirely the idea of anything fixed and immutable in human beliefs and institutions. He saw life as a continuous process of evolutionary change, in which the one unalterable law was that of the adaptation of beliefs and practices to ever-changing human needs; and of course Jewish life and Judaism were not exceptions. On the other hand, he seems habitually to have ignored the fact that change in human affairs is normally brought about by the purposive action of individuals who are for some reason or other dissatisfied with the existing order, and often by means the reverse of peaceful. He writes as though the process of adaptation came about by itself, through the operation of some impersonal force like the "instinct of self-preservation," and without any violence. Hence his *laissez-faire* approach to questions like that of religious reform in Judaism, or the future of Yiddish. He could not, consistently with his general view, have denied that a great deal of the fabric of traditional Judaism was out of date and in need of reform. In his essay on *Ancestor Worship* he laid it down as a self-evident truth that if the *Shulhan Arukh,* the medieval code of Jewish observance, had not existed, modern Jews would not have invented it; and he believed that, when once the Jewish people had regained its spiritual independence, the adaptation to modern requirements of its religious system, as of all other features of its life, would proceed by a natural process of evolution. But meanwhile his attitude towards Reform Judaism was as hostile as that of the most hard-bitten traditionalist. What the reformers were trying to do, he held, was not to satisfy an inner need, but to rid Judaism by artificial expedients of those features which stood in the way of assimilation to the non-Jewish environment. So in the case of Yiddish. He believed that in the natural course of things it must disappear within two or three generations of his own time, and he certainly shed no tears over that prospect; but he would no more countenance the attempt of the anti-Yiddishist Zionists to ban the use of Yiddish for educational and propagandist purposes than he would favor "artificial" efforts to prolong its life.

Perhaps the oddest result of this insistence on letting things take their course is seen in his refusal to encourage the use of Hebrew as a spoken language, which was beginning to make headway among the Russian Hovevé Zion when he settled in Odessa. This would have seemed to be a development after his own heart. Not only was he a Hebrew writer, but, alone among Hebrew writers of his time, he steadfastly refused to write for publication in any other tongue. He had no difficulty in speaking Hebrew, and if addressed in Hebrew would naturally reply in the same language. Yet he rarely consented to address a Hebrew meeting, and did nothing to further the cause of Hebrew speaking by practice or precept. Writing Hebrew was an established feature of Jewish life, with a tradition going back to the old days of national independence; but speaking Hebrew was something new-fangled, and had to justify itself. In the diaspora it could not be said to satisfy a real need, for it had no natural roots, and nobody was dependent on it for the possibility of communicating with his neighbor. It was therefore something forced and artificial. He was skeptical about the possibility of its taking root even in Palestine, and it was only after his visit to the country in 1911 that he had to confess that he had been beaten by the faith and persistence of the Hebrew teachers, who had determined to make Hebrew the language of the schools in spite of the formidable difficulties presented by a polyglot environment and the absence of terminology and textbooks. A dozen years later, when he settled in Palestine, he continued to speak Russian with his old friends even in the streets of Tel Aviv, where public opinion was not unnaturally sensitive in such matters. It must have been with mixed feelings that on one occasion, returning home from a walk, he found on his desk a printed injunction to speak Hebrew, which would have been handed to any less august offender in the open street. By that time it was no doubt too late to change his linguistic habits; but he of course took it for granted that, whatever he might do himself, Hebrew would be spoken in the national spiritual center. He always trusted the "national instinct of self-preservation" to do its work, with the same unquestioning faith with which his ancestors had believed that "the Guardian of Israel slumbereth not nor sleepeth."

The story of his private life is largely a record of failure and frustration. With all his intellectual brilliance and moral strength, he had not sufficient self-confidence or

power of self-assertion to be able to bend others to his will
and carve out a path for himself. Circumstances were always
too strong for him, and his very virtues, his clearness of
vision, his basic reasonableness and his consideration for
others, too often stood in the way of his self-fulfillment.
After an unhappy childhood, he was married young to a
wife whom he would not knowingly have chosen; his sense
of filial duty balked him of the university education on
which his heart was set in early manhood; ill-fortune
dogged him in business; he was never able, except for one
short period of his life, to give more than his spare time to
the things about which he really cared; his ardent desire
to settle in Palestine remained unfulfilled until near the end
of his days, and when at last he left London for Tel Aviv,
his health was broken and his active career at an end. And
to the melancholy tale of unachieved aims and disappointed
hopes must be added the catastrophe, felt by him almost as
a personal loss, of the destruction of a large part of Russian
Jewry in World War I, which followed on the heels of a
tragedy in his domestic life. The Balfour Declaration was
no doubt a ray of light in the gloom of his later years; but
that too had begun to lose its brightness before he passed
away.

His career as writer and thinker presents a very different
picture. Here there was no trace of the hesitancy and lack
of self-reliance which were his besetting weaknesses in private life. From his very first article, he compelled attention
not only by the originality of his views and the forcefulness
of their presentation, but by a certain air of authoritative-
ness, as of one entitled to be heard and obeyed. He was
always, in Bialik's phrase, "secure in his own truth," convinced of the rightness of his ideas, resolute in their defense
even when he was their sole champion, and indifferent to
misunderstanding and vilification. He took it for granted,
and expected his readers to believe, that he knew what was
and what was not consonant with the Jewish spirit.

Whereas in practical affairs he was too ready to defer to the opinions of others against his own better judgment, in the realm of ideas and their literary expression he could defy the whole world. It is characteristic that the leader of the B'né Mosheh, of whom his colleagues complained that he always asked for opinions instead of giving instructions, became the autocratic editor of *Hashiloah,* whose word was law, and who had no time to explain his reasons for using the blue pencil to those with whose articles it played havoc.

His career as a writer and leader of thought brought him a degree of fulfillment which must to some extent have compensated for his personal disappointments. Not only did he become one of the foremost Hebrew writers of his day, but—what mattered far more to him—he saw the views for which he had fought gain wide acceptance after their initial rejection by the Zionist public. Many of his ideas passed into general currency during his lifetime, and became part of the stock-in-trade of Jewish writers and public men who often had no notion of their source, and would have hotly repudiated the accusation of Ahad Ha-Amism; and the Zionist Organization in particular was permeated by the point of view which he had been the first to develop as its bitterest critic. By Zionists and non-Zionists alike he was widely recognized as a teacher whose breadth of view transcended the conflicting ideologies which threatened to disrupt the unity of the historic Jewish people, and in whose synthesis the claims of traditionalism and progress, of East and West, of religion and nationalism, were reconciled.

But though he had some legitimate grounds for satisfaction, he was temperamentally disposed to underrate the measure of his success; and he was oppressed by the knowledge that there was nobody who would carry on the fight for his ideas after he was gone. Moreover, a perfectionist like him could not but measure present achievement against a vision of the distant future, in the light of which its shortcomings were magnified and its brightness dimmed. "The

Jewish people," he wrote in his inspired essay on Moses, "has
never lived in the present. Always unhappy, always in bitter
revolt against the wickedness of the world as it is, we have
none the less retained undying hope and faith in the triumph
of the good and the right in the world that is to be. . . .
Whether the Jew is fundamentally an optimist or a pessimist is a much-debated question; but it is pointless. The
Jew is both an optimist and a pessimist; but his pessimism
relates to the present, and his optimism to the future." In
that regard, as in so many others, he was truly a representative Jew, and perhaps, in essentials, the most representative
Jew of his time.

❧ 2 ❧

With the appearance in print of his very first article, in
1889, Ahad Ha-Am leaped into fame as a Hebrew writer of
unique quality; and not many years elapsed before *yeshivah*
students in Russia were greeting each of his occasional contributions to *Hamélitz* as a kind of new revelation (the expression is Bialik's), to be read and pondered and discussed
until the last ounce of meaning had been extracted from its
every word. Bialik, who, as a young teacher in an obscure
Russian village, had received help and encouragement from
Ahad Ha-Am at the outset of his poetic career, and was
very close to him in outlook, paid glowing tributes to the
master on various occasions both in prose and in verse. For
him Ahad Ha-Am was the inspirer of everything of value
in the Hibbath Zion movement, and the first Hebrew writer
to deal with current problems like a mature and responsible
thinker. He wrote in 1897 of "the purity and holiness which
inspires his every word," and in a poem of 1902 apostro-
phized him as

the Paladin of truth

And champion of the spirit; clear of vision,
Modest and pure in every thought and deed;

Secure in thine own truth, nor caring aught
How others judge; treading thy chosen path
With firm step and unflinching gaze, as one
Who carries in his soul the sacred flame
And guards the last sole spark of heavenly fire,

and went on to liken him to

some focal star that wheels his course
On high, and draws his satellites around him,
Masters them from afar, and forces them
Into his orbit by some hidden power.

No doubt allowance must be made for the exuberance of a young poet, who was moreover under some personal obligation to the subject of his eulogy; but Bialik did but express somewhat rhapsodically what was felt by many who had not his poetic gift. It is a small but significant fact that as early as 1893, when, on his first visit to Paris, Ahad Ha-Am met the Chief Rabbi of France, Zadoc Kahn, who was a devoted Hovev Zion and had been the first to enlist Baron Edmond de Rothschild's interest in Palestine, the Grand Rabbin not only showed knowledge of his writings, but insisted on addressing him by his pen-name, thereby paying him a tribute of the kind normally offered to an outstanding rabbi by the use of the title of his most celebrated book in place of his personal name. There was a substantial measure of truth in what Bialik wrote both about his personal qualities and about his influence on his contemporaries.

His exceptional gifts of intellect and character, his vast learning, his ardent Jewish patriotism, his intense spirituality, his passionate regard for truth, and the independence and incorruptibility of his judgment, were enough to command the profound admiration and respect of his world, the world of Hibbath Zion and Hebrew literature, which had its center in Odessa. But he owed his unique position above all to something in his personality that created an impression of his being different from other men, of his

being superior to the considerations of self-interest, the ambitions, the personal predilections and antipathies by which
the judgments and the conduct of ordinary men are apt
to be affected. This impression communicated itself to his
friends and colleagues, to his readers, and to thousands who
knew of him only from hearsay. Sworn enemy as he was of
what we have learned to call "the cult of personality," he
had a host of devotees, whose attitude towards him was not
unlike that of a conventicle of hasidim towards their
Tsaddik; and even those who did not go so far as that were
wont to regard him with a kind of reverential awe, in spite
of his being always engaged in controversy, and always on
the unpopular side. He was in the thick of the battle, but
even his opponents felt that he stood above it. For a quarter
of a century his world awaited his judgments on the important issues of Jewish life as though they had something
of a canonical character. It became customary to speak not
of his views or opinions, but of his "doctrine" or "teaching."
His reasoning was too logical, and his standards too exacting, for practical men to accept his guidance; but they felt
that he was less to blame for this than themselves. He became the teacher and conscience of his generation, whose
behests were rarely obeyed, but whose words of reproof
were accepted as the "faithful wounds" of a friend.

Today the East-European Jewry in which he was born
and bred, and to which almost the whole of his original
public belonged, has for practical purposes ceased to exist.
Most of that part of it which survived Hitler and World
War II is effectively cut off from the rest of Jewry by the
Iron Curtain, and is in all probability undergoing a process
of dejudaization. The smaller remnant which had the good
fortune to escape both the holocaust and the enforced isolation from the West has found refuge either in Israel or in
one of the other countries of the free world, and in either
case has been, or is in process of being, absorbed into a

Jewish society of a very different type from that for which he wrote. As a result, some of the problems to which he addressed himself have vanished more or less completely from Jewish life. His controversy with Dubnow about diaspora nationalism no longer has any actuality. His castigation of some features of East-European ghetto life, and his battle for European standards of taste and behavior, have no present relevance except insofar as characteristics acquired in the ghetto have outlived the ghetto itself. But what he wrote about the fundamentals of Jewish life and Judaism was read by Jews all over the world while he was still alive, and its value was and remains independent of geography.

It was, somewhat paradoxically, the Zionist Organization that was responsible, directly and indirectly, for the wider dissemination of the views of its bitterest critic, which traveled westwards across the bridge built by Herzl's movement between the emancipated and the unemancipated sections of Jewry. In the early years of the Organization his attacks on its principles and policy were thought dangerous enough to call for authoritative replies in the weekly *Die Welt,* its official organ, which thus did something to bring his ideas—with or without distortion—to the knowledge of the non-Hebrew-reading Zionist public. Informal contacts between delegates from East and West at Zionist Congresses no doubt served the same purpose. On a wider front, East-European disciples of Ahad Ha-Am, who migrated to western countries in search of a freer life, were able to become missionaries of his philosophy, thanks in the first instance to the common platform provided by the local activities of the Zionist Organization. Perhaps most important of all, political Zionism forced the question of a Jewish national rebirth on the reluctant attention of assimilated Jewry, and thus provided the first incentive to the translation of Ahad Ha-Am's writings into European languages. *Slavery in*

Freedom and one of the *Fragments* appeared in Russian in 1898, and the former in French, in *L'Écho Sioniste,* three years later. During the same period Israel Friedlaender translated several essays into German, and these, published originally in periodicals, were included with others in the volume which appeared in 1904 under the title *Am Scheidewege.* That volume was reissued in 1913, and a further volume of translations by Dr. Harry Torczyner[2] (Friedlaender having meanwhile left Germany for New York) was published in 1916. The first English versions of isolated essays, mentioned on an earlier page, were followed in 1912 by a volume of *Selected Essays* translated by Leon Simon and published by The Jewish Publication Society of America; and further English volumes by the same translator appeared in England in 1922 and 1946. Meanwhile translations of isolated essays, and in some cases of collections of essays, had been published in many other languages, including certainly Italian, Spanish, Swedish, Hungarian, Russian and Polish, besides Yiddish.

Evidence of the wide interest aroused by these translations is provided by the extensive literature on Ahad Ha-Am in European languages produced during the past fifty or sixty years. His views have been expounded or criticized, briefly or at length, in dozens of articles in Jewish periodicals in many countries, and especially in the English-speaking countries and Germany; and this activity shows no sign of slackening in those western countries in which large Jewish communities still exist, least of all in the United States of America, despite the reluctance of large sections of American Jewry to acquiesce in the idea of spiritual dependence on Israel. Concurrently there has of course been a vast output of Ahad Ha-Am literature in Hebrew, and to a lesser extent in Yiddish. A bibliography compiled a quarter of a century ago listed about 430 Hebrew articles and essays on Ahad Ha-Am, and the number has grown considerably since then. No other Jewish writer of modern times can compare with him as a stimulant of thought and discussion. And it is precisely because he wrote in Hebrew, which was in his day—and still is—read as a secular language only by a small minority of Jews, that he has had so wide a public: for no Jewish thinker or publicist who used one of the European languages could have hoped to be translated into so many others.

❧ 3 ❦

Ahad Ha-Am founded no school, and most of those who are loosely called his disciples have never been blind followers who allowed him to make up their minds for them. Some of that kind there have no doubt been, but he would gladly have dispensed with them. He wished for no disciples except such as accepted his ideas in the exercise of their own independent judgment; and his philosophy was so largely the reflection of his individuality, that it was unlikely to commend itself in every detail to anybody who did not share his unusual combination of idealism, intellectualism and agnosticism. Hence most of his so-called disciples have been and are men and women who broadly accept his diagnosis of the ills of Jewry and his prescription for their remedy, but would not necessarily endorse his views on the character of Judaism and of the Jewish people, and would still less be willing to apply his exacting standards in the determination of practical policy or the estimation of its results.

In that broad sense of the term, his disciples have included many who have had a decisive influence on the course of Jewish affairs, particularly in the Zionist field, since the beginning of the present century. Under his spiritual leadership in the B'né Mosheh were the future leaders of Russian Zionism, Ussishkin and his colleagues, who were responsible for the decisive shift in the policy of the Zionist Organization after Herzl's death. Without him Weizmann's "synthetic Zionism" would scarcely have been conceivable. He was the inspiration of the group of young English Zionists who, in the years before World War I, fought against the exclusively political conception of Zionism which was then dominant in Great Britain, and who became Weizmann's first helpers in the work which ultimately bore fruit in the Balfour Declaration. In the United States of America, Judah Magnes, pre-eminently a spiritual Zionist, was a figure of importance in both Zionism and Jewish life; and later he became the principal architect of the Hebrew University of Jerusalem. At the beginning of World War II, American Zionism was powerfully stimulated by the dynamic eloquence of Shmarya Levin, whose Zionist philosophy was inspired by Ahad Ha-Am's ideas; and Louis Brandeis, whose acceptance of the leadership of American Zionism on the outbreak of the war was an event of capital importance, said afterwards that he had been "led on" by Ahad Ha-Am. Today the leading ideologist of Zionism in the United States, Dr. Mordecai Kaplan, is a thoroughgoing disciple of Ahad Ha-Am. The first High Commissioner of Palestine under the British mandate, Sir Herbert Samuel (now Viscount Samuel), owed much of his understanding of Zionism to Ahad Ha-Am; and his first Chief Secretary, the late Sir Wyndham Deedes, was a confirmed Ahad Ha-Amist. Among those who occupied key positions in the partial implementation of Zionist political aims which followed World War I, there were few whose attitude to Jewish nationalism had not been influenced to a greater or less extent by the conception of it which political Zionism had originally repudiated.

During the period of the British mandate for Palestine the position of Zionism and the Zionist Organization in the assimilated Jewish communities underwent a considerable change. The Jewish National Home was accepted as a fact, and even a welcome fact, by thousands who had hitherto shown no interest in Palestine. Most of these were still unwilling to be enrolled in the Zionist Organization, which continued to be regarded with mistrust as something exotic and outside the pale of the recognized communal institutions. But if the Zionist Organization was still cold-shouldered, conditions were much more favorable to the working of the Zionist spirit. Palestine, as a living reality, began to play a larger part in the spiritual life of the Jewish communities. There was a wider recognition of Zionism as having meaning and value for all Jews as such, and not only for the oppressed and the underprivileged. Settlement in Palestine came to be regarded as a legitimate aspiration, even for Jews not personally in need of a home of refuge from oppression or anti-Semitism. In these tendencies, which have been greatly strengthened by the establishment of the State of Israel, there are discernible the beginnings of the realization of Ahad Ha-Am's dream of the "spiritual center," at least in its psychological aspect.

Concurrently with the growth of this new attitude towards Zion, the diaspora communities have felt in various ways the impact on their own internal life of ideas which have their root in Ahad Ha-Am's spiritual Zionism. It is true that, particularly in the United States of America, the synagogue and the institutions largely associated with it are slow to respond to the new influences which are abroad, and Zionism remains peripheral to the established communities in more than the merely organizational sense; but the Zionist spirit is finding its way in through education, in the broad sense in which that term includes youth movements and classes for adolescents as well as the teaching of children. Ahad Ha-Amist ideas have profoundly influenced Jewish educationists and teachers on both sides of the Atlantic—prominent examples are Samson Benderly in the United States and Nathan Morris in Great Britain—and the Zionist Organization itself, no longer completely engrossed in its political tasks, has come to recognize as one of its essential functions the active promotion of Jewish education in the diaspora on Zionist lines, that is to say, with emphasis on the living Hebrew language and the new Jewish life in Israel. That is the most conspicuous example of the permeation of Herzl's organization by the ideas for which Ahad Ha-Am fought almost single-handed two generations ago. Mainly as a result of Zionist initiative, education is becoming more and more widely recognized as holding the key to Jewish survival in the diaspora; and the serious thought and effort now being devoted to its problems, and in particular the growth of Jewish day schools, may be expected in due course to bear fruit in a new attitude on the part of assimilated Jews to their Jewish heritage. They will come to think of Judaism as something of wider scope than a body of ancient religious rites and doctrines, of no interest, except on its ceremonial side, to any but professed students of theology or rabbinics, and to regard it as right and normal for an intelligent Jew, in whatever walk of life, to be able to speak and read Hebrew and to acquire some familiarity with the history and the literature of his own people, and some contact with life in Israel. Given favorable conditions, such a development should in the fullness of time have the most far-reaching effects on the outlook and the life of the assimilated Jewish communities, and should make the idea of a "revival of the spirit," and of that "capture of the communities" for which Herzl called, look less utopian than it did sixty years ago, or than it does today.

In Ahad Ha-Am's own mind the idea of the revival was intimately associated with that of the development in the national spiritual center of a Jewish society embodying in the pattern of its life and thought the true spirit of the Jewish people. He was not concerned to define what this would mean in concrete terms, and there is no measuring-rod by which to determine to what extent the State of Israel conforms, or is likely to conform, to any model of his imagining. It would be rash to assume that, if that possibility existed, the reality would be found to bear any close resemblance to the dream. The young State came into existence, and has struggled through the difficulties of its early years, in conditions not conducive to the development of those elements in the national consciousness which alone had value in Ahad Ha-Am's eyes as specifically Jewish. It is difficult to conceive conditions in the Middle East, or indeed in the world at large, less favorable than those of our epoch to the universalistic nationalism of the Hebrew prophets, which in Ahad Ha-Am's view is the kernel of the Jewish tradition handed down through the centuries of dispersion; and in any case it is not easy for the free-born *sabra* to recognize the essentials of his tradition through the wrappings in which the generations denied freedom have been compelled to swathe them.

Yet there is no reason to assume that Israel is destined to become "like all the nations," distinguished from the rest by nothing more than its territory and its language. The isolated position of Israel in the world of international politics has, along with its obvious drawbacks, the advantage of reinforcing the State's sense of belonging to the whole scattered family of the descendants of Jacob. The land itself, and the Hebrew language, are charged with universalist associations. In the educational system of Israel the Bible, as the nation's most precious literary possession, occupies a place such as could not be assigned to it in the state-controlled schools of any other people. There is nothing to suggest that the Government of Israel, for all its inevitable preoccupation with military and economic needs, has any bias against the spiritual conception of nationalism for which Ahad Ha-Am stands: rather the reverse. Some of his essays are still, as they were in pre-State days, compulsory reading in the schools, and many of the teachers are Ahad Ha-Amist in outlook. The recent decision to introduce instruction in "the Jewish consciousness" into the schools, as a means of counteracting the tendency of the younger generation of Israelis to turn its back on the diaspora and to lose

the sense of belonging to the historic Jewish people, is
rightly regarded as a triumph for the ideas of spiritual Zionism; and whatever may be its effects in the long run, it is
at least significant as a pointer.

If, then, we assume the continuance for some time to
come of a potentially responsive diaspora, there seems to be
no reason why Israel should not become capable of exercis-
ing the influence of a spiritual center—"a power-house of
the national spirit," to use one of Ahad Ha-Am's metaphors
—in the more strictly spiritual sense as well as in the psychological. If this does come about—and clearly we are in a
region of speculation in which the last word must be with
faith rather than with reasoned argument—Ahad Ha-Am's
campaign for the ideals of spiritual Zionism will be entitled to rank among the decisive episodes in modern Jewish
history.

❧ 4 ❧

During Ahad Ha-Am's lifetime some of his more ardent
devotees thrust upon him, in his own despite, the title of
navi, prophet, and thereby gave a handle to his detractors,
who held him responsible for the extravagances of his admirers. In modern European languages the term prophet is,
as we all know, not infrequently applied to a particularly
radical and outspoken critic of human life and institutions
with a "message" of his own; but in the language of the
prophets this metaphorical use is less easily tolerated. To
call a man a *navi* is to suggest that he is the recipient of a
direct revelation from on high, and to put him on the level
of Isaiah and Amos; and that is felt to involve a presump-
tion which borders on sacrilege. This traditional sensitiveness may help to explain the objections which were expressed to the description of Ahad Ha-Am as a *navi.* That
apart, he was clearly in some important respects very far
from conforming to the prophetic type. A prophet who does

not profess religious faith, whose normal approach to human problems is analytical and critical, whose weapon is reason, and who rarely indulges in visions of the more distant future, appears to be a contradiction in terms. In fact, in the framework of Ahad Ha-Am's own prophet-priest dichotomy, he was more closely akin to the priest than to the prophet in his absorption in current politics and his readiness to listen to the voice of reason, to bow to practical necessity and come to terms with the hard realities of life.

Yet it is not difficult to understand why he was and is so often called a prophet. There were more sides than one to his character, and he made the profoundest impact on his generation, and will be remembered by generations to come, precisely in that aspect which he himself did not consciously thrust into the foreground. The mind of a critical and skeptical realist, which normally shaped his thinking and writing, was united in him with the soul of a Jewish visionary, in which there burnt the prophet's intense moral idealism, passionate love of his people, and belief in the existence of a link between its national destiny and the ultimate triumph of righteousness on earth; and, prophet or not, he performed for his own generation a vital part of the prophet's function. It fell to him, on the threshold of the modern Jewish national rebirth, to reiterate the message of the ancient Hebrew prophets, who warned their people against succumbing to the temptation to forswear its consecration to universal ideals for the sake of immediate satisfactions; and not without right did he take for his own the words of Ezekiel with which, as with a thunderclap, he ended the noblest of his essays: "And that which cometh into your mind shall not be at all: in that ye say: We will be as all the nations. . . . As I live, saith the Lord God, surely with a mighty hand . . . will I be king over you."

GLOSSARY OF
HEBREW
WORDS

Batlan, Batlanuth. See p. 136.

Galuth. Exile: denotes the Jewish diaspora, *i.e.,* all Jews domiciled outside Palestine (Israel).

Gemara. The explanatory commentary on the Mishnah, written in an Aramaic dialect, which together with the Mishnah forms the Talmud. The name "Talmud" is often used for the Gemara alone.

Halukah. lit., "division": alms collected in the diaspora for the support of indigent Jews who used to settle in Palestine to spend their last years there in prayer and study.

Hasid(im), Hasidism. See p. 3-5.

Haskalah. "Enlightenment": the revolt against the exclusive sway of the Talmud, and the endeavor to modernize the life of the ghetto by the introduction of western education and culture.

Heder (pl. *hedarim*). Elementary Hebrew school.

Hibbath Zion. "Love of Zion": the name given to the movement, which arose in Russia in the 'seventies of the last century, for the settlement of Jews on the land in Palestine.

Hovev(é) Zion. Adherent(s) of the Hibbath Zion movement.

Humash. The Hebrew Pentateuch.

Maskil (pl. *maskilim*). A believer in the ideal of Haskalah.

Mishnah. The post-biblical code of Jewish law, written in Hebrew.

Mithnagged (pl. *mithnaggedim*). "Opponent": an orthodox Jew who is not a hasid. (see p. 4).

Melammed. Elementary Hebrew teacher.

Talmid hakham. lit. "disciple of a Sage"—a man learned in the Law.

Tsaddik. See p. 4.

Yeshivah. Talmudical college.

Yishuv. The Jewish settlement in Palestine.

Yihus. lit. "pedigree"—good social position.

BIBLIOGRAPHICAL
NOTE

Isolated essays of Ahad Ha-Am were translated into English in the early years of the present century, in England by Miss Lilian Bentwich and in the United States by Miss Henrietta Szold. The first volume of translations to appear was *Selected Essays,* translated by Leon Simon, which was published by The Jewish Publication Society of America in 1912 (and reprinted in 1936, 1938, 1944 and 1958). Two further volumes by the same translator have been published in England: *Ten Essays on Zionism and Judaism* (London, George Routledge & Sons Ltd., 1922), and *Ahad Ha-Am: Essays, Letters, Memoirs* (Oxford, East and West Library, 1946).

Literature about Ahad Ha-Am in English consists predominantly of articles which have appeared in Jewish periodicals in the United States, and to a lesser extent in England and the British Dominions. To compile a complete list of these, if it were possible at all, would involve much labor and serve little purpose. The number of English books and brochures which deal, wholly or in part, with Ahad Ha-Am and his teaching is not large, and the following list (arranged in order of publication date) is probably complete or nearly so:—

SCHAFFER, Aaron: Ahad Ha-Am, the man and his doctrines. Inter-University Zionist Association of America, 1917.

SIMON, Leon: Studies in Jewish Nationalism. Longmans, Green & Co., London, 1920. (Includes essay on *One of the People*).

BENTWICH, Norman: Ahad Ha-Am and his Philosophy. Keren Hayesod, Jerusalem, 1927. (25 pp.)

Bulletin on Ahad Ha-Am. Jewish Welfare Board, New York, 1934. (30 pp.)

GOLUB, Jacob S.: Ahad Ha-Am—nationalist. Zionist Organization of America, New York, 1939.

PESSIN, Deborah: Ahad Ha-Am. Z.O.A. Education Department, New York, 1939.

Zionism to-day, abstract and evaluation. Z.O.A. Department of Youth and Education, New York, 1941. (54 pp.)

HELLER, Joseph: The Zionist Idea. Joint Zionist Publications Committee, London, 1947.

GENSLER, Kinereth Dushkin: Ahad Ha-Am, Prophet of Cultural Zionism. A Syllabus. National Education Department of Hadassah, New York, 1949. (21 pp.)

HERTZBERG, Arthur: The Zionist Idea. A historical analysis and reader. Doubleday & Co. Inc. and Herzl Press, New York, 1959.

SACHER, Harry: Zionist Portraits and other essays. Anthony Blond, London, 1959. (Includes short essay on Ahad Ha-Am).

NOTES

[In the following notes the biographer's three volumes of translations from Ahad Ha-Am (see the foregoing Bibliographical Note) are referred to as *Selected Essays*, *Ten Essays* and *Essays etc.*, respectively.]

CHAPTER 1

1. The *Reminiscences,* apart from the final section, were published in the Hebrew journal *Reshumoth* in 1926, not long before Ahad Ha-Am's death. They appeared in full, together with a number of his letters, in a volume issued by the Beth Ahad Ha-Am, Tel Aviv, in 1931 with the title *Pirké Zichronoth ve-Iggeroth.* Some parts of the *Reminiscences* are translated in *Memoirs of My People,* edited by Leo Schwarz and published by The Jewish Publication Society of America, Philadelphia, 1943; and others in *Essays etc.*

2. The three children were: Leah, afterwards Mme. Pevsner (1879-1940); Rachel, afterwards Mme. Ossorgin (1885-1957); and Shlomo (Ginossar——b. 1889). Mr. Ginossar, now the only survivor, settled in Jerusalem after World War I, has been actively associated with the administration of the Hebrew University since its inception, and was Israel's Minister in Rome 1949-51.

CHAPTER 3

1. Translated in *Ten Essays.*

CHAPTER 4

1. Jehudah Halevi (d. 1141), the greatest of the medieval Hebrew poets, wrote a famous ode lamenting the desolation of the Holy Land, which begins (in Nina Salaman's translation): "Zion! Wilt thou not ask if peace be with thy captives...."

CHAPTER 5

1. Temkin (1861-1936), one of the earliest Hovevé Zion, was an active propagandist of the movement.

2. The Pines in question is possibly Fishel Pines, a younger brother of the more distinguished Yehiel Michal Pines (1842-1913), one of the pioneers of the Hebrew revival. Ben-Tovim is not otherwise known.

CHAPTER 6

1. Called in the original *Heshbon HaNefesh*, lit. "account of the soul." The title *Many Inventions*, under which the essay appears in *Selected Essays*, is taken from the biblical verse (Eccl. 7.16) which is prefixed to the essay by way of motto.

2. Translated in *Selected Essays*.

3. All the *Fragments* are translated in *Selected Essays*. The subtitle is by pure coincidence, almost identical with a title used by the historian J. A. Froude.

4. Translated in *Essays etc.* under the title *Progress and Anti-Semitism*.

5. S. B. Maximon (1881-1933), who had known Ahad Ha-Am before he left his native Russia, spent some years in London as a teacher of Hebrew, and in 1915 left England for the United States of America, where he did important work in the field of Hebrew education.

6. Translated in *Selected Essays*.

7. Translated in part in *Essays etc.* under the title *The People of the Book*. The Hebrew title is *Torah shebaLev*, "The Law in the Heart," with allusion to the familiar distinction between ceremonial observance which is based on true religious feeling and that which is merely mechanical.

CHAPTER 7

1. Micah Joseph Berdichevsky (1865-1921) was one of the most important Hebrew writers of the early years of modern Jewish nationalism. He also wrote under the pseudonym Bin-Gorion.

2. Haim Nahman Bialik (1873-1934), the Hebrew poet *par excellence* of the Jewish national rebirth.

3. Saul Tchernichowsky (1875-1943) ranks second only to Bialik among Hebrew poets of their generation.

4. Mordechai (Marcus) Ehrenpreis (1869-1951), Hebrew writer and scholar, and one of the earliest supporters of Herzl, was Chief Rabbi of Bulgaria, and later, from 1914 till his death, of Sweden.

5. Jacob Thon (1880-1950) was a contributor to *Hashiloah* under Ahad Ha-Am's editorship.

6. Joseph Klausner (1874-1958), a distinguished Hebraist and Jewish scholar, was Professor of Modern Hebrew Literature in the Hebrew University of Jerusalem from 1921, and later also of the History of the Second Temple Period, until his retirement in 1948.

7. Reuben Brainin (1862-1939), a voluminous and many-sided Hebrew and Yiddish writer, of Russian birth, spent his last years in the U.S.A.

8. Mordechai ben-Hillel Hacohen (1856-1936), an active member of the Hibbath Zion movement in Russia and a Hebrew writer, spent his last years in Palestine. One of his daughters is the wife of Ahad Ha-Am's son, Shlomo Ginossar.

CHAPTER 9

1. In Hebrew *Yalkut katan*. *Yalkut,* the "shepherd's bag" of I Sam. 17. 40, is used metaphorically of a collection of sayings, etc.

2. The withering comment on Reinach, entitled *A New Saviour*, is translated in *Selected Essays.*

3. Translated under the title *Ancestor Worship* in *Selected Essays;* revised translation in *Essays etc.*

4. Translated in full in *Selected Essays,* and in part, under the title *Judaism and Nietzsche*, in *Essays etc.*

5. Translated in full in *Selected Essays,* and in part, under the title *Zionism and Jewish Culture,* in *Essays etc.*

CHAPTER 10

1. Translated in *Essays etc.* (p. 273).

2. Translated in *Essays etc.* (p. 277-8).

3. *The First Zionist Congress,* one of the notes in his *Miscellany,* translated in *Ten Essays.*

4. Translated in *Ten Essays.*

5. Translated in *Ten Essays* under the title *When Messiah Comes.*

6. Translated in *Essays etc.* (p. 273-4).

7. Translated in *Ten Essays* under the title *Pinsker and Political Zionism.*

8. Judah Grazowsky (1862-1950), Hebrew educationist and lexicographer, left Russia for Palestine in his early years.

9. Translated in *Essays etc.* (p. 283-7).

10. Translated in *Ten Essays* under the title *A Spiritual Centre.*

11. A Zionist usually so well-informed as Mr. Israel Cohen, who held for some years an important position in the World Zionist Organization, and knew Ahad Ha-Am personally, seems still to suppose him not to have realized that a spiritual center could not be created and maintained "without an economic basis, a social periphery, and political security" (see p. 75 of Mr. Cohen's autobiography, *A Jewish Pilgrimage,* published in 1956).

CHAPTER 11

1. Professor Bentwich speaks in his Schechter biography (p. 324) of the offer of a Chair; but it seems clear from Ahad Ha-Am's letter to Lubarski of 30th April, 1906 (*Iggeroth Ahad Ha-Am,* vol. III, p. 236) that the headship of the institution was offered to him.

2. Israel Friedlaender (1877-1920), historian and orientalist, translated a number of Ahad Ha-Am's essays into German after he had left his native Volhynia for Strasbourg. In 1903, he was appointed Professor of Biblical Literature at the Jewish Theological Seminary of America in New York. He was active in American Zionism as well as in Jewish scholarship, and was on a relief mission in the Ukraine when he met his death at the hands of brigands.

3. Translated in *Selected Essays;* revised translation in *Essays etc.*

4. Translated in *Selected Essays;* revised translation, under the title *Judaism and Asceticism,* in *Essays etc.*

5. See the essay on Maimonides by the Rev. H. S. Lewis in *Aspects of the Hebrew Genius,* edited by Leon Simon (George Routledge and Sons, Ltd., London, 1910).

6. Translated in *Ten Essays;* revised translation in *Essays etc.*

7. His long reply to Friedlaender, dealing with this and a number of other points, is in vol. V of the *Iggeroth,* p. 57 ff. It is not available in English.

8. In Hebrew *hishtapchuth hanefesh,* "outpouring of the soul."

CHAPTER 12

1. Shmarya Levin (1867-1935), a close friend of Ahad Ha-Am, was one of the first members of the B'né Mosheh, and later one of the most effective of Zionist propagandists. He contributed much to the spread of Zionism in America in the period of World War I. He was a member of the first Russian Duma in 1905.

2. Jacob Moser (1829-1922), Lord Mayor of Bradford 1910-11, and a prominent philanthropist, was one of the early leaders of English Zionism.

3. Dr. Judah Leon Magnes (1877-1948), after a distinguished career as rabbi, Zionist and communal leader in the United States, settled in Jerusalem, and became Chancellor of the Hebrew University on its establishment in 1925. The letter to him mentioned in the text is translated in *Essays etc.* (p. 268-9).

4. Dr. Israel Abrahams (1858-1925), a prominent Anglo-Jewish scholar and man of letters, who was associated with Claude Montefiore in the editorship of the *Jewish Quarterly Review* while it was published in England, succeeded Schechter as Professor of Rabbinics at Cambridge.

5. Translated in *Ten Essays.*

6. In Hebrew *Shelilath Hagaluth*. The English translation in *Essays etc.* is called *Nationalists and the Diaspora*.

7. Translated in *Essays etc.*

8. Miss d'Avigdor had translated Herzl's *Judenstaat* into English soon after its publication.

9. The Hebrew title of the essay is *'Al sheté hase'ipim,* "between two opinions." It is translated in full in *Ten Essays* under the title *Judaism and the Gospels,* and in part in *Essays etc.* under the title *Jewish and Christian Ethics.*

10. Translated in *Ten Essays* under the title *Summa Summarum.*

11. Alter Druyanov (1870-1938) was a Hebrew publicist and historian of Hibbath Zion.

12. Aaron David Gordon (1856-1922) left his native Russia for Palestine at the age of fifty, and became the leader and inspirer of the idealists of the labor movement.

13. Mosheh Smilanski (1873-1953) was one of the early settlers in Palestine, where he made a reputation both as a writer of Hebrew stories and as an authority on farming.

CHAPTER 13

1. The English phrase appears in the Hebrew version of the letter, and was presumably used in the Russian original.

2. A translation of the Preface is embodied in the translator's Introduction to *Ten Essays.*

3. Translated in *Essays etc.* (p. 295-6).

CHAPTER 14

1. Meir Dizengoff (1861-1936) was one of the founders of Tel Aviv and its first Mayor.

2. The letter is reproduced in *Essays etc.* (p. 294-5).

3. See note 1 to chapter 1.

4. The five volumes in which the flimsy copies are bound up are for practical purposes inaccessible at present, having remained, with the rest of Ahad Ha-Am's papers, in the University Library on Mount Scopus.

5. The original edition of the Letters (*Iggeroth Ahad Ha-Am*), for the publication of which his old friend Feiwel Shapiro (d. 1960) was responsible, sold out within a few years, and the book has not been reissued. The D'vir Publishing Company, of Tel Aviv, now has in the press a second edition, with notes and some additional letters, prepared by Leon Simon and Johanan Pograbinski, whose death occurred at the end of 1959.

6. His widow died in 1929.

CHAPTER 15

1. See Professor Bentwich's *Solomon Schechter,* p. 244.

2. *Ib.*, p. 269.

3. Translated in *Essays etc.* (p. 287).

4. See above p. 229.

CHAPTER 16

1. Rabbi Arthur Hertzberg in *The Zionist Idea* (Doubleday and Co. Inc. and Herzl Press, New York, 1959).

2. Now N. H. Tur-Sinai (b. 1886), Emeritus Professor of Hebrew Philology in the Hebrew University of Jerusalem, and President of the Hebrew Language Academy.

INDEX

Abdul Hamid, 234
Abrahams, Israel, 229
Achad Cham (Asher Hinzberg, der geheime Führer der Juden), 93-94
Adler, Hermann, 71
Agricultural colonies in Palestine, 68, 89, 150, 151, 154-155, 279, 287. *See also* Colonization efforts in Palestine
Ahad Ha-Am: The Man, His Work and His Teaching (Heller and Simon), vii-x
Ahiasaf *Almanac*, 127, 128, 130
Ahiasaf Publishing Company, 90, 92, 95, 119, 127, 128, 144, 145, 146, 147, 148, 195
Ahiasaf Yearbook, 114, 116
Akedath Yitzhak, 19
Alliance Israélite Universelle, 67, 89, 232
Altneuland (Herzl), 180, 182, 183, 184, 205
'Am Olam ("The Eternal People" by Peretz Smolenskin), 288
Am Scheidewege (Ahad Ha-Am), 95, 215, 320. See also *At the Crossroads*
American Jewish Encyclopedia, 117
Ancestor Worship (Ahad Ha-Am), 312
Anglo-Jewish Association, 232
Anglo-Jewry, 215-217, 219, 221
Anti-Semitism, 101, 103, 104, 182
Antokolsky, Marc, 168
Assimilation, 41, 101, 102, 123, 173, 183, 190, 198, 216, 217, 230, 279, 286
At the Crossroads (Al Parashath Derachim), by Ahad Ha-Am, 95, 96, 175, 180, 193, 208, 234, 261. See also *Am Scheidewege*
Austria, 7

Auto-Emanzipation (Pinsker), 33, 176, 251
Autonomism, 235. *See also* Diaspora nationalism

Baal-Shem, The (Israel ben Eliezer), 3
Baku, 196
Balfour, Arthur James, Lord, 270
Balfour Declaration, 188, 254, 314; role of Ahad Ha-Am in, 252-253, 260-261, 263
Barzilai (Eisenstadt), Joshua, 57, 80, 81, 86, 264
Basle, 88, 171, 175, 186, 242
Batlanuth, 136, 137, 139, 142, 306
Batlanim, 169
Beehive, The, 39, 97
Ben-Avigdor (Abraham Leib Shalkovitz), 82, 92-93, 193
Benderly, Samson, 323
Ben-Tovim, and B'né Mosheh Society, 84
Bentwich, Herbert, 215, 291
Bentwich, Lilian Ruth, 215
Bentwich family, 216
Ben-Yehuda, Eliezer, 51, 52, 311
Berdichevsky, Micah J., 130, 135, 140, 142, 159, 160, 163, 164
Berditchev, 10, 34
Berlin, 30, 95, 96, 130, 139, 226, 252, 277
Bernfeld, Simon, 72, 139, 195
Bernstein-Kohan, J., 176, 177
Beth Ahad Ha-Am, 276
Between East and West, xi
Bialik, Haim Nahman, 134, 142, 149, 178, 224, 260, 314; poem on Ahad Ha-Am, 316-317
Blood accusation, 110, 111
Biographical Story (Tverski), vii
B'né Mosheh (Society of Sons of Moses), 42, 54, 56, 58, 59, 72, 76-94, 98,

127, 140, 174, 246, 266, 276, 315,
321; achievements, 89-90; contro-
versy over, 82-87, 92; membership,
80; object, 77-78; rules and regula-
lations, 77, 78-79; transfer to west
urged, 88
Bolshevik revolution, 59
Boycott. See *Herem*
Brainin, Reuben, 142, 146
Brandeis, Louis D., 322
Brenner, Joseph Haim, 164, 165, 246,
309
Breslau, 30
British Museum, 213, 214, 222
Brody, Galicia, 12
Buber, Martin, 5
Bund, the, 231
Burton, Sir Montagu, viii

Cairo Geniza, 221
Ceremonial, in Judaism, 231
Children of the Ghetto (Zangwill), 111
Christianity, differences between Juda-
ism and, 240-242
Collective settlements in Palestine, 244-
245
Colonial efforts in Palestine, 33, 37, 50,
58-59, 61, 62, 63, 64, 67, 69, 70,
83, 84, 89, 104, 150, 151, 169, 174,
176, 235; and political Zionism, 181.
See also Agricultural colonies in
Palestine
Constantinople, 68, 90, 171, 211

Damascus, 270
d'Avigdor, Sylvie, 239
Deedes, Sir Wyndham, 267, 322
Delegates of a Penniless People, (Ahad
Ha-Am), 155
Diaspora nationalism, 99, 235, 236,
237, 238, 292, 293, 294, 295, 296,
297, 318, 323, 324, 325. *See also*
Autonomism; Dubnow; Nationalism
Discarded Old Manuscript (Ahad Ha-
Am), 97, 247, 302
Dizengoff, Meir, 153, 267
Dr. Kohn (Nordau), 167
Dr. Pinsker and his Pamphlet (Ahad
Ha-Am), 103-104, 106
Dreyfus affair, 103
Dropsie College for Hebrew and Cog-
nate Learning, 202, 203

Druyanov, Alter, 244, 246
Dubnow, Simon, 101, 102, 196, 200,
201, 208, 216, 222, 223, 268, 277;
controversy with Ahad Ha-Am, 235-
236, 237, 238, 319
Duma (Russian Parliament), 200

East Africa, Jewish settlement in, 185-
186
Echo Sioniste, L', 320
Educational achievements of B'né
Mosheh Society, 89
Egypt, 90
Ehrenpreis, Mordechai (Marcus), 135,
159, 293
Eisenstadt, Joshua. *See* Barzilai, Joshua
Eliasberg, R. Jonathan, 113, 129
Eliasberg, R. Mordecai, 97, 113
Emancipation and Judaism, 285-286
Encyclopedia of Judaism, 75, 117-119,
148
England, 64, 72, 73, 80, 137; attitude
toward Palestine settlement, 71, 73,
74. *See also* Great Britain
English Zionist Federation, 253, 255
Erter, Isaac, 19
Evolutionist philosophy of Ahad Ha-
Am, 311-312

Flesh and Spirit (Ahad Ha-Am), 205,
206, 280
Fraenkel, Josef, xii
Fragments (Ahad Ha-Am), 103, 107-
111, 158, 212, 215, 280, 303, 320
France, 101, 137, 249
Friedlaender, Israel, 203, 204, 207, 215,
320
Friendly Attack, A (Ahad Ha-Am), 99
Frischmann, David, 47, 143, 146, 159
Fuenn, Samuel Joseph, 46

Galicia, 12
Gallipoli Campaign, 254
Galuth, 66, 68, 101 f., 160 ff., 235 f.,
285 f.
Gedera, Palestine, 60
Gemara, 10, 14, 19, 20 f.
Gerbe, La, 101, 102
German as language of instruction in
Palestine, 231-232
Germany, 80, 103, 137, 251, 276, 320
Ginzberg, Asher Zvi, name of Ahad

Ha-Am, 5, 36, 46, 48
Ginzberg, Mrs. Asher Zvi, 24, 277
Ginzberg, Hannah, 8, 13, 15
Ginzberg, Isaiah, 7, 8, 10, 12, 14, 17, 18, 19, 33
Ginzberg, Leah, 29, 196
Ginzberg, Rachel, 34, 248, 277
Glickson, M., vii
Goldsmid, Col. Albert, 64, 74
Gopitshitza, Russia, 7, 10, 11, 16, 24, 27, 30, 34, 35, 42
Gordon, Aaron David, 245
Gordon, Judah Leib, 46, 107, 111, 133
Gottlober, A. B., 27
Grazowsky, Judah, 178
Great Britain, 185, 249, 252, 255, 260, 263, 297, 321, 323. *See also* Balfour Declaration; England
Gymnasia Herzlia, Tel Aviv, 228, 230, 245, 267, 269, 302

Ha'aretz, 270
Habad, Hasidic sect, 5
Hacohen, Mordechai ben-Hillel, 147, 148, 208, 264
Hador, 146, 147
Haifa, 196, 209, 217, 226
Halevi, Jehudah, 164
Halukah, 48, 84
Hamaggid, 47
Hamélitz (*The Advocate*), 46, 47, 53, 54, 56, 57, 61, 68, 74, 82, 95, 96, 98, 101, 110, 114, 116, 129, 130, 316
Ha'olam, 244, 246
Ha'omer, 234, 235
Hapoel Hatzair, 164, 309
Hashahar, 27, 40, 51, 129, 137, 288, 289
Hashiloah, 88, 126, 130, 150, 152, 153, 155, 157, 159, 162, 164, 167, 168, 172, 176, 179, 195, 197, 206, 207, 235, 236, 238, 240, 242, 272, 310, 315; under the editorship of Ahad Ha-Am, 131-149
Hasidism, 3, 4, 5, 7, 14, 16, 17, 18, 20, 24 f., 38, 123, 220, 291, 318. *See also* Habad; Mithnaggedim
Haskalah movement, 5, 16, 18, 19, 27, 28, 29, 40, 46, 53, 55, 132, 168, 198. *See also* Maskilim.
Hatsefirah, 129, 244

Ha-tsofeh l'veth Israel (Erter), 19
Hebrew, modern, 51, 55, 89, 324, 325; and Ahad Ha-Am, 70, 114-117, 124-125, 126, 128-129, 130, 132-133, 135, 136, 142, 148, 183, 198, 204, 211-212, 219, 237-238, 288, 308, 311, 312-313, 320-321; and the new Zionism, 173; as medium of instruction in Palestine schools, 228-234
Hebrew Language, and Its Grammar, The (Ahad Ha-Am), 115-116
Hebrew Language and Its Literature (Ahad Ha-Am), 114-115
Hebrew University, 269, 322
Hebrew University Press, viii, xi
Heder, 8-10, 13
Heller, J. E., biography of Ahad Ha-Am, vii-xi
Herem, 84, 233
Hertzberg, Arthur, xi
Herzl, Theodor, 38, 39, 64, 66, 90, 91, 93, 94, 103, 104, 154, 169, 170, 174, 175, 176, 177, 178, 182, 183, 185, 186, 187, 188, 191, 244, 295, 321, 324; conflict with Ahad Ha-Am, 150, 171-172, 179-180, 183-184, 189
Hess, Moses, 288, 289
Hibbath Zion movement, 4, 33, 37, 46, 47, 48, 49, 50, 51, 53, 54, 56, 57, 62, 64, 65, 66, 67, 72, 74, 76, 77, 78, 79, 82, 83, 84, 85, 90, 95, 98, 99, 100, 110, 111, 112, 113, 114, 119, 120, 121, 122, 123, 124, 129, 150, 151, 173, 180, 181, 193, 194, 247, 279, 280, 286, 287, 288, 316, 317
Hilfsverein der deutschen Juden, 225, 227, 230, 231, 232, 233
Hirsch, Baron Maurice de, 67, 71
History, Jewish, Ahad Ha-Am's views on, 289-290
Homel, 199, 200, 208
Hovevé Zion (Lovers of Zion), 33, 40, 41, 42, 51, 52, 54, 55, 57, 58, 59, 61, 62, 63, 65, 66, 67, 68, 71, 72, 81, 82, 83, 84, 86, 88, 89, 90, 99, 100, 103, 104, 106, 113, 121, 150, 153, 155, 174, 176, 177, 181, 185, 187, 198, 287, 312, 317. *See also* Hibbath Zion.
Humanism, Ahad Ha-Am's views, 26, 132, 239

Humanists, Jewish, 132, 157-168
Humash, 8, 50
Hungary, 4

Idelsohn, Abraham, 178
Iggeroth Ahad Ha-Am, 272-276. See also *Letters of Ahad Ha-Am*
Ignatiev, Count, 11, 33
Institute of Jewish Studies, 269, 270
Intermarriage, 248
Israel, 91, 292, 297, 318, 323, 324, 325. For earlier references, *see* Palestine
Israel ben Eliezer, *See* Baal-Shem, The

Jabotinsky, Vladimir, 201, 254, 255
Jacob, Rabbi Abraham, 16, 17
Jaffa, 57, 60, 68, 79, 80, 82, 87, 88, 89, 278
Jaffa Schools, The, 153
Jerusalem, 66, 83, 86, 216, 234, 248, 266, 267, 270, 271
Jewish Agency, 91
Jewish Colonial Trust, 181, 186
Jewish Colonization Association, 154, 178
Jewish Legion. *See* Legion, Jewish
Jewish National Fund, 89, 226
Jewish Publication Society, viii, xii, 320
Jewish Quarterly Review, 238, 240
Jewish State and Jewish Problem (Ahad Ha-Am), 172, 180, 193
Jewish Theological Seminary of America, 202, 221
Judaism, Ahad Ha-Am's views, x, xi, 49-50, 97, 105-106, 111-114, 116-117, 122, 123, 124, 132-133, 135, 158-159, 164-165, 189-190, 206, 208, 212, 216, 217, 228-229, 230, 231, 238-241, 279-286, 287, 288, 289, 290-291, 294-295, 296, 297, 302, 303, 306-307, 311-312, 319, 326, 327; difference between Christianity and, 240-242; and the Gospels, 280; and humanism, 160-162, 163, 166, 167, 168; and Zionism, 164-165, 324. *See also* Prophetic Judaism; Reform Judaism
Judenstaat, Der (Herzl), 64, 104, 169, 176
Juedischer Verlag, 215
Justice and Mercy (Ahad Ha-Am), 109

Kahn, Zadoc, 71, 317
Kaminka, Aaron, 179
Kant, Emanuel, 307
Kaplan, A., 145
Kaplan, Mordecai M., 322
Karlsbad conference, 269
Kastinieh, Palestine, 60
Kiev, 5, 7, 12, 43
Kishinev, pogrom, 199
K'lal Israel, 290, 291
Klausner, Joseph, viii, 119, 140, 149, 164, 178, 188, 218, 227, 301
Kohan-Bernstein, S. *See* Bernstein-Kohan, S.
Kokesch, Dr., 154
K'tavim balim, 36-38

Law out of Zion, The (Ahad Ha-Am), 164-165
League for the Attainment of Equal Rights for the Jewish People of Russia, 200-201
Legion, Jewish, in Palestine, 254-259
Leipzig, 30
Leningrad. *See* St. Petersburg
Letters of Ahad Ha-Am, 72, 280, 299, 303, 310. See also *Iggeroth Ahad Ha-Am*
Letters on Judaism, Ancient and Modern (Dubnow), 235-236
Levin, Shmarya, 224, 225, 230, 232, 322
Lewin-Epstein, E. W., 79-80, 86
Lex Talionis, 112, 307
Life of Tchernichowsky (Klausner), viii
Light of Dawn, The, 27
Lilienblum, Mosheh Leib, 53, 54, 80, 82
Lithuania, 88, 236
Little Miscellany, A (Ahad Ha-Am), 157, 158
London, x, 59, 70, 71, 72, 73, 165, 203, 211, 234, 252, 254, 264, 268, 276, 277, 291, 308, 310, 314; Ahad Ha-Am in, 218-247
London *Jewish Chronicle*, 70, 215
Lo Zeh Haderekh ("The Wrong Way"), 47, 48, 49, 50, 53, 55, 58
Lubarski, Abraham, 57, 195, 202, 203, 204, 227

Magnes, Judah L., 229, 270, 294, 322

Magnes Press. *See* Hebrew University Press
Maimonides, 17, 18, 163, 206, 207, 208
Man in Private, A (Ahad Ha-Am), 107
Mandate for Palestine, 271, 297, 322
Many Inventions (Ahad Ha-Am), 97-98, 107-108
Maskilim, 18, 19, 27, 32, 46, 102, 107, 129, 218. *See also* Haskalah movement
Maximovski (Maximon), S. B., 110
May Laws of 1882, 12, 33
Melitsah, 124, 125
Men of Conviction and Men of Action (Ahad Ha-Am), 83
Mendelssohn, Moses, 102
Minsk, conference at, 177, 178
Miscellany (Ahad Ha-Am), 238
Mithnaggedim, 4, 5, 17, 20
Montefiore, Claude, J. G., 220, 221, 238, 239, 241
Montefiore, Sir Moses, 74
Morris, Nathan, 323
Moscow, 209, 211
Moser, Jacob, 228
Moses (Ahad Ha-Am), 205-206, 212, 280, 315-316
Moses, or The Three Prophets (Ben-Avigdor), 82
Munich, 169
Mystères de Paris (Sue), 16

Names That Have Lost Their Meaning (Ahad Ha-Am), 239
Nathan, Paul, 225, 227
Nathanson, Rabbi Joseph Saul, 20, 21
National Education (Ahad Ha-Am), 199
National Morality (Ahad Ha-Am), 167
Nationalism, and Judaism, 164-165, 229, 230, 231; Ahad Ha-Am's views, 172, 173, 174, 279, 281, 282, 285-286, 287, 288, 290; Ahad Ha-Am and Herzl viewpoint, 189-190, 191-192; controversy with Dubnow over, 235-236. *See also* Diaspora Nationalism; Zionism
Negation of the Diaspora, The (Ahad Ha-Am), 236
New York (city), vii, 5, 127, 202, 221, 229, 320
Nietzsche, philosophy of, 160, 161, 163

Nissayon shelo hitzliah (Ahad Ha-Am), 246
Nordau, Max, 154, 158, 167, 172, 175, 176, 184, 185, 205, 278

Odessa, 28, 34, 35, 40, 41, 42, 43, 45, 46, 47, 57, 59, 70, 74, 79, 128, 130, 131, 139, 149, 150, 152, 165, 196, 198, 201, 207, 208, 209, 211, 213, 214, 218, 220, 234, 289, 308, 312, 317
Oliphant, Laurence, 51
Ossorgin, Michael, 248
Otzar. See Thesaurus of Judaism

Palestine, 4, 7, 32, 34, 35, 39, 41, 42, 47, 48, 50, 51, 52, 53, 54, 57, 58, 59, 68, 70, 72, 74, 78, 80, 82, 84, 89, 90, 100, 104, 105, 106, 120, 139, 149, 150, 151, 154, 155, 169, 170, 172, 174, 178, 180, 181, 182, 184, 185, 186, 187, 188, 191, 192, 193, 194, 196, 223, 224, 225, 226, 227, 232, 233, 234, 235, 237, 242, 243, 244, 245, 248, 251, 265, 266, 268, 288, 295, 296, 297, 309, 310, 313, 314, 317, 322; Ahad Ha-Am's early views on rebirth, 60-66, 68-69, 120-121; Ahad Ha-Am's mission to, 209-210; as spiritual center, 104, 105, 106, 191, 192, 242-243, 287-288, 289, 292, 293, 296-298, 323-324; question of Jewish legion in, 254-257; and the Versailles Peace Conference, 261, 263. *See also* Agricultural colonies in Palestine; Balfour Declaration; Colonial efforts in Palestine; Mandate for Palestine. For later references, *see* Israel
Palestine, National Society for, 64, 65
Pardess, 103, 107, 110, 111, 113, 128
Paris, 71, 101, 103, 317; Ahad Ha-Am's mission to, 150-156
People of the Book, The (Ahad Ha-Am), 159
Petah Tikvah, 52, 60
Pevsner, S., 196
Philadelphia, 202
Pines and B'né Mosheh Society, 84
Pinsker, Leo, 33, 41, 58, 67, 103, 104, 105, 106, 176, 251
Pirogov, Nicholas, 9

Pisarev, Dimitri, 28, 35
Pograbinski, Johanan, xii, 272
Pogroms, 12, 29, 38, 41, 52, 199, 200, 201, 265
Poland, 3, 4, 88, 236
Political Zionism and the Jewish Colonial Trust (Ahad Ha-Am), 181-182
Political Zionism and Palestine Colonization (Ahad Ha-Am), 181
Priest and Prophet (Ahad Ha-Am), 110, 212
Priests and People (Ahad Ha-Am), 98-99
Prophet, Jewish type of, 92-93, 205, 212
Prophetic Judaism, 282, 283, 284, 285
Protocols of the Elders of Zion, 93-94

Rabbinism, traditional, 3
Rapoport, Shalom, 18
Raszviet, 40
Ravnitzki J. H., 104, 128, 130, 138, 171, 177, 216, 237, 271, 272, 276
Reform Judaism, 109, 112, 288, 294, 312
Rehovoth, 60
Reinach, Salomon, 158
Religion and nationality, 228, 229. *See also* Judaism
Remazim (Ahad Ha-Am), 246-247
Reminiscences of Ahad Ha-Am, 5-6, 9, 12, 13, 14, 18, 21, 22, 23, 24, 26, 30, 31, 32, 34, 38, 43, 48, 59-60, 66, 67, 68, 72, 83, 152, 202, 242, 276, 289, 299
Reventlow, Count Ernest zu, 94
Rishon le-Zion, 60
Rival Tongues (Ahad Ha-Am), 237, 238
Rome and Jerusalem (Hess), 288
Rothschild, Baron Edmond de, 48, 53, 64, 69, 71, 89, 151, 153, 317; difference with Ahad Ha-Am, 154-155, 156
Rumania, 4, 202, 220
Russia (czarist), 4, 5, 7, 10, 12, 41, 61, 68, 69, 71, 80, 88, 89, 90, 98, 101, 130, 151, 154, 169, 171, 195, 196, 199, 200, 204, 209, 214, 223, 225, 249, 316; fight for equality in, 200-201

Russian Jewish Encyclopedia, 197
Russian Jews, in England, 218, 220
Russian revolution, 200
Rzhevutski family, 10, 11, 33

Sach Hakol (Ahad Ha-Am), 242, 244, 245
Sacred and Profane (Ahad Ha-Am), 109
Sadigura, Galicia, 16, 17
St. Petersburg, 46, 129, 179, 197
Samuel, Herbert, 267, 322
Schechter, Solomon, 202, 203, 220, 221, 225, 230; and Ahad Ha-Am, 290-291, 307
Schiff, Jacob, 225, 227
Selected Essays (Ahad Ha-Am), 320
Self-defence. *See* Legion, Jewish
Shalkovitz. *See* Ben-Avigdor
Shimkin, Esther, 7, 8, 11, 12
Shneerson, hasidic family, 21
Shulman, Kalman, 16, 19, 301
Simon, Aviva, xii
Simon, Oswald John, 239
Singer, Isidore, 117
Skvira, Russia, 5, 8, 12
Slavery in Freedom (Ahad Ha-Am), 101, 183, 319-320
Smilanski, Mosheh, 247, 248
Smolenskin, Peretz, 27, 40, 51, 102, 103, 129, 288, 289
Socialism, Ahad Ha-Am's attitude, 245, 309
Society for the Support of Jewish Agriculturalists and Workmen in Palestine and Syria, 58, 61
Society of Sons of Moses. *See* B'né Mosheh
Sokolow, Nahum, 129, 250, 253, 256, 258
Some Consolation (Ahad Ha-Am), 110-111
Spiritual center. *See* under Palestine
Spiritual nationalism. *See* Autonomism
Spiritual Revival, The (Ahad Ha-Am), 167-168, 177, 194, 212
Studies in Judaism (Schechter), 221
Sue, Eugène, work by, 16
Supremacy of Reason, The (Ahad Ha-Am), 205, 207, 208, 234
Switzerland, 264

Sykes, Sir Mark, 252
Synoptic Gospels (Montefiore), 238, 239
Syria, 58, 60, 90

Talmid Hakham, 300, 308 f.
Talmud, 35, 45, 303
Tchernichowsky, Saul, 134, 164
Tchlenow, Yehiel, 171, 225, 227, 232, 252
Technical school in Palestine, Wissotzky bequest for, 224-228
Tel Aviv, vii, 6, 96, 149, 153, 156, 164, 228, 245, 266, 309, 313, 314; Ahad Ha-Am in, 267-278
Tel Aviv Gymnasia. *See* Gymnasia Herzlia, Tel Aviv
Temkin, Zeev (Vladimir), 84, 85
Territorialism, 185-187. *See also* Zangwill
Theory and Practice (Ahad Ha-Am), 176
Thesaurus of Judaism (*Otzar*), proposed by Ahad Ha-Am, 116-119
Thon, Jacob, 135
Those Who Wept (Ahad Ha-Am), 186
Three Stages (Ahad Ha-Am), 193
Tiflis, 196
Time Has Come, The (Ahad Ha-Am), 216, 234-235
Torczyner, Harry, 320
Transvaluation of Values, The (Ahad Ha-Am), 163
Trumpeldor, Joseph, 254, 256
Truth from Palestine (Ahad Ha-Am), 60, 62
Truth from Palestine II (Ahad Ha-Am), 68-69
Tsaddik, 3-4, 5, 10, 16 f., 21, 24 f., 123, 163, 318
Turkey, 37, 51, 63, 65, 67, 68, 71, 169, 171, 185, 187, 234, 251, 254, 256
Tverski, Johanan, vii
Two Masters (Ahad Ha-Am), 103, 109-110

Uganda, 187 f.
Ukraine, The, 5, 250, 265
Union of Jewish Literary Societies, *Annual,* 215-216

United States, 52, 62, 204, 223, 320, 322, 323
Universal History (Shulman), 19
Ussishkin, Menahem, 90, 153, 169, 171, 187, 226-227, 244, 260, 265, 321

Versailles Peace Conference, question of Palestine at, 261
Vienna, 29, 30, 41, 129, 154, 177
Vilna, 196
Volhynia, Russia, 10
Voschod, 70, 101, 201

Wailing Wall, Jerusalem, 66, 69
Warsaw, 27, 67, 78, 79, 85, 127, 128, 130, 147, 154, 177
Weizmann, Chaim, 91, 129, 185, 188, 218, 223, 251, 252, 253, 260, 261, 269, 321; and a Jewish legion, 254-260. *See also* Balfour Declaration
Welt, Die, 184, 319
Wissotzky, David, 225
Wissotzky, Kalman, 116, 117, 118, 119, 128, 137, 144, 224, 225
Wissotzky firm, 148, 195, 197, 202, 204, 214, 215, 217, 265, 277, 310
Wolffsohn, David, 178
Words and Ideas (Ahad Ha-Am), 192, 194
World War I, 150, 221, 233, 249, 254; effect on Ahad Ha-Am, 250-251
World War II, 236, 297

Yeshivah, 123
Yevreiska Jizn, 251
Yiddish, 184, 204, 308, 311, 312; as national language, 237-238
Yiddishkeit, 168, 218
Yihus, 22
Yishuv, 63, 74, 151, 153, 154, 155, 156, 225, 242, 254, 263, 267, 269, 278
Yishuv and Its Patrons, The, 153
Yivo Institute for Jewish Research, xii
Young Turks, 234, 235

Zangwill, Israel, 111, 187, 188. *See also* Territorialism
Zederbaum, Alexander, 46, 47, 74, 130
Zeitlin, J., 137

Zhitomir, Russia, 21, 26

Zion Mule Corps, 254

Zionism, 38, 39, 40, 42, 48; fore-
runners of, 51-53, 57-65, 68-69, 71,
74, 76-94, 99-100, 129, 288, 289.
See also B'né Mosheh; Hibbath Zion;
Hovevé Zion; Nationalism

Zionism, modern, beginnings, 169-171;
attitude of Ahad Ha-Am, 171; and
Judaism, 324; post-Herzl policies,
243-244; and socialism, 309

Zionism, political, 59, 62, 64, 67, 90,
158, 169-194, 295, 319, 322; opposed
by Ahad Ha-Am, 150, 172, 173, 174,
179, 180-181, 182, 183, 184, 186,
191-194, 198, 205, 208, 213, 216,
279, 280; and colonization efforts in
Palestine, 181; and diaspora nationalism, 235, 236

Zionism, spiritual, of Ahad Ha-Am, x,
xi, 48, 54, 67, 98-100, 102, 103,
104-106, 120, 121, 122, 123, 124,
188, 189, 192, 193, 234-235, 243,

245, 263, 287-298, 307, 315, 323,
324, 325, 326

Zionist Archives, xii

Zionist Central Archives, xii

Zionist Congress, first, 88, 169, 171,
271; Ahad Ha-Am's views on, 169-
170, 171, 172, 180

Zionist Executive, 176, 252, 253

Zionist General Council, 269

Zionist Organization, 90, 91, 94, 96,
129, 151, 154, 167, 176, 177, 187,
188, 233, 234, 242, 243, 253, 257,
258, 315, 321, 323; and Ahad Ha-
Am, 150, 174-175, 177-178, 183-
184, 185-186, 191, 319; and Hebrew
culture, 183-184; and Territorialism,
185-187

Zionist Organization of America, xi

Zionist Quarterly, xi

Zionist Revisionist Organization, 201

Zozovski, Golda, 8, 11

Zozovski, Jacob, 8

Zozovski, Rachel, 8

ABOUT THE AUTHOR

The author of this biography, Sir Leon Simon, C.B., was born at Southampton (England) in 1881 and educated at Manchester Grammar School and Oxford. After graduating in "Greats" in 1904, he entered the British Civil Service and served in the General Post Office until his retirement in 1944 after attaining the rank of Director. After his retirement he was for some years Chairman of the Executive Council of the Hebrew University of Jerusalem, and is still a member of the University's Board of Governors. His Zionist activity began over half-a-century ago, and he was among the original members of the Zionist Commission to Palestine in 1918; but his main interest has been in the cultural aspect of Jewish nationalism, and particularly in the Hebrew revival. A disciple of Ahad Ha-Am since his student days, and a personal friend from 1908 onwards, he has published three volumes of translations of Ahad Ha-Am's writings, and is joint author of the Hebrew biography of him published in 1956.

The author's other publications include *Studies in Jewish Nationalism* (1920) and a Hebrew volume of *Essays on Ancient Greek Literature* (1951), as well as translations into Hebrew of John Stuart Mill's essay on *Liberty,* and of several of Plato's *Dialogues* for which he received the Tchernichowsky prize.